ALSO BY DAVID FAIRBANK WHITE

*True Bearing*

# BITTER OCEAN

## The Battle of the Atlantic, 1939–1945

DAVID FAIRBANK WHITE

SIMON & SCHUSTER
NEW YORK  LONDON  TORONTO  SYDNEY

SIMON & SCHUSTER
Rockefeller Center
1230 Avenue of the Americas
New York, NY 10020

For information about special discounts for bulk purchases,
please contact Simon & Schuster Special Sales at
1-800-456-6798 or business@simonandschuster.com

*Designed by Kyoko Watanabe*

Manufactured in the United States of America

1   3   5   7   9   10   8   6   4   2

Library of Congress Cataloging-in-Publication Data
White, David Fairbank, date.
Bitter ocean : the Battle of the Atlantic, 1939–1945 /
David Fairbank White.
p.      cm.
Includes bibliographical references and index.
1. World War, 1939–1945—Campaigns—Atlantic Ocean.
2. Naval convoys—Atlantic Ocean—History.   I. Title.
D770.W44 2006
940.54'293—dc22                    2006042312
ISBN-13: 978-0-7432-2929-6
ISBN-10: 0-7432-2929-0

*For Margaret Stanback White*

# Contents

# BITTER OCEAN

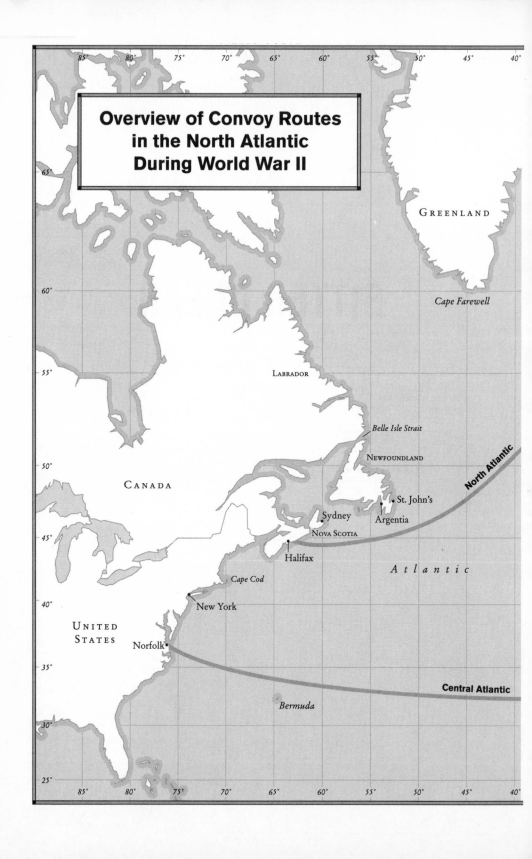

# Overview of Convoy Routes in the North Atlantic During World War II

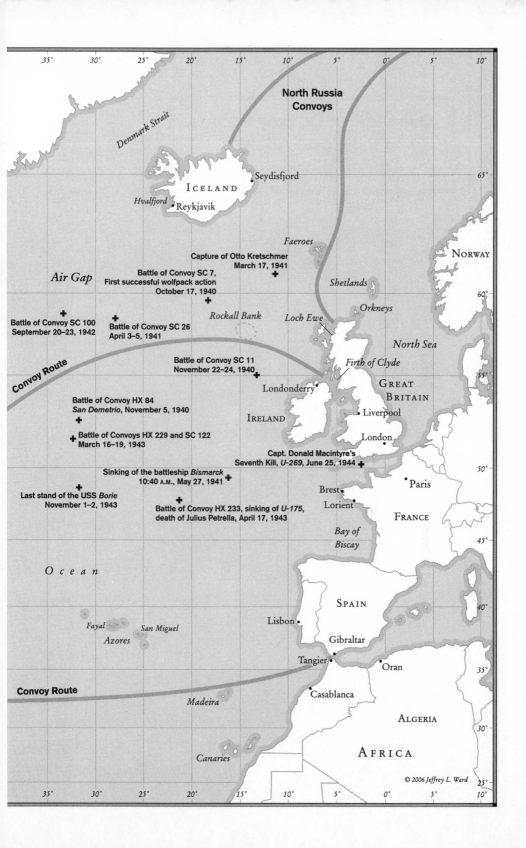

35°  30°  25°  20°  15°  10°  5°  0°  5°  10°

**North Russia Convoys**

*Denmark Strait*

Seydisfjord — 65°

ICELAND

*Hvalfjord* • Reykjavik

*Faeroes*

NORWAY

Capture of Otto Kretschmer
March 17, 1941 ✝

*Air Gap*

Battle of Convoy SC 7,
First successful wolfpack action
October 17, 1940 ✝

*Shetlands* — 60°

*Orkneys*

✝
Battle of Convoy SC 100
September 20–23, 1942

✝
Battle of Convoy SC 26
April 3–5, 1941

*Rockall Bank*

Loch Ewe

*North Sea*

Convoy Route

Battle of Convoy SC 11
November 22–24, 1940 ✝

*Firth of Clyde*

55°

Londonderry•

GREAT
BRITAIN

Battle of Convoy HX 84
*San Demetrio*, November 5, 1940

IRELAND

• Liverpool

✝
Battle of Convoys HX 229 and SC 122
March 16–19, 1943

London

Capt. Donald Macintyre's
Seventh Kill, *U-269*, June 25, 1944 ✝

50°

Sinking of the battleship *Bismarck*
10:40 A.M., May 27, 1941 ✝

Brest•
• Paris

✝
Last stand of the USS *Borie*
November 1–2, 1943

✝
Battle of Convoy HX 233, sinking of *U-175*,
death of Julius Petrella, April 17, 1943

Lorient•

FRANCE

*Bay of
Biscay*

45°

*O c e a n*

SPAIN

40°

*Fayal*  *San Miguel*

*Azores*

Lisbon•

Tangier•

Gibraltar

Oran•

35°

Convoy Route

*Madeira*

• Casablanca

ALGERIA

30°

© 2006 Jeffrey L. Ward

*Canaries*

AFRICA

25°

35°  30°  25°  20°  15°  10°  5°  0°  5°  10°

# WINTER, NORTH ATLANTIC

O UT HERE ONLY WEATHER EXISTS, AND THE IMMENSE field of the sea, wide as a wilderness all its own, white-flecked, deep blue, marked by the endless waves that march away in perfect, receding uniformity. The spot at latitude 42° 80' north, longitude 37° 20' west on the Atlantic Ocean is vacant, blank, chilly, grooved by the layers and furrows of the mid-ocean currents, precisely identical to every other mile around it. Beneath these waters lie the countless graves of navy sailors and merchant seamen who perished at the hands of German U-boats to keep the supplies flowing to feed World War II. There are no headstones out here, no markers, no monuments. For sailors lost at sea, there are no tablets. There is only this place, the wind-whipped, empty, anonymous ocean. A modern containership passing by in 2002 hustles past the froth, and the waves turn to marbled swirls of aqua, blue, white, mingling and turning and folding into frigid pinwheels of color.

More than 36,200 Allied sailors, airmen, and servicemen and women went to their death on this ocean, or in the contest centered around it, between 1939 and 1945, in Lightning Class destroyers, tiny corvettes, and B-24 Liberator aircraft, or at land installations ashore.

Alongside these, some 36,000 merchant ship sailors were lost, many dying terrible deaths, plunging to the bottom of the Atlantic in ships which disappeared from the surface with all hands in less than twenty seconds, many others succumbing to isolation, exposure, or starvation in open lifeboats or on rafts.

The Germans paid a high price, too. One thousand one hundred seventy-one U-boats went to war between 1939 and 1945. Six hundred sixty, almost 57 percent, were lost. The loss in men was far greater; the casualty rate for the German U-boat service is the highest for any military unit since the time of the Romans. Forty thousand German officers and men went to war in U-boats. Only 7,000 came home.

The Battle of the Atlantic was fought all across the 32 million square miles of the pitching, heaving Atlantic Ocean, in the frigid, green wastes up by Iceland, in the empty waters off the Azores, in the gray, quick approaches to the English coast. It saw lone, knifelike U-boats surface in the pit of night on heaving seas to set, aim, and slam torpedoes into aging merchant ships; it saw wolfpacks of ten or more U-boats gather to maul convoys of forty or fifty merchant ships in battles that stretched over three or four days; it saw the development of advanced, futuristic Type XXI U-boats which could race along underwater at phenomenal speeds. The conflict was Hitler's ambitious bid to win the war on the Atlantic with his U-boats, long, tapered, bristling with guns.

The battle—it was not really a battle but a struggle that lasted the entire war—was a six-year effort of fundamental importance to every other engagement of World War II. On this battle hinged the effort to bring massive convoys of merchant ships across the Atlantic, carrying the provisions, food, raw materials, and oil to keep solitary England alive during the years she stood alone against the Germans until 1941, and later every tank, gun, tent, helmet, bomb, all the troops, gasoline, coffee, wheat, rations to feed, fuel to supply the Allied armies sprawled across Europe. Without the men and ordnance on the ships, no battle, on any front, in any country overseas could be fought. The Battle of the Atlantic was the confrontation upon which the rest of World War II depended.

The convoys—eastbound formations were designated HX, for Halifax, Nova Scotia, and SC for Slow Convoy; westbound formations were dubbed ON, for Outward Bound North, and ONS for Outward Bound North Slow—originated in the East Coast ports of Canada and America, formed up in Nova Scotia, and then followed the great circle route, up across the top of the globe, then came into the North Channel above Ireland after a crossing of about two weeks.

On the side of the Nazis, Admiral Karl Dönitz, commander of the German submarine service, meticulous, possessed of a punctilious memory, presided over the flotillas of low, dark subs which hurried everywhere across the Atlantic. An accomplished submariner himself in World War I, Dönitz had been given the task of rebuilding Germany's submarine arm in the aftermath of the crippling terms of the Versailles Treaty. Above Dönitz was Grand Admiral Erich Raeder, commander-in-chief of the entire German navy. Raeder had come up through the ranks in heavy surface ships. These two men spearheaded the German submarine war.

From the catacombs of his headquarters, secreted in a bunker in a villa in Lorient, Occupied France, Admiral Dönitz oversaw his worldwide fleet of U-boats chiefly by means of an advanced radio network that carried as many as seventy messages a day to his U-boats at sea. Almost alone among the German High Command, Dönitz, convinced of the supremacy of his submarine weapon, grasped that if his subs could sever the Atlantic convoy chain, the Allies would be crippled.

By November 1940 the war in Europe had grown to frightening dimensions. Germany had overrun France, Poland, Czechoslovakia, the Low Countries, and now threatened to roll over all of Europe. The British now stood alone.

Then, too, there was the peculiar darkness of Nazi Germany, which made the conflict so important and desperate. Adolf Hitler, appointed chancellor of Germany on January 30, 1933, had risen to power on the fanatic appeal of his National Socialist German Workers Party and its weird proselytizing on the ideas of extremist nationalism, Aryan supremacy and a German master race, and absolute, authoritarian power. Later, after Hitler's rise, the Nazi Party had developed the plan for the war to advance and perpetuate the Thousand Year Reich. From this had grown the militant and bizarre specter of Nazi Germany, a state in which fervid, warped totalitarianism prevailed and the doctrine and figure of Hitler held complete sway. Under the Nazi state, the systems of society—art, culture, media, education, every social institution down to the Hitler Youth and the League of German Maidens—all these were manipulated and controlled by the state. Under the rule of the Third Reich, life by the tether was the law. The vision of Hitler and the Nazis was to export this horror by war.

Eventually, of course, came the midnight event of the Holocaust. In an attempt to eliminate Jews and Judaism, more than six million people—nearly two thirds of the Jews in the countries overrun by Hitler's armies—were shot in mass graves or marched into gas chambers and exterminated with Zyklon B gas in an act that was not only genocide, but also religiocide, an attempt to kill a people, a faith.

To counter Nazi Germany's attempt to propagate the Third Reich, the Allies had to go to war against the Reich at sea.

The endless, pitching, rolling, unforgiving conflict called the Battle of the Atlantic was waged on a vast scale—across the void, windswept, yawing wastes of 2,500 miles of open Atlantic Ocean. It unrolled on huge dimensions—some 1,000 warships belonging to numerous navies marshaled to decide the outcome of the war. Its significance was enormous, determining the fate not only of Britain but of Europe and the Western world. It was won almost entirely by the British Royal Navy, 300 years old, the blade of Jervis, Nelson, and Jellicoe, England's "Wooden Wall," which had defended her throughout her history. Until 1943, the United States, for the most part, was tied up in the Pacific winning an equally stunning triumph over the Japanese. After 1943, when the U.S. Navy took up a significant role in the engagement, most action and battles took place in the British sector of the Atlantic. The cost of the effort was staggering; British Commonwealth forces suffered more than 33,600 casualties on the sea and in the air; by comparison, the U.S. Navy and Army Air Force, alongside the British, lost roughly 2,600 servicemen. The British, to all intents and purposes, were the overwhelming factor in the immense contest that unfolded across the wide, vacant wilderness of the Atlantic Ocean.

The names of Trafalgar, Jutland, Omdurman, are names which rise from the gorge of time and stand as monuments to

British military achievement. At these places, Englishmen won great battles which were not only victories, often against far superior odds, but also displayed ingenious strategies. So, too, the Atlantic victory should stand alongside them. In substance and stroke, the Atlantic victory was British, Royal Navy, Union Jack.

In terms of almost every phase of the war's prosecution—the makeup of the enormous fleet which fought the struggle, the officer and rating corps which manned the ships, the celebrated aces who racked up the top tallies, Captain F. J. "Johnnie" Walker; the crisp, ever-correct Captain Donald Macintyre; the superbly talented Commander Peter Gretton and his fabled B-7 Escort Group; in terms of the tactical thinking and strategic planning which underlay the triumph; combat victories; the command apparatus overseeing the effort—the victory on the Atlantic was overwhelmingly Britain's, with great assistance from its stout cousin, the Royal Canadian Navy. Up to 1943, virtually all confirmed combat victories in the Atlantic conflict were scored by British and Canadians. After 1943, when America took on responsibility for the South Atlantic, roughly 75 percent of the combat victories were still British Commonwealth.

But Britain did not win the Battle of the Atlantic alone. U.S. Navy and Coast Guard units did join in the war, fighting straight across the ocean alongside the British. Beyond the naval battle, U.S. shipbuilding pumped out a boggling total of some 27 million tons of shipping and in the end flooded the Atlantic with ships faster, literally, than the Germans could sink them, helping to swing the outcome of the war. American advances in science and technology—including radar, communications, and aviation—all helped to win the day.

◆　◆　◆

All record begins with the gleaming new tanker *San Demetrio*, shoving through the ocean 700 miles west of Cape Clear, Ireland, one in a thirty-eight-ship convoy, HX 84, departed Nova Scotia October 28, 1940. She was an oil-burning ship, 463 feet in length, carrying 11,200 tons of oil. She had two deckhouses midships and aft, and nine cavernous tanks. Before her journey was done, she would tell a remarkable tale of men and survival. That was in the future, however, far ahead across the great distances which lay before her. Now she was just a plodding, anonymous merchant ship, registered in London, pushing east across a bright sea.

She nudged through the broad, quiet distance, a hobo, workhorse ship, 8,073 tons, her Kincaid 8-cylinder engine chugging on, plowing through the sea. Finally, during the morning, the Kincaid broke down, so she had to drop out of the convoy on the open, broad Atlantic and come to a stop on the blank face of the ocean for engine repairs. She slipped out of drive, steadily, slowly lost way, and drifted to a halt on the trackless ocean expanse. The *San Demetrio* sat as the engineers went below to the engine. They tinkered, worked on the engine—burning oil, not coal. The repairs took sixteen hours; after that, she got underway, her big propellers biting into the deep green water, and she picked up head, rejoining the convoy that night.

The next day was November 5, 1940, by coincidence Guy Fawkes Day, a British holiday onboard; the *San Demetrio* was a British ship. Now, on the great, flat, Atlantic terrain, thousands of miles away, HX 84 proceeded, shedding the miles of open sea which dropped behind. It was as peaceful a day as any sailor could remember. The convoy commodore, the officer commanding the merchant ships, was well satisfied with the progress of his charges, spread over the Atlantic. The convoy proceeded east across the empty, unending distance. In time, evening descended, a wash of hue against the horizon. It was a tranquil, pale dusk; the *San Demetrio*'s engine rumbled in fine health.

They saw it just after sunset. They saw it on the horizon, small as a fleck of pepper. At first it was no more than a speck, but unmistakable, a mast on the horizon. Then they saw quite clearly it was the mast of a warship. Then they saw a superstructure, a forward turret, a bridge; finally the huge battle cruiser was in sight: the Nazi raider *Admiral Scheer*. Captain George Waite, the master of the *San Demetrio*, sprang into action. He signaled all ahead full to the engine room below and ordered the lifeboats readied. The gun crews manned the 4.7-inch low-angle gun and the 12-pounder. No one onboard the *San Demetrio* needed to wonder what would happen next. The ships of the convoy and the German battlewagon closed slowly across the water, drawing nearer and nearer. Now the *Scheer* was clearly in sight, bearing in upon the flotilla. The raider drove down on them, getting larger and larger, plowing through the sea. She continued, steaming in, a big sash of bow wave in her teeth— then, all at once, she opened fire. Crashes rocked the evening. Thuds and whumps of salvos shook the sky. Thundering echoes and sharp cracks filled the distance. Onward came the *Scheer*, lobbing salvo after salvo onto the convoy; now the men on the *San Demetrio* commenced firing. The immense *Scheer*, big as a fort, kept coming.

The convoy now proceeded to pour fire onto the German battlewagon; the sea shook with shellfire. The commodore of the convoy, its senior merchant officer, ordered his ships to scatter and make off at full speed. The roar of the guns continued, the reverberations shuddering through the tints of the evening. What followed next was a selfless and remarkable act of bravery so extraordinary that every *San Demetrio* crewman who witnessed it remembered it forever.

Outgunned and outpowered by the German raider, mounting only 6-inch rifles against the *Scheer*'s 11-inch armament, E. S. F. Fegen, the captain of the armed merchant cruiser escorting the convoy, the *Jervis Bay*, proceeded to make directly for the *Scheer* and challenge her. Tied up all at once by the *Jervis Bay*, the *Scheer* now commenced firing at the *Jervis* at 18,000 yards, far beyond the range of the British warship's guns. The *Jervis* was suddenly hit and burst into flames; still Captain Fegen drove on, not yet shooting. He closed on the *Scheer*, and only when his guns were close enough to score direct hits did Fegen let loose with his barrage. He did not have a chance against the battleship. His ship was hit again and again, but his guns kept roaring, the two ships firing back and forth. The guns rocked with their thundering salvos. The duel went on. The *Jervis* was finally outstripped, and ablaze. At last, with flames enveloping her from stem to stern, her ensign still flapping from her rigging, the *Jervis Bay* went under. She was gone, but her action, distracting the *Scheer* without any consideration for her own chances, had given most of the convoy time to escape. Captain Fegen, mortally wounded, had given his life and his last defiant fight to save the convoy and allow the ships to pass on.

The German raider now turned on *Cornish City* and *Rangitiki*, two other ships in the convoy. *Rangitiki*, turning through the seas, managed to escape through her own smokescreen. Aware that the *San Demetrio* was next in the line of attack, Captain Waite at this point ordered a course change, as the *Scheer* opened fire.

The first shells missed, nearly, sending up columns of water on either side of the ship. The second salvo slammed into the tanker, ripping into her amidships and blasting through her port bow. The wireless operators were killed instantly. The lookout was killed as well. Waite, whose first thoughts had been for his cargo and his ship, now turned his concern to the lives of his crewmen. He signaled "Abandon Ship" and rang down to the engine room "Finished with Engines," a prearranged signal to take to the lifeboats. The engineers, who would die trapped in their steel catacombs if the ship went down, lost no time in abandoning their gauges and wheels, and ran across the cat-walks, up to the deck.

Fire was ripping overhead with a whine, and steel fragments tore through the air. Speeding through the hail of volleys, the men raced to lifeboat stations. Charles Pollard, the chief engineer, took charge of one lifeboat; Samuel Wilson, the first officer, took charge of the other. The crew lowered away, let go the falls, and dipped their oars into the dark water. At any moment the *San Demetrio*, fully laden with a highly volatile cargo, could blow up. Tracers like red flashes were whizzing across the night; the *Scheer* sent up flares to illuminate the dark. The men took hold of their oars and began desperately to pull away from the ship. There were sixteen men in Mr. Pollard's boat, and they pulled, their arms pumping like pistons until they were free and the tanker well behind. Then they were away, alone. The other ships in the convoy had long since moved on. They were not to see Mr. Wilson's boat again. Chief Pollard's sixteen men stroked slowly along. Not a sound stirred. Behind them, the pyre of the ship lit up the night.

They rowed, slipping in silence across the water. Soon they were safe. They had nothing now but the immense void stretching out in all directions around them. They huddled over their oars, rowing quietly in the dark and the cold. Calum Macneil, a young sailor who was an expert at handling small boats, chanted out a rhythm for the stroke. They had little hope of making land or being rescued. What morning would bring would stun even the most hardened of them. But tonight they had only the small, open boat, on the black, inky sea spreading away.

The *San Demetrio* had been obliterated by the *Scheer* and her 11-inch guns; the *Scheer* was typical of the heavy surface ships on which the Germans had depended in the first years of the war. In 1940, the German navy's High Command looked to big battlewagons like the *Scheer*, the *Bismarck*, and the *Scharnhorst* as a key piece of their strategy to devastate Allied shipping. The U-boat would come next. After the humiliating defeat of the *Graf Spee* in 1939 and the *Bismarck* in 1941, Hitler would turn away from a strategy centering on heavy surface ships, and take up the U-boat as his chief naval weapon. The day of Dönitz's blunt, dark raptors would come. The long, gray subs would multiply, and spread out all across the ocean in dozens of flotillas.

# PART ONE

# THE BRITISH MACE

# 1

THE LONG, CLIPPED BOW OF THE SUBMARINE HURTLED across the waves, shooting through the night, transferring fast across the water. He was on the bridge of *U-99*, peering through his binoculars, clear-eyed, with a pronounced brow, clad in his gray leather U-boat commander's coat with large collar, slash pockets, and silver buttons embossed with anchors. He was trim, lean, liked to smoke small cigars, and now he could see it, off in the distance, a convoy heading home in the dark pit of the night. Earlier they had picked up the smoke trail, now, just past ten o'clock at night, they were up on it. Kretschmer focused his glasses on the dim forms of the ships, calculating to himself in the windy black. At twenty-eight, Kapitänleutnant Otto Kretschmer was no ordinary sub commander. He was the top-scoring German U-boat ace, with thirty-one victories to his credit, making him the silver bullet of the Kriegsmarine, the German navy. Otto Kretschmer had also earned a distinct reputation for keeping to himself, rarely speaking to others, rarely chatting. The submarine raced across the distance, gobbling up the yards, her black silhouette invisible in the night. Now, as was his wont, Kretschmer was silent.

*U-99* dashed along, closing the distance between the convoy and herself, and they all kept quiet. There were two other men on the bridge with him; they watched; no one spoke. It was November 5, 1940. Earlier that night, the *San Demetrio* had been devastated by the immense guns of the *Admiral Scheer*. Now, hundreds of miles away, the crewmen of the *San Demetrio* were bent over their oars, rowing slowly, thrown by chance into the same common vortex of chronology as Kretschmer, closing on his quarry. *U-99* galloped across the waves, narrowing the distance, closing on the attack. The dark veiled everything, Kretschmer hunched against the bridge bulkhead, peering through his glasses. The sub raced forward, cutting through the sea. Kretschmer said nothing. The men on the bridge watched in the windy night. Kretschmer looked, made final calculations. The final preparations and settings for the torpedoes were given. Kretschmer peered through the dark, made last adjustments, and shouted, "Fire!"

A hiss of compressed air shot the torpedo out of its tube. The projectile streaked through the water. A stopwatch ticked. Seconds passed. The torpedo shot under the surface. They waited. Nothing happened. The stopwatch ticked. Then all at once, a huge explosion thundered and rocked the air and the British tanker *Scottish Maiden* erupted in a column of water and steel. Slowly the wreckage settled. In the emptiness of the dark, another Allied ship slid to her agonized, groaning death.

Kapitänleutnant Kretschmer had just claimed his thirty-

second victory. He had every reason to be proud this November 5. He had just come from a patrol which had netted
him six sunken ships. Upon his return, he was to be awarded
the Oak Leaves to his Knight's Cross decoration. To top off
events, the führer had invited Germany's number one skipper
to lunch.

This was the U-boat, a 220-foot, 761-ton tube of cold, narrow
steel armed with twelve torpedoes, an 88mm deck gun forward,
and a 20mm antiaircraft mount on its conning tower. In an
emergency it could disappear completely from the surface in
thirty seconds. The narrow, bristling U-boat was the long, slender knife which nearly cut the Allied convoy supply chain in
two. Through the war, in shipyards and design offices, the Germans developed thirty-four separate types of U-boat varieties,
including the large Type IXs, the Type X minelayers, and Type
XIV tanker supply subs, but the most common were the Type
VII and the Type IX. The Type VII, a medium open-ocean boat,
was the most numerous class of sub. With four bow torpedo
tubes, one stern tube, it was capable of 17 knots on the surface,
and 6 knots submerged. This animal, long and low, thick with
ballast tanks like a cobra, called a "Hearse" in slang by U.S.
Navy sailors, was the venom-tipped fang of Dönitz's effort to
disrupt Allied shipping.

These voracious predators, grouped into wolfpacks with
names such as *Pfeil* (Arrow), *Stürmer* (Stormer), or *Dränger*
(Pusher), were a deadly weapon administering a summary,
lethal blow. In the worst year of the war, 1942, U-boats bagged
a total of 1,006 Allied merchant ships, roughly the equivalent of
four good-sized national merchant navies. The U-boat service

was considered an elite branch of the military; its success in the climactic years of 1942–43 made for a torturous test of Allied resolve. "The Battle of the Atlantic was the dominating factor all through the war," said Winston Churchill, the promontory who stood unbuttressed against the Nazis for more than two years. "Never for one moment could we forget that everything happening on land, sea and in the air depended ultimately on its outcome and amid all other causes, we viewed its changing fortunes day by day with hope and apprehension."[1]

The U-boat theory which guided the war was simple, basic, strikingly straightforward. Over twenty-five years it had evolved from the experience of the First World War, refined in a kind of collaborative process half centered at U-boat Command, half taken from the observations of the commanders at sea themselves. U-boat theory was based on a set of remarkably ruled, regimented lessons; they formed the fundamental scheme for U-boat operations from the first years of the war to the later elaborate phases.

The classic attack called for approach on the surface, at night, behind the moonlight, so you would be hidden by the darkness. According to the pattern, the commander took station ahead of a convoy, so it would sail down upon the sub, and then, when it did, the submarine skipper fired a spread of torpedoes into the convoy. This was the classic maneuver; individual skippers made up their own variations. Kretschmer spun his own tactics—to penetrate the defense screen of a convoy and pop up smack in the middle of it, then "one shot per ship." Kretschmer's trick went against the school; it was maverick— and it earned him the top score in the navy.

The mother arch of all submarine strategy was wolfpack tactics, or *Rudeltaktik*. Wolfpack theory was the master strategy from which all types of combat action descended. Intricate, involved, pack action was like a complicated dance and became the basis for every type of action from the Western Approaches of England to the mid-ocean reaches. In pack theory, a long string of U-boats, separated by twenty miles between boats, was dangled in hiding across the path of a convoy. When one of the subs picked up the oncoming formation, the other boats slowly assembled at the fix of the sighting sub. Then the attack went off. Revolutionary, groundbreaking, the wolfpack concept governed all U-boat battle order, was the standard exercise for attack. It had first been hatched by Admiral Dönitz himself in World War I. Stringing together pieces of combat experience, Dönitz had observed: "The greater the number of U-boats that could be brought simultaneously into the attack, the more favorable would become the opportunities to each individual attacker."[2] The strike power of submarines was exponentially increased when they were massed into groups.

Dönitz brought his wolfpack idea to U-boat Command even before 1939, and sought to institute it at once, at first with little success. On October 13, 1939, he attempted to corral nine subs into a pack to attack Convoy HG (Homeward from Gibraltar) 3 off Ireland. Then snafus entered the picture. Only three subs were prepared when the action commenced and problems with faulty torpedoes and the coordination of the three subs fouled the operation. On September 7, 1940, Dönitz attempted again to gather four U-boats into a pack to strike the fifty-three-ship convoy SC 2, bound for Liverpool. A Royal Air Force antisubmarine aircraft arrived overhead out of the blue, however, forcing the U-boats under. These efforts characterized Dönitz's early attempts at pack actions. But finally, on the night of October 16, 1940, a window of opportunity opened wide. Headquarters managed to assemble seven subs into a team, all targeted on inbound Convoy SC 7, the group led by submarine aces Kretschmer and Heinrich Bleichrodt. The ensuing battle lasted three days. Kretschmer penetrated the inner rows of the convoy formation and went on a shooting spree which potted six Allied ships. Of Convoy SC 7's total roster of thirty-five merchant vessels, twenty were sent below. The wolfpack was born.

The formation of dangling patrol lines, coordination, communications, the careful gathering of subs to form strike groups, all this was a delicate, dark ballet choreographed by Dönitz in the dim catacombs of his headquarters, Befehlshaber der Unterseeboote, BdU, located in the villa of a sardine merchant in Lorient, Occupied France. The nerve center of all worldwide fleet operations, the lair consisted of two rooms, a situation room, and, across the way, a data room with charts and graphs showing the progress of the U-boat campaign.

Here, the man called by his crews "The Diva" orchestrated distant patrols, all boats in the field, and the course and shape of the U-boat war. On the walls of the situation room were sea charts, maps showing the positions of Germany's U-boats and the locations, as known, of Allied convoys at sea. Convoy cross-ocean routes were shown here; also on the walls were tide charts, current charts, charts showing ice and fog, the data, readings, intelligence from the sea. Dominating the room was a huge globe three feet in diameter.

Amid these surroundings, Dönitz's team presided over subs from the North Sea to the Indian Ocean, assigned U-boats to their sectors, and directed the strategic thrust of the Battle of the Atlantic. The team was young; British naval experts considered it incredibly small. Most important was Captain, later Admiral, Eberhard Godt, chief of staff, Dönitz's right-hand man. Under Godt was a 1st staff officer and a 1st staff officer for operations. Beneath this trio was a tiny roster of six other men. From this lair, the U-boat admiral and his staff coordinated the Second World War on the Atlantic, and the gambit to smash the British.

That was later, at the apogee of the U-boat campaign. The war had started with a bare growl, with an almost ridiculous pocket armada of fifty-seven operational submarines. Long before hostilities had commenced, since 1939, Dönitz had argued vociferously, repeatedly, for a massive fleet of subs. With a fleet of 300 boats, he had insisted, he could bring Britain to her knees. The Royal Air Force would run out of petrol. The British would run out of iron ore, steel, food, supplies.

"In our present situation the one essential thing is that we should . . . set about the task not only of raising the number of our operational U-boats to the highest possible total, but also that we should do it as quickly as possible, while . . . enemy anti-U-boat measures . . . are still inadequate. The opportunity we miss today will never occur again," Dönitz said of his idea for a war to sever the ocean convoy supply lines.[3] The führer had been lukewarm to Dönitz's concept. Prone to seasickness, with little aptitude for things nautical, Hitler had once said, "On land I am a hero, at sea I am a coward." Hitler had rejected Dönitz's concept of a submarine war at sea.

The reality of the submarine situation was far worse than that. Cold logistics winnowed the U-boat fleet far below the fifty-seven number. The laws of maintenance and administration dictated that one third of the fleet was tied up in port undergoing repairs, one third was tied up in transit to and from the combat areas, leaving only a third on patrol. The simple fact was that Germany's effort to rupture the convoy chain started with no more than twenty subs patrolling, more often twelve or fifteen.

Germany's fleet of submarines was small; the blunder, though, was to underestimate the pocket armada, as the British Admiralty understood. First action, first taste of war, showed that Hitler's small band of commanders was proficient far beyond its number. At sea, the Germans were racking up victories at an astonishing rate. Through the twelve months of 1940, U-boats had sunk 375 ships amounting to 1,804,494 tons. That roughed out to a formidable twenty-five ships sunk by each boat, better than two ships every month. The Germans were good, they were bull's-eye good.

By 1940, the Southern Approaches to England, through the Channel, had been eliminated as too perilous, and the convoys now came in high, over the top of England, through the North Channel. The U-boats waited off the coast of the British Isles, where they could find the lumbering flotillas; then the scene was the same: a hover, the final aim and torpedo settings; the shoot—another merchant ship going up in a thundering explosion, its back broken by a torpedo. It was a scene that happened all too often. The number counters at the Western Approaches Command and in the Admiralty's Submarine Tracking Room in London counted. Hitler's sea raiders were more than a side show; they were raising the curtain on a long, draining war.

The first sally disturbed Churchill, it disturbed the other Allied leaders—Greece, the Free French, the Dutch and Poles who had escaped occupation forces, others—who dreaded what they felt must follow: a major offensive. Churchill, in the gloomy apprehension of these early years, compared Britain to:

... the diver deep below the surface of the sea, depending from minute to minute on his air pipe. What would he feel if he could see a growing shoal of sharks biting at it? All the more when there was no possibility of being pulled up to the surface. For us there was no surface.[4]

The U-boat was out of the cage; it was goring the North Atlantic convoy system.

# 2

THOUSANDS OF WINDY MILES FROM THE POINT WHERE Otto Kretschmer was hurrying home through the inky black of the Atlantic night to a hero's welcome, and thousands of miles from the spot where the *San Demetrio* survivors sat in their open lifeboat, pulling on their oars, rowing slowly through the water, November 5, 1940, had an entirely different meaning across the United States of America. Before the day was done, the diaphanous shroud of history would slip silently across America, the Atlantic, and the world.

From the foggy hills of San Francisco, to Chicago, with its honking lakefront drives, to the farms of Kansas and Ohio, the American people were leaving their homes, gathering at polling places, coming together as one. November 5, 1940, was election day.

High in the obscure thermosphere of politics, the decision of the American people took shape all day long, crystallizing in the cloudy medium of millions of single votes, slowly taking form. This election day had presented voters with a dramatic choice: whether to return President Franklin D. Roosevelt to an unprecedented third term in office. Opposing him was Wendell Willkie, a popular Wall Street lawyer. While the campaign began as a debate on Roosevelt's New Deal anti-Depression program, the war in Europe bulged before the election like a giant, bloated abscess. Norway had been invaded by the Germans. Denmark was occupied. Using their armored blitzkrieg tactics, the Germans had rolled across France in a matter of weeks with their mechanized panzer divisions. Now America's closest ally, Britain, was besieged; U-boats marauded all across the Atlantic, the war seemed to be at the very doorstep of America, the slumbering giant. Would it awake? Isolationists who opposed committing American lives to war rallied in Congress, in the press, and in the streets to keep America out of Europe's crisis. Opposing the isolationist view was William Allen White's Committee to Defend America by Aiding the Allies. White's committee had organized a massive grassroots movement calling for U.S. aid to Britain. Roosevelt, privately, in his own thoughts, had drifted from doubt about entering the war, to conviction that arms and material support for Britain would be necessary. Publicly, however, Roosevelt had been forced to hide his beliefs in the face of widespread opposition, and assure Americans their sons would not have to fight overseas. Willkie also played on the isolationist question.

Against the backdrop of this dense swirl of opposing views, election day stole forward as the clock wound through hour after hour on November 5. From coast to coast, America awaited its outcome; so, too, did statesmen in London, Berlin, and Tokyo.

Of all the world leaders who awaited the outcome of the American election in foreign capitals scattered across the globe, none waited more anxiously than Winston Churchill, Britain's prime minister, embattled, implacable. Churchill, lone, indomitable, the very backbone of Britain's defiance to Nazi aggression, had led England's redoubtable stand against the advancing German onslaught.

In July, some 715 British pilots in banking, soaring Hawker Hurricanes and Supermarine Spitfires, considerably outnumbered by German ME-109 Messerschmitts, had cut the Luftwaffe down out of the skies in the famous Battle of Britain, the storied triumph of the RAF, establishing crucial air superiority over England, and resoundingly besting the Germans. Now, though, Britain barely clung to survival and viability in the darkest hour of its trial, enduring the siege of Hitler. England hung on, beleaguered, battered by the Nazi broadsword.

In June 1940, Britain's army had almost been trapped in the disastrous retreat from Dunkirk following the fall of France. Then had come the Blitz, the unrelenting bombing campaign of Hermann Göring's air force. On the night of September 7, 1940, a fleet of 200 Luftwaffe bombers had rained down destruction upon London. For one month after that, night after night, London had endured the hammering of the German raids; the attacks soon shifted to the west coast ports of Liverpool, Glasgow, and Bristol.

At sea, the war went little better. The ever multiplying groups of U-boats were deadly effective with their strikes. In 1940, sinkings for the year had passed the 1.8-million-ton level. In February 1941, shipping losses reached an alarming 300,000 tons. In all, dock tallies showed, by mid-1941, Britain was losing ships three times faster than shipyards could replace them.

Across the ocean, Roosevelt watched the stubborn stand of

Britain from his distant remove. Churchill watched Roosevelt and America, and wondered, would the sleeping giant stir? The British prime minister sought with all urgency and guile to move the American president.


Britain endured in the rubble of Göring's bombing. At sea, the war seemed to stall in the face of mounting losses. The rush to arm did not go well. All across the parade grounds, fields, and anchorages of England, lack of ships, men, and effective equipment hampered the ability to mount an offensive. The Royal Navy and RAF Coastal Command, the navy's adjunct in the air, were ensnared in squabbles over command jurisdiction, interfering with combined operations. The Royal Navy, the greatest in the world at the time, counted but 245 escort bottoms in early 1940. Though it would swell to 336 escort ships by 1941, it was badly strained now by lack of hulls. Norway, invaded that spring, had drawn off even more ships. On RN destroyers, sloops, and corvettes, training was a critical weakness. Recruits frequently had no training at all; ships often counted no more than a handful of experienced seamen in their crews. Weekend yachtsmen rounded out many ships' companies. As 1940 came on, the venerable Royal Navy was compromised by lack of training, a shortage of escort hulls, most critically excessive reliance on sonar. Sonar had been developed in the First World War; it was a pod that projected an underwater beam which could detect a submarine. Yet U-boats, aware of the device, had come to attack on the surface, where they were out of reach of the underwater probe.

RAF Coastal Command also struggled to gather its mobilization. Coastal Command's long-range aircraft were critical for far-flung reconnaissance flights and attacks on U-boats, but the air arm was compromised by deficiencies. The service had only recently introduced the Sunderland, its first really effective, combat-proven antisubmarine warfare (ASW) aircraft. Bombs and detection devices mounted on the air arm's planes were badly outdated. Coastal Command fumbled, as well, to respond.

Thus, Britain lurched off to war in the Atlantic, a slouching, stumbling Quasimodo. As sailors and airmen raced to hone their defenses, Dönitz's U-boats roved the ocean wastes, crossing the offshore waters of England, chalking up ever more victories. German skippers called it "The Happy Time." The convoys shoved across the empty, rolling, white-capped Atlantic and the British mustered along their coasts, and guardedly waited, watching the sleeping giant, America. Would it wake up?

Roosevelt won the election of 1940 by defeating Willkie with a vote of 27,243,466 to 22,304,755. FDR captured thirty-eight states; the tally, though far narrower than in 1936, was still broad enough to give him decisive leadership of the American people.

The president could now turn his mind to the great, waiting question of the war in Europe; the president was free to embark on his cautious march to action. It had started long before, in a halting series of gestures, each one betraying Roosevelt's real concern over the specter of the Thousand Year Reich and its war.

Months before, amid the hot summer clamor of the baseball season, and the debate of isolationists and interventionists, Roosevelt, in a show of support for the British, had dispatched to England twelve merchant freighters loaded to the gunwales with a bulging array of arms. The whopping payload had included 93 bombers, 184 tanks, 500,000 Enfield rifles, 76,000 machine guns, 25,000 Browning Automatic Rifles, 895 75mm guns, and 100 million rounds of ammunition. The shipment had weighed in at 70,000 tons.

Then, in September, Roosevelt had responded again to Churchill's urgent pleas. Acting without congressional approval, he had given the British fifty surplus destroyers in a ships-for-bases deal that netted the U.S. rights to use Britain's airstrips in the Atlantic.

Now, in November, the decision of the American electorate was past; Roosevelt could move forward with somewhat more freedom. Here, presently, with victory in hand, FDR at this point proceeded to confound all about him as well as leaders on three continents by taking off on a cruise alone in the Caribbean aboard the cruiser USS *Tuscaloosa*.

For ten days in December, the *Tuscaloosa* steamed through the bright, azure waters of the Caribbean, the president diverting himself, but all the time weighing the difficult predicament of the nearly bankrupt British. Sixteen months into the war, Great Britain could no longer afford to pay for arms. Her coffers strained at each new purchase. Roosevelt fished, enjoyed movies, entertained a retinue of British dignitaries, and considered the intricate question of arms and money. By the time the cruise ended, the elaborate elements of the president's thinking had meshed and he had come up with an answer.

The solution—the Lend-Lease program—was unveiled at a press conference back in Washington not long after the *Tuscaloosa*'s return. The ingenious arrangement called for Britain to receive American arms, and then repay the U.S. not in cash but "in kind" after the war was over. The program, part banking, part contract, removed a major hurdle to American support for Britain.

Then, on December 29, the president took a decisive step in his long journey toward war. In a fireside chat broadcast to the American people, Roosevelt for the first time cast the conflict directly as an American concern. In the talk, broadcast coast to coast on the radio, the president declared to listeners gathered close in kitchens and living rooms that "the Nazi masters of Germany have made it clear that they intend not only to dominate all life and thought in their own country, but also to enslave the whole of Europe, and then to use the resources of Europe to dominate the rest of the world." Roosevelt had brought the specter of Nazi Germany directly to the doorsteps of American homes. In London, Britons had tuned in on the speech and listened with relief to his message as bombs had rained down on the heaviest night of the Blitz.

Fully one year before Pearl Harbor, Roosevelt had suggested for the first time that the strife across the sea must come to concern all the great, sprawling, square-shouldered American nation. Thousands of soldiers, sailors, and airmen could read the headline plainly: the thunderheads of war would soon crack before them. Aboard battleships and cruisers, aboard destroyers and submarines of the U.S. Navy, men and officers could clearly see how the skies crossing the horizon were changing.

Among these thousands of capable young officers was a straight-cut, dark-haired, tough-minded commander named Paul R. Heineman, forty-three years old. As a twenty-year-old midshipman schooling at the U.S. Naval Academy, Heineman had served in battleships during the First World War, then logged other sea duty before being given his first command in 1933, of a minesweeper, the USS *Robin*. Now, in December

1940, Commander Heineman was one of a flurry of young officers lost amid the byzantine corridors of the U.S. Navy's Bureau of Ships, or Buships, tinkering with the technicalities of ship design and construction. Heineman was a digit, almost unseen. Later on, the Atlantic battle would come to him with an enormous importance. But now, he was a desk driver lost amid the maze of navy bureaucracy.

So, with Commander Heineman tucked away in the corridors of Buships, Roosevelt freshly reelected to lead the "Arsenal of Democracy," and the British navy and air force rushing to marshal their ranks and mount an effective offense, the convoys kept coming across the Atlantic, across the marching, white-capped, rippled swells. The Royal Navy was struggling to respond, the weather blustery, the destroyers and sloops strained. There was a shortage of escort hulls. Radar had not yet come in. Sonar was useless against submarines attacking on the surface, as they were now. The fall of 1940 was a difficult, thankless time for the British on the Atlantic. The U-boats were hitting hard, the Royal Navy laboring, still assembling its cohorts. The convoys toppled across the expanses. There were many hard-luck convoys that year. One of them was Convoy SC 11.

# 3

THE SEA IN NOVEMBER WAS CHILLY, CARVED WITH identical rows of blue, whitecapped waves, spray-tossed, and as far back as he could see, Commander Alan K. Scott-Moncrieff, senior officer escort, aboard HMS *Enchantress*, was pleased with the progress of his charges, thirty-four merchant ships spreading back in a wide field behind him. Ten years hence, Scott-Moncrieff would rise to the rank of rear admiral and become commander-in-chief of all British naval forces in the Korean War, but today, at forty, he was one of many young, promising escort group leaders. The ships pitched along, rolling in the green swells: the determined British *Fintra*, carrying lumber, only 2,089 tons; the *Brask*, a Norwegian ship, in number two position of the third column; next the Greek *Panaghis*, carrying corn, the other ships stretching behind.

Now they plunged ahead, the weather clear, the sea playful

no more. Visibility was fine, a good wind blowing, and the entire procession was coming up northeast on the last leg into the North Channel, which would take them in to England. Vice Admiral F. M. Austin, the convoy commodore, had noted: "SS *Henry Mory.* . . . Engine trouble . . . was a menace to convoy through bad station keeping. . . . *Vicia*—Finn [Finnish]. . . . Was never in station. Never answered any signals."[1] So they continued, a motley pack, lumbering and pitching on their way. The sky was clear and blue all the way down to the horizon.

The weather came up in the afternoon, Friday, November 22; by evening it was blowing full gale force. The winds shrieked out of the west, tearing the tops off the seas, and the great waves were now combers, the wind ripping spume from their crests, making a field of hills and ditches through which the thirty-four ships of Convoy SC 11 rose and fell. All afternoon they kept on, heading to the northeast. Evening descended, darkening the face of the heaving sea and the dome where sky and sea are indistinguishable. Many of the ships switched on their navigation lights so they would be more visible to each other. This was a mistake. U-boats saw these lights, too.

At 10:30, with the seas convulsing, the convoy made an 18 degree turn to port, left. In the howl of the wind and the water, it was awkward; some of the ships became separated from the convoy and fell astern. Now squalls came in, bringing violent rains. The ships plugged on.

All at once, blowing the night apart and splitting the black, an explosion roared through the dark, coming from one of the ships that had fallen behind, the 4,740-ton British freighter *Bradfyne*. She had been hit just aft of her bridge, at just about the point of her No. 2 Hold. She was new, modern, one of the most efficient ships in the fleet, had been built in 1928. She would sail no more. The *Bradfyne*'s days were done.

Somewhere about the darkened yards of the convoy, an intruder had just launched his first fish, first torpedo, of the evening. The Germans called them *Aale*, eels. Commander Scott-Moncrieff would have been very interested in the identity of the stranger. He was Kapitänleutnant Joachim Schepke in *U-100*, one of the leading aces of Germany. One of the black virtuosos had stumbled onto Convoy SC 11.

As it was, Scott-Moncrieff was unaware of the torpedoing. The *Bradfyne* was well astern, in the group of ships which had become separated behind, out of sight and earshot of the commander. Alone, in the black pit of the night, the *Bradfyne*, smoking, slipped from the surface and dove below, her short service done. Of forty-three men aboard her, only four would survive.

The rains continued. The winds were blowing at Beaufort Force 7, gusting to 33 knots. The convoy swung on, leaving a trail of smoke behind. The sheets of the downpour slanted across the ships; the wind flapped and shook through the rigging and masts of the darkened merchantmen. They pitched on. Then, forty-five minutes later, at 11:45, another deafening roar rocked the air and split the calm. Now, the 4,562-ton freighter *Justitia* had been hit. She was British as well, carrying steel and lumber. The *Justitia* was also in the group well astern; again, no one in the main body of the convoy was aware that she had been attacked. Of thirty-nine men aboard the ship, only twenty-six would be accounted for. The *Justitia* was just six years old, gleaming new. She had given her last in the fight to bear her cargo to England. Schepke's log records the moment of her destruction. Requiem for a hobo freighter: "Torpedo firing. Tube IV, 7e [electric torpedo], hit amidships. Steamer stops with strong list; not observed further because preparing for next attack. Sinking assumed."[2]

It was shortly after one in the morning. Schepke, the mae-stro, had bagged two invaluable Allied ships for openers. He had only begun the dark tarantella of mayhem he would dance that night. He was not alone. One other intruder had joined Schepke at this point. Kapitänleutnant Claus Korth, in *U-93*, had responded to Schepke's alert on finding the convoy. Con-voy SC 11 now had two wolves running amid its ranks. The rains lashed down. The seas swept to the east in the pitch black.

The main body of the convoy was still unaware of what had happened. Commodore Austin, looking out from the bridge of his ship, SS *Llandilo*, kept the wandering herd of merchant ships in line—twenty-two of thirty-four vessels in the convoy had no signal lamps and had to communicate by the rude means of sig-nal flags. They stumbled on, the rain pelted down, dribbling across bridge windows, making trails along the glass. For three and a half hours nothing happened. The wind howled east.

Then, at once, out of the blue, from the fourth ship in the fourth column, came another deep rumble and a deafening blast at 3:35 in the morning. This time, the little Norwegian *Bruse*, 2,205 tons, registered in Oslo, had taken a torpedo. She was modern, had been built in 1933. The *Bruse*'s call sign, the ready identifier of a ship in wireless traffic, had been Lima, India, Tango, Hotel, LITH. It would call no more. Schepke had struck again. His log records: "Torpedo tube firing, tube I (G 7e) on a tanker of approx. 7,000 tons. [He badly overestimated the ton-nage.] Characteristics: forward mast fairly far forward, very large and very broad bridge, with two derricks . . . aft very large stack. Hit in the engine room." Schepke had bagged his third hull; he would go on to rack up an even more extraordinary number of victories during the night.

Now, Scott-Moncrieff wound up into action. He swung around in the dark. He gave helm and engine orders. A personnel fitness report had said of him: "[An officer] of great merit and ability, he leads and handles his flotilla with skill and dash. He is admired with affection by his subordinates, over whom he retains a firm and paternal hand. Fit and strong, cheerful under adversity, and possessing a high moral standard." Scott-Moncrieff had seen a white rocket go up, presumably from *Bruse*. He lunged forward. His fast, 282-foot sloop, *Enchantress*, was a legend in the British navy. Before the war, she had served as the Admiralty yacht, painted a beautiful royal blue.

Now the commander and his tiger, *Enchantress*, immediately took off at flank speed and surged through the darkened rows of ships toward the white rocket they had seen.

Suddenly, as they crossed through the shadowy masses of the ships, a second explosion split the air and rocked the convoy with a thundering roar. The Norwegian *Salonica*, 2,694 tons, carrying pit props, wood frames for coal mines, had been hit. She had been built in 1912; the *Salonica*'s good life had ended. Schepke again. He was pumping torpedoes into SC 11 like a sniper with bolt-action reflexes.

Now the full chaos of a convoy battle broke into life. Commander Scott-Moncrieff, running up between columns one and two of the convoy, began firing starshell, bright white, illuminating projectiles, and started to search for submarines.

Schepke's log reads: "While a destroyer comes straight at us, [we are] still able to get off a quick torpedo shot. Torpedo tube firing tube II (G 7e) at a medium sized freighter of 5,000 tons, stack and bridge separate, hit amidships. Immediately afterwards target of repeated firing of star shells from destroyer while approaching rapidly."

Now Scott-Moncrieff signaled two Canadian escorts, *Ottawa* and *Saguenay*, to stay close by the convoy. To a third escort, the Canadian destroyer *Skeena*, he sent a request for a starshell to display her position. As *Enchantress* drove through the confusion, her sonar pinging, Scott-Moncrieff peered through the dark for signals.

"He had a pair of leather sea boots that came up to his knees," recalls James Woodhead, chief yeoman of signals aboard *Enchantress* at the time of the battle of Convoy SC 11. "We all had rubber sea boots. He had leather . . . and a towel around his neck and his hat slightly to one side. He was a commanding figure."[3] The escort leader, on his open bridge, looked in the dark for his cohorts. The reports were not good. *Saguenay* indicated she was many miles out of the picture. *Skeena* responded that she was four miles astern. At this point, with a full convoy battle breaking wide open, *Enchantress* was left with one other ship, the Canadian destroyer *Ottawa*, to fight off the subs. *Skeena* returned to the convoy. *Ottawa* took up station close by. The storm blew, lashing the ships with rain.

Commander Scott-Moncrieff, lone armored maw in the night, now took off, up the convoy ranks. He jumped ahead, lunging forward to hunt for the submarine which had attacked *Salonica*. At the rear of the convoy, *Skeena* was now on to the track of another U-boat. She tracked, caught up, and attacked with three depth charges. Nothing showed; nothing came to the surface. She had missed. She pressed her search with starshell, but finally the sub was gone. Schepke and Korth had evaded the entire group.

The battle now fell into a lull. The U-boats, for a time, held off. Scott-Moncrieff diverted to pick up survivors from the torpedoed ships. In the heavy weather prevailing, the crew of *Enchantress* had enormous difficulty with the rescue. *Skeena* picked up one boatload of men; Lieutenant Roger P. Hill, a senior officer aboard *Enchantress*, now began to lead his crew in recovering survivors amid the heaving waves.

Then the bizarre, smoky aftermath of combat closed in around Scott-Moncrieff about six o'clock in the morning. First he came upon the strange sight of the bow section of *Bruse* still floating, with the master and four men aboard it. He ordered *Skeena* to assist.

The following scenes drifted by: a straggler, SS *Hilversum*, in the damp dark of the morning, which Scott-Moncrieff ordered to get to England on her own as best she could; the bow of the sinking *Salonica*, settling fast, with pit props in the water all about her shattered hulk. The destroyer *Skeena*, with survivors from *Salonica* and *Bruse*, and *Enchantress*, now headed back to the convoy formation.

For a time, the calm following action settled in over the flotilla. The storm had quieted down. The wind fell off to Beaufort Force 5, gusting to 21 knots. The ships of SC 11 slugged on through the early hours of morning. The convoy was smaller by four ships, the remaining thirty straggling along; they were now about 200 miles from the coast of Ireland. The ships rolled along through the seaway, nine columns, most four rows deep. Nothing marred the quiet of the early morning hours. The ships steamed ahead in their precise formation. One hour passed.

Then, all at once, at 7:10 in the morning, another explosion tore through the convoy and split the air, coming from the third ship in the second column. The Canadian *Ottawa* responded, taking off at full speed, jumping off onto a depth charge attack. The 3,136-ton British *Leise Maersk* had swallowed an "eel." H. E. E. Pedersen, the third mate of the *Leise*, "felt a terrific shaking and I was thrown out of my bunk. I heard a noise like the crack of a gun."[4] The *Leise* had been hit at No. 3 Hold, which had blown up.

Schepke had bagged his fifth ship of the night. He shucked

his position and sped off again. He was having a marksman's night.

Onboard the sinking *Leise*, Pedersen struggled to get to the bridge, but could not get there with the beams and debris from the explosion blocking his way. In the confusion, several men in the crew tried to lower lifeboats, but failed.

Men now jumped from the ship into the water, one after the other. Pedersen swam around in the cold of the morning until he sighted a raft, toward which he made his way. Two men were already on the raft; five others were picked up before long, making eight in all. In the chill of the waters, the float drifted away. Soon the men lost sight of the ship. All day, in the storming weather which still prevailed, the eight clung to the raft as best they could, cold and exhausted, marooned on the sea. Once in the building swells, the raft turned over and the chief mate, exhausted, drifted away despite all efforts to retrieve him. Now reduced to seven, including Pedersen, the men on the raft held on in the rain, riding like a sled over the waves that came. Three times, airplanes flew over them, but did not see the float. Twice, ships passed nearby, one to port, one far ahead, but these, too, failed to see the raft. At last, the next day, after eight hours on their makeshift platform, the seven were picked up by a Dutch tug. They were the only survivors of the *Leise Maersk*. Seventeen men perished with the ship.

Back on the field of battle, with the *Leise* torpedoed, the destroyer *Ottawa* now moved out, firing starshell, hurrying up past the rows of ships. *Skeena*, too, was on the move. She had picked up a contact, and now attacked and swept thoroughly, but by the end of her hunt, nothing had turned up. The subs still eluded. She broke off.

◆  ◆  ◆

Morning at last spread over the convoy, a wash of robin's-egg blue at first, then brilliant, quiet, spreading over the surface of the Atlantic. The ships lumbered on, making their slow, determined way toward Ireland. Once more, the lull between action settled in on the ships. On the decks, along the rails, in the compartments of the tired, lifting escorts, depth charge crews stood down, sailors gathered at their stations, men waited, tense, some talking, mostly silent. The convoy lumbered on, heaving east, due east now. Day passed. Evening fell, bringing the gentle curtain of dusk. The twenty-nine ships of SC 11 swung through the seaway, toppling across the waves, plunging on. The escorts pitched across the combers. The convoy shoved ahead. Nothing marred the quiet of the pale sky.

Then, as the ships rocked along, at 8:05 in the evening, as darkness descended across the horizon, a huge explosion three quarters off *Enchantress*'s port bow shattered the twilight. The sloop jumped ahead in a split second and sprinted toward the sound at flank speed, making a beeline for the blast. Five minutes later, a red flare went up in the air. The Dutch *Bussum*, fourth position in the ninth column, had been torpedoed. She was 3,636 tons, carrying grain. Schepke had struck again, number six.

Once again, the escorts turned to. The immense dynamo of an escort group of five ships and a thousand men slowly cranking up into gear began to turn. *Enchantress* altered course to 360 degrees, due north, and took off in pursuit of the sub which had struck at *Bussum*.

Once more, the full fury of convoy battle broke into havoc. Ships began firing starshell. *Ottawa* lunged ahead, searching the right side of the convoy. Scott-Moncrieff launched a depth charge attack. At this point, around 9:00 P.M., still on the 23rd, the weather-beaten *Enchantress* had only one starshell left, having expended thirty in twenty-two hours of continuous combat. The ships chased contacts in the night. Shadows and hulls crossed in the dark. Finally, around nine o'clock, Scott-Moncrieff broke off, having found nothing, and fell away to rejoin the armada.

The convoy returned to course in the full black, and *Enchantress* assumed position ahead of her flock, the flotilla moving on, now reduced to twenty-eight. Night had come on, and the shroud of darkness fell across the dutiful ships, peace once more spreading throughout the long, neat columns.

The battle, most of it, had passed. Six ships totaling 20,972 tons had been sunk in two days. Schepke had pranced through a stunning dance of devastation lasting more than twenty hours, picking off ships like clay pigeons. Korth, in *U-93*, had unaccountably failed to score. Schepke tried to approach for one more attack, but failed. He retired with a rich day under his belt.

Convoy SC 11 plodded along. In the windy gusts of the night, the weather moderated, a light swell ran to the east. The procession was no more than ninety miles from Ireland, shoving east in the darkness, coming up on the big, inbound approaches which would take them into the Irish Sea and the cluster of ports to which they would scatter. But the Germans had prepared one last surprise.

At 4:30 in the morning, in the impenetrable black of the early hours, as the ships scuttled home, still dogging east, a sudden roar tore through the convoy and shattered the calm of the neat rows and columns. Once more, havoc had struck.

The *Alma Dawson*, the first ship in the second column, had hit a German mine. Both forecastles were wrecked. No. 1 Hatch was blown off. The main deck between No. 1 and 2 Holds was completely buckled and No. 1 Hold was full of water. No. 2 Hold was leaking.

Captain P. D. Townsend of the *Alma* and his crew took to the boats and made away. There were no casualties. The *Alma Dawson*, which had served twenty-two years in the British Merchant Navy, was finished. She settled slowly by the bow, her stern raised in the air, and finally she plunged below.

There was no more action. The Battle of Convoy SC 11 was over. A quiet fell over the flotilla. The rusty ships hobbled on to Bantry Bay. Twenty-seven of the original thirty-four ships were still left. The wind blew from the west, dawn broke, spreading a wash of ocher across the vacant sea. The combat had lasted more than twenty-eight hours, from Friday night until early Sunday morning. Scott-Moncrieff had brought twenty-seven of his flock to the barn.

"He kept us all safe crossing the Atlantic and coming back," recalls Woodhead. "Sometimes we thought we'd never get back, seeing all the ships sunk around us. But *Enchantress* seemed blessed by Commander Scott-Moncrieff."[5]

The morning sun spread across the extent of the ocean, rising over the silent, blank surface. The wind died to a whisper. The sky was an arc of color, falling down to the horizon. Convoy SC 11 broke up in the Irish Sea. Commander Scott-Moncrieff had hacked his way through a long ordeal.

At 5:15 P.M. on November 24, the corvette *Bluebell* picked up twenty-four survivors from the *Justitia* at sea.

At 2:02 P.M. on the 25th of November, the tug *Thames* arrived in the Scottish harbor of Campbeltown with the seven survivors from the *Leise Maersk*.

On November 30, the tugs *Seaman* and *Thames* arrived with the bow section of *Bruse*.

Convoy SC 11 had endured a devastating trial. Nearly 110,000 tons of general, breakbulk cargo, pulpwood, iron ore, phosphate, grain, sugar, newsprint, and lumber, had made it. A relentless nightmare was over. A grateful England desperately needed every ton of the cargo that had crossed with Commander Scott-Moncrieff. He was one of dozens of ready, tough, hard, tempered commanders fighting a war that was proving all too costly.

# 4

He was standing about, looking, in the element that suited him best; the sprawl and whirring and yards and docks of a great harbor stretched behind. Standing atop the gear-studded bridge of his 323-foot destroyer, *Hesperus*, Lieutenant Commander Donald G. F. W. Macintyre cut the clean figure of a Royal Navy officer. Macintyre was alert, legs akimbo, his hat perched to one side, a thick duffle coat heavy about his shoulders. In his pictures, he was always smiling, beaming in fact. This was deceptive. Macintyre was a stickler for rules, in many respects a drill major out of the old school. Now he was on the bridge of his ship, looking out over a compass. Beneath his feet was a stallion of weaponry and speed, an ex-Brazilian H Class destroyer, HMS *Hesperus*, delivered only months ago to Brazil but taken back for the war, mounted with three main 4.7-inch guns, seven antiaircraft guns, eight torpedo tubes, and depth charge racks. On first seeing her, Macintyre had described *Hesperus* as "the ship that I knew I could lose my heart to."[1] Soon they were on their way.

Sailor and ship were one on this November day in 1940, as *Hesperus*, with a plume of bow wave in her teeth, raced past Oversay light in the North Channel to form up with her charge, Convoy WS 4, bound for Suez, by way of the Mediterranean. Seventeen ships made up the formation.

Something of an enigma, a man of many talents, he had trained first as a pilot and flown off aircraft carriers; he was an expert pistol shot. A mishap had disfigured his face, adding to the impression of sobriety he made. He had had to ditch a plane in the sea early in his career; this had left one side of the face paralyzed, "which meant that even a smile appeared grudging, quite erroneously as one later found out," according to David Lord Mottistone, a junior officer on *Hesperus* during the war.[2]

Pilot, ship captain, pistol shot, later author of naval histories; alternately rigid disciplinarian, yet not beyond moments of humor, Lieutenant Commander Macintyre was something of a riddle. He was correct, careful, but capable of moments of ample warmth. Macintyre was, if anything, practiced. Much loomed over Macintyre on this day, and he would play an important role in the years of warfare ahead. Today, he was concealed to himself as a thirty-six-year-old junior officer, one of dozens under the Western Approaches command, the command which oversaw the Battle of the Atlantic.

Seven hundred miles to the south, along the curve of the Biscay coast, as Convoy WS 4 and its escort slipped to the open sea, leaving Scotland and the land behind, Otto Kretschmer and his sleek, long *U-99* glided into port, coming off patrol in Lorient, where military brass bands and crowds of pretty young women always waited to greet the homecoming U-boats. Lorient was a big sub base; following the fall of France, Dönitz had moved U-boat operations 500 miles west from Kiel and Wilhelmshaven, Germany, to France's Atlantic coast; boats would operate from Lorient, Saint-Nazaire, Brest, La Pallice, and La Rochelle. Dönitz's headquarters at BdU was at this time sited in Paris, on the Boulevard Suchet; it, too, would later shift to Lorient.

Now Kretschmer, poised, watched coolly as the 220-foot sub eased up to her pier. Other boats lay close by, in from patrol at sea, or readying to go out; *U-99* glided in, then went to dead slow ahead. She drifted up to the pier, then idled up to her space at dockside. Kretschmer had finished off six ships on this last sortie, and damaged two others; he was the top ace of the German U-boat service. He watched the dock now as *U-99* closed the gap to her slip. The sub eased up to the wharf. More than brass bands and pretty girls waited for the young sub captain today; a sheaf of telegrams had arrived:

In grateful acknowledgement of your heroic achievement in the battle for the future of our people I bestow on you, on the occasion of the sinking of 200,000 BRT [tons] of enemy merchant shipping as the 6th officer of the German Wehrmacht, the Oak Leaf to the Knight's Cross of the Iron Cross.

— Adolf Hitler

To *U-99* for the Commander

My best congratulations, with proud acknowledgement of your achievement, on your being awarded the Oak Leaf to the Knight's Cross.

— Commander-in-Chief [Grand Admiral Raeder]

To *U-99*

Congratulations. Carry on the same way.

—Your BdU[3]

The water between her hull and the dock narrowed; at last *U-99* was alongside. Kretschmer leaned over the side of the conning tower, looking at the dockside bustle. He was finally on leave, he could rest now from action.

The next days were a jumble of sights, relaxation, far places, rest, and honor from the Reich High Command. The day after his return, Kretschmer flew up to Paris to see Admiral Dönitz in his headquarters on the Boulevard Suchet. Dönitz debriefed Germany's top sub commander on his last patrol: operations, ships sunk, analysis of his kills.

At last, on November 12, Kretschmer flew on to Berlin, where he was to receive the Oak Leaf to the Knight's Cross from Hitler himself. As the plane winged its way east across Germany, Kretschmer could only bask in satisfaction at this achievement, and look out on the broad fields passing below. He was traveling to the highest summit of power. In Berlin, an official car was waiting to take him to the Kaiserhof Hotel, reserved for the most important state guests. He unpacked and washed. The twenty-eight-year-old ace had reached the inner lair of the Nazi labyrinth. He changed and left on his tour.

Kretschmer's first stop was the Navy Department, where he had an audience with Grand Admiral Raeder. The two had a high-level discussion of the war at sea, and the importance of aerial reconnaissance, which the U-boats badly needed at that time. They talked fully, discussing many subjects. The two parted cordially. Kretschmer noticed that Raeder seemed weary.

Then, at 11:30, Kretschmer's car came to take him to the Reichschancellery for his decoration ceremony. The car drove the short way to the building, Kretschmer keyed up—he was to meet the führer for the first time. The driver drew up to the chancellery; Kretschmer had arrived at the citadel. Hitler's naval adjutant, Captain von Puttkamer, was waiting, and together the two walked up the steps through the magnificent entrance to the structure, emblazoned with a huge German eagle. Puttkamer and Kretschmer walked through the stately lobby and into the imposing, vaulted reception room. Finally, all was ready for the ceremony. Then, as author Terence Robertson recounts:

> At noon punctually, von Puttkamer left him for a few minutes; huge swing doors opened and Hitler walked in, accompanied by the adjutant. Von Puttkamer presented Kretschmer to the Führer and the formal investiture took place immediately. With a few words of praise, Hitler handed his leading "ace" the gold-edged box opened to reveal the glittering Oak Leaves. They sat down on a settee and after a moment of silence, Hitler began talking.[4]

The two discussed the conquest of the French Atlantic ports—U-boats had been able to operate from the Bay of Biscay bases since the fall of France in June, cutting 500 miles off their journey to the hunting grounds. They discussed the progress of the war, the need for better air reconnaissance, and a boost in submarine production.

Hitler took note of Lieutenant Commander Kretschmer's comments, then stood and said, "Thank you, Commander. You have been admirably frank, and I shall do what I can for you and your colleagues." Then the führer shot out, "You will be lunching here with me."[5]

Lunch followed immediately, with about a dozen civilians

and military officers as guests. The servants attending were all SS personnel. Kretschmer enjoyed the conversation; the fare was excellent. After lunch, Lieutenant Commander Kretschmer retired with some of the guests for coffee, brandy, and cigars. He left in the afternoon. That night, his private car took Kretschmer to the State Opera, where he sat in the State Box, filled with flowers, reserved only for Hitler and the most distinguished state representatives. After a glittering performance of *Tannhäuser*, Kretschmer returned to the Kaiserhof.

On the 16th, four days after his arrival in Berlin, Kretschmer flew back to Lorient in an airplane of the "Führer Squadron," one of Hitler's own aircraft.

He flew first to Kiel to gather some of his own effects, then it was off to a small retreat outside Lorient frequented by German officers, for several days in the French countryside and fields. The other two great aces of the U-boat service, Joachim Schepke and Günther Prien, both friends, joined Kretschmer, and the troika of glittering champions had a dinner of the finest food available on the Atlantic coast, to celebrate Kretschmer's decoration. The dinner was memorable, there was champagne. Then the days of peace and fun ebbed to a close, the fading dusks began to slant west toward Lorient, and it was back to sea.

*U-99* put out, pointing her prow north once more, on November 27. She sortied, hailing north and west, marauding the empty leagues of the North Atlantic once again.

They were alone. They were alone in an open boat. There were sixteen of them, pulling on their oars, pulling, drawing, their backs bent over their oarlocks. The face of the sea was blank and empty and vast all around. The survivors of the *San Demetrio*, which had been attacked by the *Admiral Scheer* in convoy one day before, rowed along, not speaking, stroking, back, dip, raise, back. There was nothing to be seen, anywhere around, in any direction, for hundreds of miles. They pulled, hauling by rote, leaning over the thwarts of their open boat, as small as a dot on the huge face of the sea. Calum Macneil kept up a steady chant to give them a rhythm for their beat, back, dip, raise, back. Nothing showed anywhere on the horizon, not a smoke trail, not a mast, not a speck. They dipped and stroked; Macneil chanted. They were hundreds of miles from land, from any-thing. The sky was an empty dome of blue. All around were only the traveling swells of the Atlantic.

In the evening a storm came up. The wind began to build, then mounted to a blow; soon it was howling, the waves as big as bluffs. The little boat pitched and toppled to the tops of the waves, then bounded down into the gray, undulating troughs. They spent the night at their oars, shivering, soaked, pulling, bucking, and bobbing over the mountainous seas.

In the early morning, the weather slackened, falling off to a gentle blow. Mr. Hawkins, the second officer, carefully doled out biscuits and a dipper of water to each man. They resumed their rowing, drawing on their oars, pulling, stroking, their backs bent low under the sun. The sea was vacant and vast and empty again. The sky was clear and blue. They kept shoving, keeping the pace of Macneil's chant. The wind blew across their necks, off to the north-northwest, out to sea. The ocean around was empty and shimmering. They stroked, not thinking, just pulling, dipping their oars in the water. They pumped; they said nothing. They drew; they rose to the top of a swell; and just as they got to the crest—on the rise of the afternoon—they saw it: a burning hulk. It was there, an apparition, a phantasm—a hulk burning in the distance. At first it was just a form, then it was clearly recognizable: a tanker. First one of them recognized it, then a few more, then their jaws dropped; then all at once the rest of them saw it: it was the *San Demetrio*. She hadn't gone down.

They went back to their oars like beggars before a pirate's treasure. They pulled with new life in their shoulders. They pulled, and she drifted down upon them. They drew nearer and stood off. She was a ghastly sight. Two fires raged and every time she rolled, the low, huge oiler shipped green water across her well decks.

They spent one more miserable night in the launch; in the morning the tanker was nowhere in sight, but soon she drifted into view. They rigged a passable sail; Macneil took the tiller, the wind caught, and they set out on a kind of bounding sleigh ride, speeding and tumbling over the waves to the wreck. The sail tugged, the bow of the boat raced through the waves. They drew up, and at last at 9:30, on the morning of November 7, they slowly came to and maneuvered up on the starboard side of the hulk of the battered, immolated, ruined M/V *San Demetrio*, 850 miles due west of Ireland, out in the middle of the Atlantic, cast away on the ocean.

There was a damaged Jacob's ladder dangling down her side; Mr. Hawkins and Chief Pollard climbed aboard, then the others slowly pulled themselves up the ladder; and at last, all of them stood in a dazed, stooped circle on the deck of the tanker. They were exhausted. John Lewis Jones's lips were blistered, badly swollen. George Willey, the third engineer, had feet disfigured due to exposure. John Davies, the storekeeper, and John Boyle, the greaser, had damaged ribs and could not move without great pain. The salt-stained, weary, drooping men stood on the buckled decks of the giant, slick with oil.

She was a terrible sight to see. The midships housing was destroyed; the navigation bridge atop the deckhouse was gone, with the wireless, compasses, steering gear, charts, and signal flags. Forward, all the superstructure had been crumpled. The only accommodations left were starboard, aft. Of key importance, the steward's stores with all the food they might find on the ship were completely gutted. The main freshwater tanks were gone, too, but two tanks aft had survived. The whole, long alley of the main deck was pocked with holes, studded, a field of twisted metal. Two vast fires blazed from the London-registered tanker, the worst one from the meat room at the stern, another on the foredeck, above No. 7 Port Tank.

The situation was grim; they had much to do. They put their heads together immediately, and conferred. They divided tasks. Some would have to see to the many holes in the deck. They would have to get bucket parties and extinguishers ready to fight the fires. They stood by the deckhouse; all the way forward, the oiler was a derelict. They finished up, finalized arrangements. Then Chief Pollard went down to the engine room to the heart of the mammoth which must power them.

In the catwalks, levels, and cavernous companionways of the engine room gloom, Chief Pollard and his men waded through the pools of water that had accumulated and made the space a lagoon—and rapidly ascertained certain things. The engine room was a mixed picture. The ship's generator, one boiler, and the electrical cables sending power through the ship were all out of commission. But the starboard auxiliary boiler was working; the lubricating system and water-cooling array for the engine were in order; and, best of all, the main engine itself was sound. This was critical. Their plan was to resurrect the *San Demetrio* and sail back, all the way across the wide, unending ocean, to Britain; the engine was indispensable to the plan.

Chief Pollard immediately got the starboard boiler fired up and connected a hose to the ballast pump, so hoses could be used to fight the deck fires. Now the men above on the buckled decks of the 463-foot ship fed the hoses up from below, leading them forward and aft. Astern, they trained the nozzles on the flames, playing the hoses over and over across the billowing smoke and the blaze, sending gallon upon gallon jetting onto the fire threatening their ship. Forward, at the blazing inferno on the foredeck, over No. 7 Port Tank, the bucket and extinguisher party threw bucketload after bucketload onto the conflagration there, firing the six extinguishers, and the thirty-six refills they had, keeping a steady chain of buckets coming up from below. Other teams plugged holes in the deck with cotton waste and blocks of soft wood, pumped out the engine room, then repaired and reconnected the damaged electrical cables. At last, a crew was able to get in and cut away the cork and cement insulation in the meat locker, so the hoses could get at the core of the fire there. All day long, the fires raged and the men toiled on their endangered, isolated ship.

The battle for the *San Demetrio* went on through the day on the 7th of November. In the middle of the day, to the great delight of the men, four cases of blackened eggs were found and John Lewis Jones, the apprentice, came across a joint of beef burnt to a crisp. Chief Pollard boiled some water for tea; and the first food the men had eaten in three days was served out, a royal banquet of blackened eggs and charred beef, with tea. To the sixteen men, the spread was finer than a feast of Tournedos Rossini, served with vintage Bordeaux.

Finally, as a lavender evening fell across the ocean, by eight o'clock on the 7th, the fires were out. Not a spark or a cinder flickered anywhere on her hull. The *San Demetrio* was sound. She was safe. The sixteen survivors stood depleted, slack-shouldered from exhaustion. They were covered with soot; they were filthy. They were also among those very few men who fumble across the line of last capability to the extreme zone of bare survival. They were standing, they were alive. The evening fell like a vast curtain of darkness, dropping to that state where the sky is just three shades lighter than the ocean, closing over the sea.

Later that night, on November 8, with the sea flooding wide and full to the east, the ship was in order and secure. The *San Demetrio* was regained. They were ready to test the engine—and the improbable notion that they could sail the ship back to England.

Above all in importance to their plan, the bridge was destroyed, so there was no means of communication with the engine room. To set up some means of passing orders, Chief Pollard rigged a system of light bulbs overhead in the engine room; the lights, when certain ones lit, signaled "ahead," "astern," or "stop."

Almost as vital, the steering system, which guided the whole assembly of pumps, rams, and rudder post, had been completely destroyed as well. The men tackled the breakdown, and finally managed to get the "trick steering," the emergency system, functioning adequately. Only the hub, four spokes, and some of the rim were left on the trick wheel, but they got it rigged again. On top of the steering situation, the binnacle, containing the compass, had crashed through two decks. It was recovered and set in place. This was critical. If they were to make their way back home, they needed a compass by which to steer.

At last, at 2:30 A.M., in the pitch black of the night found only far out at sea, the moment for which they had worked over three unending days had arrived. The ship could be sailed. They were ready to test the engine, and, if it would start, begin their long voyage across the sea to Britain.

Chief Pollard went below, down the catwalks and ladderways and levels of the engine room, got everything ready, and summoned his men. Then he went through the starting procedure, cranked up the rig—and the massive engine jumped, roared, and thundered to life in a peal of turning, drive, and power. He took it to 90 revolutions per minute; it was go all the way; a helm order went to the helmsman—and the *San Demetrio* set off, shoving and plunging and driving across the open Atlantic.

They were airborne. She raced over the seas, taking the brunt of the swells, battering through the waves as she slid. It was 1,013 miles to home, a long, flying, arcing distance of ruffled waves, temperature, and sky—a long, winging, windy span across the sea to Britain. They figured they had every possibility of hitting Ireland; but without navigation equipment it was just as likely they would hit France, which was occupied by the Germans.

So they went, plunging across the waves, the bow sluicing across the seas, and parting them as they came, throwing sheets of spray to the side, the *San Demetrio* riding like a toboggan over the hillocks of water. Her forecastle and deckhouses cut a dark, stenciled silhouette against the sky, her port bridge wing a dark lattice against the clouds, the sea gray and blown spume all around, the sky overcast in a slate wash.

The odyssey was more than incongruous; it was a wonder. They had no charts, no compass—the binnacle had proved unworkable—no navigational instruments, no aids, not even a set of dividers; they were sailing by bare fist and naked will, blind, back 1,000 miles across the sea.

Even their most rudimentary attempts at dead reckoning were frustrated. The ship's chronometer was destroyed and the men's watches were waterlogged. Without knowing the time, they could not establish their position. The conundrum worked the other way, too—without knowing their position, they could not determine the correct time. They had to depend on the sun's progress.

They sailed by guesstimate and sense. They could determine their course only by the dim glow of the sun, in the west when it set, by sightings of the stars in the great, silky ceiling of the heavens by glimmer of night, then by the faint tint of light over the horizon, in the east when the sun rose.

Later a school geography textbook turned up, but the maps were too rudimentary to help.

The ship kept making 9 knots; the *San Demetrio* held up seam and keel; and they drove across the Atlantic, running through the big, following swells that carried the tanker along. They made just over 200 miles a day, far from top speed, but about convoy speed, the ship leaving a white wake behind.

On Sunday, November 10, a bad gale blew and seas were breaking across the main deck, but Mr. Hawkins gave a short religious service. There was no prayerbook aboard, but one of the seamen, Oswald Preston, a Canadian, produced a Bible given to him by his children. The men gathered together, and Mr. Hawkins read the Lord's Prayer and recited what he remembered of the Form of Prayer to Be Used at Sea.

"Look down, we beseech thee, and hear us, calling out of the depth of misery, and out of the jaws of this death, which is ready now to swallow us up. Save, Lord, or else we perish. The living, the living, shall praise thee. O, send thy word of command to rebuke the raging winds, and the roaring sea . . ."

Boyle died. The compact little greaser, whose ribs had been injured, died in his bunk. He collapsed in the engine room; they had to lay him up in a surviving cabin; try as they did to force condensed milk down his throat and keep him warm, he finally failed after his long struggle. Having done his share of toil from the lifeboat to the engine room, despite the pain of his injured ribs, he succumbed in his sleep, going to the lee of final harbor.

For two more days, the *San Demetrio* hauled east, ever east. She drove along, bucking the seaway, sailing straight through U-boat country. The crew stood half watches, so the others could sleep, and the ship could be sailed around the clock, keeping their sightings by the sunset, by the stars, by the dawn. The *San Demetrio* did her part and left the gray, wind-blown miles behind her. Finally, the great trans-ocean passage began to close and they drew nearer to land.

On November 12, Mr. Hawkins took the momentous step of setting double lookouts; he expected they would sight land that night or the next day. The men stood to their watches, half in disbelief at their progress, half in suspense as to where they would find themselves.

On the afternoon of Wednesday, November 13, at precisely 1:30, the break: they sighted land. It was elevated, green. The spit before them had high bluffs with green grass on top. As they neared the coast, they could see black rocks leading out from the shore to the sea. At length, they found a small, sheltered bay where they could put in safely, and spent most of the night making the *San Demetrio* secure. It was a big ship with much to tend to.

In the morning they gave Boyle a burial at sea. They covered his body in the Red Ensign, the flag of the British Merchant

Navy, and, standing in a lone cluster, they committed him to the deep. The second officer said the Lord's Prayer and the 23rd Psalm out of Oswald Preston's Bible.

"The Lord is my shepherd; I shall not want. He maketh me to lie down in green pastures: he leadeth me beside the still waters . . ."

Then they returned his body to the waters.

The rest of the morning, they worked, preparing the ship for harbor. They had tried for a long time to raise a response from the shore, with no success. There was a lighthouse, but it was impossible to signal to it since the signal flags had burned in the fire. They shut down the engine room, watched the land and waited. An hour passed. Then, suddenly, steaming up the bay came a naval tug, *Superman*. Someone ashore had seen them, and summoned help.

They were in Ireland. It was November 14, 1940, and they were in Blacksod Bay, Ireland.

# 5

THE SIXTEEN MEN OF THE *SAN DEMETRIO* CAME TO hold a distinct and celebrated place in history; thousands of other burly, rude seamen went mostly unheralded—Greeks, Dutchmen, Swedes, Americans, Lascars (Indian and other Asian seamen working for lower pay), Chinese, British, Nigerians, many more—the bandy, rugged merchant marine sailors who played a role as important as that of the navy gobs, crewing the freighters and tankers which bore the cargoes that fueled the armies in Europe. Strapping men, able, ready to serve, they were ordinary seamen of no special title, no embellished place or privileged station, tough men, dirty men who kept the cargoes going through torpedo, gun, the most unimaginable dangers. Displaying brass and moxie, merchant seamen faced U-boats, aerial attack, surface attacks, mines, and much more.

In the most basic terms, the merchant seamen were, when all

was said and done, the linchpin of the Battle of the Atlantic. Ordinary naval battles were about warships slugging it out for control of the seas. But the Battle of the Atlantic was about cargo. It was a fight to sink—or defend—these vital supplies borne by the merchant ships: it revolved around the indispensable stores hauled by the "heroes in dungarees."

One succinct analysis estimated that the loss of two 6,000-ton ships and one 3,000-ton tanker meant the loss of forty-two tanks, eight 6-inch howitzers, eighty-eight 25-pound guns, forty 2-pound guns, twenty-four armored cars, fifty Bren carriers, 5,112 tons of ammunition, 600 rifles, 428 tons of tank supplies, 2,000 tons of stores, and 1,000 tanks of gasoline.

No wonder Dönitz so wanted to enlarge his fleet of submarines, no wonder he so prized the sinking of one of these merchant ships.

The great globe-straddling convoy operation, which impelled the convoys over the vast, climbing track of the North Atlantic, 2,500 miles across, was, quite simply, the greatest cargo-lift operation in history. To derive some sense of what a convoy was like, it is necessary to consider the bare facts of the North Atlantic convoy operation.

On any given day, four to five convoys were in motion on the sea, heading for Britain or returning to America. They were huge. It took about two weeks for a convoy to cross. A typical convoy had some forty ships in it, arranged in eight columns, each five rows deep. There were 1,000 yards between columns, 400 to 600 yards between a ship and the ones ahead and behind her. When fully spread out on the face of the sea, each flotilla covered a tremendous area, perhaps twelve or fifteen square miles.

The ships were the plebeian, workman heroes. Many were gleaming and new, like the *San Demetrio*; others were black tramps long into their years, aging, their square bridges still functional. There were sleek house liners with fresh paint, Luckenbach, Moore-McCormack, American Export Lines; ships near breakdown, ships with outdated machinery, others with finicky steering gear; still others had a weather helm—they tended to steer in one direction. They were of every class and category. Breakbulk ships, with their masts and rigging, sailed alongside bulk ships, with their long, clean hulls; World War I Hog Islanders (ships built under the emergency ship production program at Hog Island, Philadelphia) steamed next to tankers, passenger ships, trawlers. The average convoy of ships ran the gamut from the finest, the most modern and efficient, to the oldest beasts, with their creaking cross heads and tender engine plants. The convoy commodore's ship stood at the vanguard of the formation, in the middle position of the first row.

Consider then the almost incredible skill of the masters who steamed for two weeks across the Atlantic, holding position faithfully and constantly, adjusting speed, advancing and backing, staying just 1,000 yards from the ships to the left and right, 500 yards from the ships in back and in front. With a thoroughly varied cross section of differing engines, varying steering qualities, different hull characteristics, the ships nudged forward, dropped back, yawed, bobbed across the ocean. The infernal job of the shipmasters in staying on station demanded the seamanship and competence of a Columbus, crossed with the calm and patience of a Confucius. It is doubtful that the herculean feat of the convoys, precision sailing in formation across the sea time and again, through six long years of war, will ever be repeated.

The conduct, safety, and order of this motley armada with its international mix was the chief province of the convoy commodore. Generally retired Royal Navy officers who held the rank of rear admiral, these men led in noble service. Of the abiding goodwill and capabilities of the convoy commodores, it may be noted that only one acquired a bad reputation for ill temper and crankiness. His crusty qualities were put to invaluable use elsewhere: he was Vice Admiral Gilbert O. Stephenson, who went on to head the escort training program at Tobermory.

Commodores, and most ships, used signal flags as the primary means of communication; ships learned fast what signal pennants meant. The pennant for the letters "V, D" meant "You are ahead of station." "V, E" was for laggards who were falling too far behind, "You are astern of station." "V, H" was one nobody liked to get. It stood for "You are keeping station badly. Endeavor to do better."

There were bleaker ones than that. "T, D" meant "If you cannot maintain present speed, you will have to proceed independently unescorted."

The most important signal of all was the number "1" pendant with six short blasts of the siren. It meant: "Submarine in sight . . . or track of torpedo . . . on starboard side." The number "2" pendant with two groups of six short blasts was for torpedoes on the port side.

So the convoy progressed, passing through five time zones, proceeding across the Atlantic wastes, shuffling to England in tandem, a city of grimy hands checking deck fixtures, hatches, anchor rigging, cargo stowage, or, in the amber catacombs of the engine room, oiling, repairing, stoking furnaces, minding Scotch boilers (early, primitive ship boilers), tending to the jungle of engines, generators, pumps, and piping which made up the gloomy, glimmering kingdom of a transatlantic, deep-sea engine room. But everything stopped when the number 1 pendant and the six short blasts of the siren came along. A white rocket or a telegraphed "SSS" meant the same thing: "Submarine attack."

Joseph E. Bodner of Massapequa Park, New York, was a twenty-two-year-old ordinary seaman on his first trip out on SS *William Gaston* when the ship was torpedoed off Buenos Aires on July 20, 1943.

At 8:20 that night, in the vast, void black of the South Atlantic, a torpedo slammed into the *Gaston* aft of her bridge, exploding suddenly with a deafening roar. The entire ship ran with tumbling feet as men rushed for their life jackets. "I was doing my laundry and one of the armed guard gunners . . . says, 'Joe, on a Sunday night?' One minute later—BOOM. The thing blows up. I was doing my laundry and it knocked me on my ass. It didn't dawn on me that it was a torpedo. I didn't want to think it was." [1]

The lights dimmed, then went out. Bodner groped his way through the dark ship to his bunk to get his life jacket, then escaped with the ship's carpenter via an escape hatch. They wound up on the afterdeck in the cool pit of the night. Debris was still falling through the air. Every time the ship rolled, a geyser of water would shoot in through the torpedo hole, at the rate of thousands of gallons a minute. The carpenter and Bodner knew they were in trouble and ran for the boat deck. There, men were gathering to abandon ship. In the press of sailors, one of Bodner's friends turned to him and said, "Joe, I come from Philadelphia. If I don't survive and you do, will you stop and tell my folks I loved them?" Bodner said he would, and then asked the same favor of his friend. Then an officer came down— and the ship's whistle sounded seven blasts. Bodner made it into one of the lifeboats.

The boat was lowered, the sailors cut the lines free, and they rowed away from the *Gaston*, rowed for their lives, rowed into the night. Behind them, as they left, their ship went down. They would spend four days in that open lifeboat.

That night a storm was blowing; it would go on for two days. In the wind and the blowing spray, the little boat struggled to the tops of the waves, then slid down the faces into the troughs. The darkness was soaked and impenetrable and thick, and they could see nothing but the phosphorescence of the waves. Two of the men in the boat had no clothes so the chief engineer and another sailor gave them a jacket and a sweater; three of the men in the boat were injured. The seas shipped in and they bailed constantly. "You go up and down," recalls Bodner. "The seas were six-foot seas, so you go about four or five feet, because you don't go as far as the sea, you just go part way up. It was a ride, anyway. We were all wet. Hypothermia was hitting us, so by morning we'd become zombies."

The sun rose, gray and grim. They were wet, cold. They had a keg of water and some pemmican, dried meat mixed with lard. They had two blankets and a sail. They had a reliable lifeboat compass, which enabled them to steer a course and keep heading west across the desolate tract of the South Atlantic. They talked to pass the time; they fished some, but without any luck. By day they rowed and sailed under the hot sun, which had finally come out; by night they took turns resting. All around them, the sea was blank and bare, a flat mesa marked only by unending distance. "We were bailing all the time. After a while, everybody was so tired, we didn't even bail. There was water left in the boat," Bodner recalls. At night they hung a lantern at their masthead. Day after day, the small boat pitched across the sea.

Then, on the afternoon of the third day, in one of those seemingly interminable hours of slow rowing, one of the injured sailors said to Bodner, "Joe, could I hold your rosaries?" The man had seen Bodner praying with his rosaries on the *Gaston*. "So I reached in my pocket and gave them to him. And he's laying there and about fifteen minutes later he said, 'There's a plane.' We thought he was delirious. He said, 'There's this plane on the horizon.' So I turn around, and sure enough, there's a plane this far off the horizon. It was a PBM Mariner. So I said, 'Mate, there's a plane on the horizon.' The mate says, 'What?' So he looks over there and says, 'Break out that signaling mirror.'" They grabbed the signal mirror and began wildly flashing it at the plane. The plane kept approaching. They flashed the signal mirror, the plane kept coming in. Then all at once, the aircraft started flashing its lights. They could see it plainly. Over and over, a U.S. Navy PBM was flashing its lights. They had been seen. They were saved. The plane roared past them overhead, then droned away out of sight. It finally disappeared, a speck in the sky. But they knew they had been spotted.

The next day, the seaplane tender USS *Matagorda* hove into sight. At first she was just a chip on the horizon, then a tiny form, then a vessel with masts and a bridge. She was enormous, a castle, flying the Stars-and-Stripes. The *Matagorda* approached. Then she pulled up, eased forward, and drew alongside them.

Bodner was the last man out of the boat. He refused any assistance getting onto the ship, at which point, being unsteady after four days sitting in a lifeboat, he almost fell into the water. The sailors caught him and hauled him aboard. The thirteen men from the *William Gaston* had survived their ordeal. The *Matagorda* steamed on; she left the Gaston survivors in Florianopolis, Brazil.

From Florianopolis, they got a ship to Rio de Janeiro. They

flew by C-47 transport to Recife, then by C-46 to Trinidad, and finally home to Miami. Their wearying ordeal was over.

Torpedoes were not the only dangers merchant mariners confronted. Others faced V-2 rockets and Luftwaffe attacks. George Goldman, then a twenty-one-year-old mess boy on the oil tanker *Patrick J. Hurley*, faced *U-512*, commanded by Kptlt. Wolfgang Schultze.

At 8:30 at night on September 12, 1942, Schultze approached the *Hurley* on the surface and all of a sudden began machine-gunning the bridge. He peppered the fort with numerous fusillades, then he opened up with his 88mm deck gun. Goldman, belowdecks, at first thought the machine gun fire was a pail rattling on the deck. Then the lights went out. The engineers came streaming up from below, leaving behind the engine room. The ship kept hurtling on, blasted away as she was. Goldman rushed to the boat deck, a sailor cut loose a life raft, which slid into the water. Goldman didn't hesitate another moment. He plunged from the ship into the sea and began swimming. There was fire on the water where oil had spilled, but the mess boy kept going. He made it to the life raft, climbed aboard—and then passed out.

He came to the next morning, others on the life raft with him. They clung to the float, adrift on the sea and marooned without hope, but soon they came upon an overturned lifeboat. The men worked on the boat and managed to get it righted and bail it out. They had no oars or mast and sail, but later in the day, Goldman spotted two oars, jumped into the water, swam out, and brought them back. The men lashed the oars together to fashion a jury-rigged mast and sail, and the twenty-one stranded men in the salvaged lifeboat began a grueling, stark, week-long journey, 485 miles across the ocean.

The ruined *Hurley* had gone down 850 miles northeast of Barbados. Now, sailing back west again, they hoped to make the Bahamas, if they stayed on course. They had biscuits, pemmican, and a keg of water. The fierce sun was their worst enemy. Goldman today plays down any drama. "It was just a matter of sitting, yakking, trying to keep busy; the thing that I recall that was the worst was the wooden thwarts that we were sitting on. We were all skinny young fellows . . . and [the thwarts] just seemed to be grinding into our bones. I had no clothes, I think I just had on . . . a pair of drawers and my eyeglasses. Most of the guys were about the same, so it would be a little cool at night." [2]

So they persisted, half naked under the sun, the boat slowly sailing west, all of them resolute. In the morning they got one ounce of water in a tin can and one fifth of a small can of pemmican; in the evening they received the same ration. The hunger never bothered Goldman, but the terrible thirst did. "After a couple of days, you don't feel the hunger, but you feel thirsty," he said. Eating the crackers was "like trying to eat sand." Often they found tiny creatures, krill, lodged in the clumps of seaweed they passed. The men spent hours picking the tiny crustaceans from the seaweed and cracking them with their teeth for a tiny squirt of fresh water. The constant farming of krill became a ritual of their saga.

On they trailed, slipping across the waves. They had a compass, and so they could bear slowly west, riding over the lapping waves. The stronger ones took turns steering and keeping a lookout. The days passed and the sun bore down on their backs. Once a storm came up. Goldman says they "had to practically beat some of the guys up" to get them to put on life jackets.

"They became very lethargic." It was a wet and woolly ride, but the storm passed. On they sailed, running with the trade winds, west toward the Bahamas. Each morning they had a ration of pemmican and water; each evening another was given out. Sometimes they fished; in the night they kept a chilly vigil. Goldman says they never despaired; it was too short a time for them to become truly desperate.

"I guess we were worried and that kind of stuff, but we were all pretty much young fellows and we were sure we were going to be picked up . . . maybe in another week or two." The *Hurley* survivors kept on in their open boat, day passing to night, and back to day.

On the seventh day of their journey, at night, they sighted the lights of a ship. The ship came closer, approached; it slowly circled the boat a couple of times to be sure it wasn't a trap. Then it drew up. The ship was Swedish, named the *Aetna*. Their wearying odyssey was over. The *Aetna* took them aboard, headed on; she was bound for New York, where she dropped them, and where they were reunited with American soil.

The American Merchant Marine was rough, ready, burly, indispensable in filling the convoys. American merchant mariners by the tens of thousands volunteered for sea duty, many as young as sixteen, spewing out of training schools and academies in Brooklyn, the Great Lakes, and San Francisco. But nothing was equal in importance to the British Merchant Navy, immense, covering the range of the seven seas, reaching to the four corners of the earth. At the start of the war, the British Merchant Navy approached something on the order of a constellation, with 3,000 ships and 1,000 coasting vessels, aggregating a huge 20.4 million tons, as opposed to the U.S. fleet, which comprised just under 9.4 million tons. British deckhands, stokers, wipers, oilers, donkeymen (engineers who maintained machinery), and water tenders manned furnaces, boilers, winches, deck tackle on a tremendous fleet of ships scattered worldwide. A population of 159,000 British seamen and officers manned the Commonwealth's ships, compared to a 1940 strength of 55,000 U.S. sailors. Although by war's end, the U.S. Merchant Marine surpassed the British Merchant Navy with a strength of 215,000 men, British tars manned the gunwales of a truly magisterial fleet.

The U.S. and Britain were the major fodder and fill of the convoy effort; that effort was polyglot. A broad array of other Allied nations provided tankers, tramps, and men to the sealift. The Greek merchant navy provided 650 ships to the convoy span; one gauge of Greece's enormous sacrifice is that more than 500 of these ships were lost during the war. The Dutch, Norwegians, Belgians, Finns, Swedes, others sailed in the convoy ranks; the crews were of all races, colors, nationalities. Casualties were high. The British Merchant Navy suffered 30,000 lost; in addition 6,000 American sailors went to their deaths. The job was tough, the pay was low. A British ordinary seaman in 1942 earned 22 pounds a month—about $45—including a danger bonus. The U.S. merchant seamen's union drove a hard bargain, and American mariners made roughly $90 a month, or twice as much, plus a bonus for North Atlantic duty and full life insurance. It was hardly lavish compensation for the dangers the merchant marine faced.

Why did men, of any nation, who were poorly paid, little respected, under no military obligation, completely free in choice, go back to sea time and time again of their own accord to face torpedoings, trials in lifeboats and on rafts, the prospect of death by starvation or exposure, and the many other dangers merchant seamen confronted?

Most went for one reason. It was their billet, their work, their part of the war. "It was my job," says Goldman. "There was a war on. It was a personal job, being Jewish. I felt I was contributing something."

Like Goldman, most sailors went back to sea because they felt it was their duty, some kind of personal obligation, an imperative to return to the struggle against the Nazis. "It was wartime. So you gotta keep sailing," says Joe Bodner. "Life goes on. That's the attitude. So we shipped out in those days," he recalls in a view voiced by many.

The merchant mariners always went back. They went up the gangplanks, stowed their duffel bags under their bunks, took up the hawsers, the rigging, the coal shovels, and they turned to. The ships set out, from Halifax or Cape Breton in Nova Scotia, they shoved in their columns across the sea, swaying and bobbing in their formations; if they were lucky the tars came ashore in Liverpool or Clydebank for a few days in the blacked-out harbors which by 1941 had been devastated by bombing raids, where no hero's welcome awaited them. If they were not lucky, they took a torpedo. A deafening roar split the night; a ship went up in flames, they abandoned ship and spent days in lifeboats until they were picked up. But if they survived, the merchant mariners always went back to sea again.

# 6

ON THE WALLS OF BdU, IN PARIS, BEHIND THE ornate facade of the building on the Boulevard Suchet that fall of 1940, the charts and graphs pinned up in the warren of rooms told a satisfying story. Admiral Dönitz could strut by the data and tables content; Captain Eberhard Godt, the chief of operations, could be confident. The U-boats of Nazi Germany now lay in an arc off the waters of England, descending in a big, curving crescent from the Hebrides, just off northern Scotland, down to the gentle shunt of Cape Clear, Ireland. The picture was one of accumulating successes; the sea war was entering its second year, unfolding with promise. In September, all across Europe, across the belt of the Low Countries, the territories to the east, Germany occupied the lands which her armies had overrun. A Greek counteroffensive had pushed the Axis powers back; Greece, though, would fall in May.

Britain was embattled. Britain persisted in the face of Göring's bombing. Londoners and their countrymen all across England persevered, accustomed now to the rubble they saw in the streets, to the hardships the war had brought. The German battle at sea, like the jaws of a vise pressing closed, had begun to choke supplies more seriously. Total imports would fall from 55 million tons in 1939 to 30 million tons in 1941. Food imports had plummeted from a prewar 22 million tons to under 12 million tons, the minimum needed for Britain to survive. The losses in shipping had begun to seriously affect the food supply. Since January 1940, rations on bacon, ham, butter, and sugar had steadily diminished. Meat and cheese were in short supply, eggs virtually nonexistent. That March, facing the losses in the U-boat war and the crisis of supply in Britain, Churchill had proclaimed "The Battle of the Atlantic"—the term by which, forever after, the conflict on the Atlantic Ocean during World War II would be known. In March, also, Churchill established a top-level "Battle of the Atlantic Committee," chaired by himself, to deal with every aspect of the U-boat situation. For the moment, the Atlantic war went on, ever tightening the clamp around Britain. Hitler's U-boats continued to hunt, to rove and attack and devastate the plodding, tumbling convoys which came in now over the top of Ireland, into the North Channel.

Thus, to the planners at BdU, poring over their maps, collating their reports from commanders at sea, sifting through the data from German intelligence, the success of the U-boat war lay in the jabs the subs could throw throughout these northern approaches to England. Dönitz's crews were scoring there steadily, successfully. "The Happy Time," as commanders called it, went on.

Out at sea, notably, on the quick, gray face of the Irish approaches, new aces now stood at the head of the service.

Joachim Schepke would account for thirty-seven ships, would be awarded the Oak Leaves to the Knight's Cross. Heinrich Bleichrodt would sink twenty-eight ships, would also receive the Oak Leaves to his Knight's Cross. And the Golden Ace of the U-boat fleet, Otto Kretschmer, hunted on, hailing, hailing, ever north, stalking his quarry across the gray and fickle sea.

"Silent Otto," "Wise Otto," "Immortal Otto," they called him. The bow of *U-99* hurtled along, clipping through the waves, hurrying through the sea, racing across the Atlantic at 17 knots, leaving a boiling wake behind. It was March now, spring of 1941. There were two lookouts on the bridge, and Kretschmer, and they could see nothing. A thick fog cloaked the ocean all about; even the bow of the boat was invisible. Kretschmer was in his gray leather U-boat commander's coat, leaning into the bridge bulkhead with a pair of fine, high-optical-quality binoculars minted specially by Zeiss for the top U-boat aces. He said nothing, kept to himself, his intense brow nearly hidden by the glasses. Germany's top ace was, most discernibly, a prism, hard, clear, faceted.

Kretschmer, icy, was something of a mystery. By 1938 his fellow officers had reckoned he was the best torpedo shot in the German navy. After the war he would become an admiral in NATO. Once, in an accident, he had been left topside when his submarine dove unexpectedly. Kretschmer had taken a swim in the Atlantic, then been fished out of the water when the sub resurfaced. He had faced his commanding officer with the rather unruffled remark: "Reporting back on board, sir."

Admiral Karl Dönitz had written of him in a 1939 report on his character:

For his age he is of unusually quiet but inwardly strong and definite character. Very sympathetic, modest and well-bred in manners and appearance. Never tries to make much of himself. . . . Mentally alert, varied interest, well read, interesting to talk to, once he has gotten over a certain shyness and reserve. Inclined to be a lone wolf and make up his mind on all things for himself, but in spite of this popular with his colleagues, through his basically cheerful and comradely manner, as well as his dry humor.[1]

With a rounded brow, clear eyes, a strong jaw, and thin face, Kretschmer was hewn from a different timber, cool, private—notably, not very favorable toward the Nazi Party. He refused to write his memoirs for the propaganda machine of Joseph Goebbels. A British report on him commented: "He gave the impression of being a quiet, deliberate man, and looked more like a student than a U-boat captain. His political views were less extremely Nazi than had been assumed."[2]

Kretschmer was an anomaly in the compassion he was capable of feeling for his enemy, which prompted him to remark once, "The war at sea was always fought with chivalry." The young lieutenant commander was in the habit of stopping by the lifeboats of the merchant ships he torpedoed, whenever possible, to make sure the men had a compass course to land, bread and water. Kretschmer was insular, belonged to himself, a virtuoso, one of gallantry.

Far out to sea, on one patrol in September 1940, Horst Elfe, the second watch officer under Kretschmer on *U-99*, recalled picking up a survivor from a torpedoed merchant ship, the *Baron Blythswood*, about 500 miles off the British Isles. The waterlogged man was brought aboard, then taken below, into the narrow spaces of the submarine.

"Kretschmer said to me, 'Let us try to help the poor fellow.' He said: 'Elfe, you go help him.' He [the survivor] was already nearly stiff and quite exhausted from standing on the raft."[3] Elfe and the crew of *U-99* brought the man into the berthing spaces below, and gave him a blanket and a cup of tea.

The man woke up, groggy, drenched; then he began to talk. "I must tell you I am a lucky guy," he said. "I was . . . on the steamer *Baron Blythswood* and we carried iron ore and we were sunk by one of those German Nazi U-boats. The ship went down like a stone."

"I said, Yes," Elfe recalls, "quite natural if you are an iron ore boat."

The British sailor then went on: "I am the only survivor. And now I am so lucky that a submarine of the Royal Navy came and picked me up."

Elfe, president of the Berlin Chamber of Commerce after the war, recalls thinking: "Oh boy."

"I went to Kretschmer and said, 'He thinks he is onboard a submarine of the Royal Navy.' Kretschmer said to me, 'Elfe, you tell him the truth.' Oh my God . . . I tried." Elfe finally got through to the sailor, made him understand that he was on a German U-boat.

The man said, "You're pulling my leg."

Elfe said, " 'No, no, no.' And I tried to then, since we on-board were all wearing overalls with no swastika and no badges, no nothing on the submarine, I said to [myself], try to find a swastika or something like that to show to the man," Elfe recalls. "He broke down. He said, 'My God.' " Elfe told the man, "Be quiet, you will not be killed. You will not be shot, be quiet, you will be all right."

Later that day, *U-99* continued on her way. She slid through the waters, picking up way, heading out on patrol again. Before long, she stumbled across the lifeboat of another torpedoed merchant ship, the British tanker *Invershannon*. The crewmen in the boat were Chinese, with a lone British officer at the helm, who did not speak, watched silently and showed disgust as *U-99* approached. The Chinese, terrified that the submarine had come to kill them, started crying, "Heil Hitler, Heil Hitler!"

Elfe replied, "Oh my God. Shut up, shut up. We just want to give you one of your men. You have the chance to come to Ireland. It's not too far from here. You take him, because we do not want to make prisoners."

Elfe and his men then handed over the exhausted crewman of the *Baron Blythswood* to the Chinese and the officer in the lifeboat. Then the *U-99* crew asked, "Have you got a compass?"

"Yes," the men in the lifeboat responded.

"Have you water?"

"Yes," came the reply. The *U-99* crewmen looked down from the submarine.

"Okay. We give you some water." The sea was open, calm.

"And now bread."

The lifeboat had no bread. The submarine stood by.

"We gave them [a] provision of that. All of a sudden the British officer turned to us, and said, 'Thank you.' " And then, to return the favor, the crewmen in the lifeboat tried to pass the *U-99* crew some packets of British armed forces cigarettes, Woodbine. Alas, it was impossible to smoke on a submarine. *U-99* and the lifeboat parted. The lifeboat pulled away, the men cheering the crew of the looming submarine. "This was even such a situation during the war, one side wished to the other good luck, good hope. They said to us, 'Good luck to you'; and we said to them, 'Good hope to Ireland. Good luck to you also.' This happened in the war; it's still in my memory. It was typical for Kretschmer."

◆   ◆   ◆

He was, too, "The Wolf of the Atlantic," a virtuoso who accounted for 238,327 tons of Allied shipping, the most dangerous foe the Nazis put forth. Now he roved on, ranging across the sea, hustling fast, driving across the empty Atlantic in search of Convoy HX 112. The submarine hurried on, leaving a trail of wake behind her, sluicing through the ocean, the waves coming across her bow. Up they hailed, on to the reported location of the convoy, Kretschmer keeping a vigil on the bridge when he came above. On March 16, they found HX 112; bingo, right on the mark, forty-one ships headed for Liverpool.

Kretschmer followed the convoy through the day. After dark, he began to move in. He headed up the side of HX 112, sneaked forward, and slipped into the convoy between two escort warships. Silently he crept forward. He selected a large tanker on the outward left column of the convoy, moved into attack position, gave torpedo settings for the shot, then he watched, calculated—and fired!

A torpedo shot out of the bow tube, sped through the waves, and slammed into the tanker, the Norwegian *Ferm*, which exploded into flames roaring high into the air. The blaze lit up the whole night sky. Kretschmer scuttled away, out of the light revealing him, retreated. Later he entered the middle of the convoy. He picked out another large tanker, the *Bedouin*, also Norwegian—and shot. The torpedo socked into the *Bedouin* and she, too, erupted in flames as the torpedo exploded against her hull.

"Self-control. His capacity. He had judgment of the situation. Brave. He was always clear in attacking," said Elfe of Kretschmer. "He was very sober in his decisions. And he had a good crew. He had trained his crew very thoroughly in the

Baltic before we went into the Atlantic. Very good training. Hard training. But always fair, and correct. Quiet. Real quiet. Absolute quiet. Decisive in his decision. Perfectly clear in his orders. No trouble and no discussion. In action, his highest quality was that he was quiet, sober, and never got excited or out of his mind."[4]

This was Kretschmer, calculated boldness carried to that narrow, thin zone that exists in the maximum extent just short of doom.

Now, with the flames from the two torpedoed tankers lighting up the sky, Kretschmer stole into another lane of the convoy. He ran along amid the ships for a time, covered by the thick black of the night. He picked a third target—a large tanker. He prepared, made calculations, pulled all the elements of the attack together—and fired. The torpedo slammed into the British *Franche Comte* and she went up in billows of black smoke and orange flames. Time passed. Kretschmer kept dogging the convoy. In time he entered another lane, and picked a fourth target. He moved slowly ahead into the attack position, gave torpedo settings, depth, speed, waited and fired at a large freighter. In a column of smoke and water, the 5,728-ton *Venetia* blew up as the torpedo found its mark. Kretschmer's fifth attack was as precise, deadly, but difficult. He lined up the 7,375-ton Canadian steamer *J. B. White* in his sights, plotted the attack, set, and fired again. The torpedo went speeding through the water and smacked into the *White*; she settled, but did not sink. Kretschmer fired again; he missed. It took a third shot to send the big Canadian breakbulker down. Slowly she settled beneath the surface of the waves. Now Lieutenant Commander Kretschmer was well behind the convoy and he surged ahead to catch up. He hunted, searched, in time he came upon a fourth tanker, his sixth target of the night, the *Korsham*. This time a shot from his stern tube broke the steamer in two, and slowly she settled beneath the waves to an agonized death. She had carried her last cargo. HX 112 moved along, shoving ahead through the ocean, pushing through the inky blackness of the sea at night.

In a matter of hours, "Silent Otto" had accounted for six more ships. His fuel was low, he had expended all his torpedoes, his crew was exhausted from some forty-eight hours at action stations. He set a course north and disappeared.

*U-99* passed Lousy Bank late, running ahead, surging forward, sliding through the satiny waves, leaving the miles behind. Kretschmer went below to talk, to count tonnage, to debrief. A watch officer and two lookouts remained on the bridge. Then it was night, and the enormous frame of the surrounding darkness, and the sub sliding through the sea with nothing else around her. She was clipping through the waves and had much to report back to BdU in Lorient when she arrived. Then later, the watch officer spotted a destroyer, suddenly, unexpectedly; and here, at this sighting, the watch officer made a mistake. Ignoring Kretschmer's standing orders to remain surfaced in the event of a possible attack, he dove. Half a minute, and *U-99* was gone from the surface. She reached a comfortable depth, and then she evened up, crawling through the dark fathoms of the sea, invisible, deadly, creeping through the gloom below the surface.

He did not know exactly what was around him. Standing silent on the bridge of his destroyer, he peered through the dark. He had a pair of binoculars around his neck, and was watching, scanning the surface. It was pitch black, early morning, but what it was exactly, the young Royal Navy officer did not know. He turned, looked at his men, then continued gazing. Commander Donald G. F. W. Macintyre—he had been promoted—the crisp, rulebook escort skipper who had trained as a pilot, had a sonar contact. Macintyre was not sure it was a sub, perhaps a disturbance in the water, a school of fish, who knew what; but then his sonar operator was confirming that it was indeed a sub, and Macintyre knew all he needed to know. He swung his destroyer, HMS *Walker*—he had transferred from *Hesperus*—around and drove in for the kill. The ping of the sonar kept sounding. Macintyre closed in, homing in on the contact. Now he dashed in, the sonar pinging regularly; he primed six depth charges—all that could be gotten ready—and, just as the destroyer crossed over the point where the sub should be, Macintyre loosed his six charges in a pattern into the water.

The sub crept through the gloomy fathoms of the ocean deeps. No one could see her; she was lost in the depths. She crawled on. Her motors barely turned over. She was hidden by the silent leagues. *U-99* edged ahead. Then, all at once, detonations from the six depth charges crashed through the deep, slamming the submarine's hull. The lights went out. The glass dials on the gauges shattered and the chronometers were broken. The men watched each other, not speaking, silent, horrified. The explosions had jarred the hull. Water began streaming into the sub from a broken pipe; oil poured into the control room. The men said nothing, sat motionless in the smell of bodies and diesel fuel. Suddenly, the sub began to dive toward the bottom of the ocean, plunging out of control. The men, aghast, looked with bulging eyes.

"These depth charges were the end of *U-99*, these six depth charges. . . . We went down to a depth that normally would destroy a boat, 220 meters, 270 meters," recalls Volkmar König, a midshipman aboard *U-99* that night. "Normally at 150 meters, you would say, please, not deeper."[5]

The crewmen sat in tense silence as *U-99* plunged through the gloom. The first watch officer read off the depth as the sub continued sailing down, 150 meters, 160 meters, 170 meters. "He had a pale face. . . . He had a white face," recalls König.

Kretschmer reacted with the cool of a pool hall sharpie. He said gently, "Come on and blow," blow the ballast tanks, blow air into the ballast tanks to clear them of water so the boat would go up on its buoyancy.

The tanks were blown, and gradually the sub responded, 140 meters, 130 meters, 120 meters, 100 meters, 90 meters. At 90 meters, Kretschmer ordered, "Stop blow." The blowing stopped; the submarine stabilized—and then, horribly, *U-99* began to dive down again through the fathoms, losing buoyancy. All stared in desperation at the depth meter. Kretschmer had no choice now but to blow to the surface. He used the last air to blow his tanks; *U-99* rose through the water, climbed and broke through above water.

Immediately, gunfire poured upon the sub from *Walker* and HMS *Vanoc*, another escort. Enter Commander Macintyre. Fierce 4.7-inch gunfire and pompom tracers tore into the wounded sub. Kretschmer, in the black of night, summoned the crew onto the main deck: they would have to abandon ship. König was standing next to the commander on the decks, now slanting; Kretschmer told him, "We are going to die a hero's death." From his bridge, Kretschmer now flashed Macintyre a message across the dark by semaphore: "CAPTAIN TO CAPTAIN. I AM SUNKING [sic]. PLEASE RESCUE MY CREW."

At this point, in the midst of a running convoy battle, Macintyre took the highly unusual step of stopping HMS *Walker*, so the German crew could be picked up.

One by one, holding on to each other, the crewmen of *U-99* jumped into the icy waters and began swimming toward *Walker*. König recalls the night vividly. "I was already tired. This is the first step to die. The cold creeps up your body. If you're tired, you fall asleep, that's it. But then there was a searchlight glaring in my face. I was wide awake." With König and the others swimming across the distance between *U-99* and *Walker*, Kretschmer suddenly realized that the submarine was still afloat and could be captured. At once, he told the chief engineer to go back and open valves so the sub would fill with water and sink. The chief engineer swam back, got into the sub, opened the valves, and *U-99* began to slowly settle by the stern, then plunged below. The chief engineer was never seen again. "This must have haunted Kretschmer all his life," says König.

The Germans kept swimming across. *Walker* had rigged scrambling nets down her side and the *U-99* crew began hauling themselves up the net. They struggled, and one after another emerged from the frigid sea. Some were so exhausted and drained they could not negotiate the nets, and a British seaman named Prout immediately went fully clothed into the water to help them up. Slowly the Germans were dragged aboard, up the side of the *Walker*. The last man out was the commander. To the astonishment of all on board the *Walker*, it was Otto Kretschmer, the Golden Ace.

Commander Peter Sturdee, then a sub-lieutenant aboard *Walker*, was at the rails when Kretschmer came aboard. "I could see old Kretschmer hanging on. He was going to see all his chaps aboard. He was tired. He had always said, 'No enemy will have my boat or have these glasses [the special Zeiss glasses minted for the aces].' We got him over the guardrails, absolutely exhausted."[6]

All at once, Kretschmer realized he still had the Zeiss binoculars hanging around his neck. He moved to throw them into the sea. "I took the binoculars," recalls Sturdee.

Macintyre, who had watched all this from the bridge, now saw a gilt-edged trophy of the capture. He barked down from the bridge: "Sub. Bring those up. They're mine—a prize of war."

A prize they were, marking a stunning victory. Macintyre, the crisp, polished rulebook officer, had fished out of the North Atlantic Germany's top ace. Otto Kretschmer was now a captive of the British. For a thirty-six-year-old escort leader, the victory was a dazzling triumph. For any officer of any age or station, it was an extraordinary coup. Macintyre, who came to be nicknamed "Bulldog Drummond of the Atlantic," had bagged "Silent Otto."

Overnight and the next day on the trip back to Liverpool, an unusual development unfolded. Enemies in war, the crewmen of *U-99* and *Walker* made friends. They shared bunks, talked, exchanged thoughts. "We got on well with them," recalls Roy Hemmings, a sailor aboard *Walker*. The Germans said, "If you win the war, you look after me. If we win the war, I'll look after you." Hemmings promised to contact a German sailor, Jupp Kassel, when the war was over, writing his address on a package of cigarettes.

Life proceeded quirkily onboard the Admiralty W Class destroyer, full of odd scenes. The chief engineer of *Walker* got a bridge game going consisting of himself, Kretschmer, and two officers from the *J. B. White*, whose crew had been rescued by *Walker*. Chief Osborne said it was the only decent bridge game he got in during the war.

Elsewhere, other unusual scenes played out through the ship. Sturdee interrogated the German survivors and impounded their personal possessions. Later, after the Germans had left, he noticed a rosary and a medallion of the Virgin Mary on his bunk. Jupp Kassel had remained behind in the cabin; he and Sturdee were talking, when two shy young sailors came down the stairs. Sturdee asked them what they had come for; Kassel intervened. He explained they had come to collect the rosary and the medallion. The two were Catholics, and such was the religious intolerance in Nazi Germany, not simply against Jews, that "if they had taken [the religious articles] in front of the others, they might have been molested or even killed."

Later, Sturdee, a correct officer who spent thirty-one years in the Royal Navy, took up the matter with Kretschmer, and commented that he had had two Catholics aboard *U-99*. So great was Kretschmer's shock that he snapped out, "I haven't." *Walker* steamed back to Britain with its motley cargo of a British crew, German prisoners of war, and Canadian merchant seamen from the *J. B. White*.

On March 18, 1941, Commander Macintyre, sporting his usual broad grin, and *Walker* proudly sailed into Liverpool harbor and Gladstone Dock, where the escorts tied up, with their celebrated captive. *Walker* was berthed at Prince's Landing Stage, reserved usually for bigger ships. A cheering crowd, including the commander-in-chief, Western Approaches, Admiral Sir Percy Noble, who oversaw all the Atlantic battle, was waiting at dockside to hail the victors. The crowd celebrated; the *Walker* men beamed; the day was memorable. The legendary ace Günther Prien had already been sunk on March 7; Joachim Schepke, who had so ravaged SC 11, had been sent below the same night as *U-99* had been sunk; the capture alive of Kretschmer marked the elimination of Germany's three top aces, a remarkable achievement. In Germany, the news came as a serious morale setback and marked the end of the "Happy Time." For the British, the event marked a considerable coup. Donald Macintyre was an instant hero. Liverpool hailed its Ajax.

# 7

WHAT WAS SHAPING UP AT WESTERN APPROACHES was a scrambling war, a scattershot war of hundreds of individual battles, fought all across the Atlantic, everywhere, from Land's End to Rockall, by dozens of small units, splayed out across the ocean.

Since the age of Nelson and the Battle of Trafalgar in 1805, the British navy had been the "Big Ship" navy, founded on mass, firepower, and might. The Big Ship domination of the Royal Navy, which had brought forth fleets of ponderous, towering forts of steel like *Dreadnought* (1906), *Iron Duke* (1914), and *Hood* (1920), had lasted through the Battle of Jutland in World War I—the greatest naval engagement in history, in which an extraordinary battery of no fewer than thirty-seven British capital ships had met the German High Seas Fleet of twenty-one capital ships in a stark, bloody face-off that represented the high-water mark of the Big Ship era.

The principle of surface action, the heavy surface ship, had compelled certain fundamental laws. Wars were centered around decisive battles, which determined the course of nations. Ships fought in fleets, the basic unit of navies. These fleets were commanded by admirals, leading squadrons.

Now, all this had been replaced by a new map of war with few defining moments or characteristics. There were no decisive battles. Instead the conflict was composed of a hundred small, scattered battles, each centering around a hundred dispersed convoys, each one contributing a notch to the British and Allied cause, off England, up by Iceland, in mid-ocean, everywhere. There were no fleets. Instead there was a flurry of isolated convoys guarded by escort groups, the largest of which consisted of a mere eight ships. Most escort groups were led by nothing higher than a lieutenant commander. There were no admirals at sea. The Big Ships, for the most part, played a small role. It was a small ship war—intended for fast, light destroyers, frigates, sloops, and corvettes, so much better than the Big Ships at hunting submarines.

The British had fought a submarine war in World War I— but it was limited, narrower in scope. Convoys had not been instituted until one year before the war ended, in 1917. Moreover, the Germans had had far fewer U-boats at sea—only about fifty at the height of their strength. These had been clustered in the waters immediately off England. There had been no field, no splay of battles across the vast, ruffled expanse of the Atlantic. The submarine war of 1917–18 had been reduced, limited in geographic scale and scope.

The map of the new war was entirely different. It was the buckshot war, thirty terriers chasing 100 foxes, hither, yon, up, down, everywhere. The Battle of the Atlantic was a war on the chase, fought in a blizzard, across a thousand scattered skirmishes.

The Allied command center from which the buckshot war was fought was Western Approaches Combined Headquarters, housed in the basement of a grimy office building on the stately Liverpool waterfront called Derby House. Western Approaches had taken up quarters there in February 1941, transferred from Plymouth, on the English Channel, which had the twin disadvantages of being under daily watch by the Luftwaffe and being far less suitable for control of the immense traffic coming into Clydebank and Liverpool.

If one were to choose a building where the Second World War was won, the White House in Washington, D.C., might be a choice; the British Ministry of Defence in London might be a possibility; or one might very well choose this building—Derby House in Liverpool. Here, the planning, tracking, and prosecution of the Battle of the Atlantic was carried out.

The elaborate workings of the command revolved under the hand of the commander-in-chief, Western Approaches, Admiral Sir Percy L. H. Noble. Urbane, possessed of a sharp intellect, fastidious, popular with his staff, the sixty-one-year-old Noble in his youth had served on the royal yacht, *Victoria and Albert*, then in cruisers, then in command of the China Station. Noble took charge on February 17, 1941, just after the command had moved from Plymouth to Liverpool.

Four hundred people worked at Western Approaches. It was the nerve center for all intelligence, battle reports, planning, the direction of daily combat, and the mapping out of strategy in the war.

The command center was a labyrinthine maze of underground passages, rooms, offices, and cubicles, supporting a central Operations Room. There were communications areas with telephones and gray decoding machines, alcoves with banks of teleprinters, a vast main switchboard with six consoles of innumerable telephone lines, a radio room, and dozens of other offices where ganglia of wires brought field reports, intelligence, weather data, ship positions, and other information into the center.

All this fed the vast Operations Room, which was the heart of the headquarters. At the front of the command center was an immense black chart of the Atlantic, with the land masses in white, displaying the current positions of convoys at sea. The huge chart, fourteen feet by ten feet, had a ladder running up its face so staff could update these positions daily, or hourly. In the cockpit of the room, at its center, were two tables with sea charts and maps of England. Dotting these charts were wood pieces which were moved about to give the known positions of U-boats. Before the chart tables, on the back wall of the Operations Room, was a row of twenty-three pegs, each holding a clipboard keeping the vital statistics of battle at any given moment. To the right of the huge convoy map were blackboards giving the time of dawn and dusk, the moonrise and setting; wind direction, wind force, visibility, and other meteorological data for Shannon, Rockall, Fastnet, and the rest of the sea frontier. To the left of the big black convoy chart up front was a chalk board giving the readiness status of RAF squadrons throughout England.

Above the clipboards, two large glass windows, for a naval controller and an air controller, looked out on to the room; above these were windows from Admiral Noble's office and the air commander's office, also giving out on to the room. Outside Noble's office was a room with two bunks where the admiral and his deputy could sleep. A red hotline was nearby, on which Noble could raise the War Cabinet in London directly.

From these catacombs, Noble, understated, soft-spoken, dignified, the man who would see Britain through one of the darkest passages of the Battle of the Atlantic, gathered intelligence and formed his picture of what was happening at sea; commanded the immense assets of the Royal Navy and the eleven other navies—from the Royal Netherlands Navy and the Royal Indian Navy to the Polish Navy and the Free French Navy—under his authority, and conducted the action and advance of the Battle of the Atlantic.

Western Approaches Combined Headquarters was gas-proof and bomb-proof. It was known as "The Citadel."

In 1941, as the chill autumn winds blew up past the stately government houses of Whitehall in London, there were gathering signs that the war at sea, ever changing on the rolling, marbled expanse of the ocean, was shifting, slipping and passing to the British. There were no great departures, no signal advances, but gradually, bit by bit, growing signs and indications emerged that the battle was moving, if not yet tipping, to the British finesse. It was evident at the Admiralty's Submarine Tracking Room in London; it was apparent in the shape of the statistics accumulating at Western Approaches Combined Headquarters.

The apparent turn of events followed eighteen months of toil, of preparation, of strenuous effort to marshal Britain's assets. On land, at sea, in the air, she had drilled to move ahead her new "buckshot" offensive.

In the town of Tobermory, on the island of Mull in the Hebrides, a training course for escort ships had been established under the demanding eye of Vice Admiral Gilbert Stephenson, the curmudgeonly figure who earned the nickname "The Terror of Tobermory." For one month, ships and crews underwent an intensive workup in the basics of escort warfare—submarine attacks, firing guns, landings, boarding parties, lowering boats, fire drills, and much more. The course immediately addressed the dire training problems which the Royal Navy had faced.

As Tobermory milled out class after class, two other new initiatives began to shape the North Atlantic escort groups, further honing the response to lack of training. Standing escort squadrons, which trained and remained together as permanent units, were instituted. Previously, these groups had been thrown together at random for each assignment, leaving ships and crews without any working knowledge of their cohorts. Escorts now went to sea coordinated, jointly trained in team exercises.

And in 1941 there were new ships. Through 1940 and 1941, British shipyards turned out thirty-eight new destroyers, and the nimble little corvettes began to appear, 112 of them. The fresh hulls were a welcome reinforcement. The Canadians, too, were building dozens of small antisubmarine corvettes.

At this time, science, too, had begun to scrawl the signature of a new age on the face of naval tactics. An entirely unheard of kind of technological warfare had begun to transform war at sea, more than any other shift since the rise of ironclads and the move from sail to steam. The impact of the new technology began to show everywhere, on the convoy routes, in the air, all across the war the British were fighting. It brought a battery of innovations that turned naval warfare into a whole field of blips, screens, radio waves, transmitters, and receivers.

Radar, which could see over great distances, through fog or

night, was introduced on board ship in 1940. Type 286 radar used a fixed antenna, so a ship had to turn to track its target. The first sea battle in history using radar was fought on March 17, 1941, 400 miles off the Shetland Islands, when HMS *Vanoc*, using Type 271 radar, another early version, sank *U-100*, with the ace Joachim Schepke, who had raided Convoy SC 11, on-board.

High Frequency Direction Finding (HF/DF or "Huff-Duff") first appeared in 1941. With it, an operator could fix the bearing of a signal being sent by a U-boat. If two fixes or bearings could be achieved, an intersecting point establishing the exact position of the U-boat could be determined. Huff-Duff had been introduced on U.S. Navy ships prior to 1940, on British ships in 1941.

Aviation, too, was transformed by a flurry of new devices. ASV radar (Aircraft to Surface Vessel) for aircraft was developed, at first so primitive that crewmen in some aircraft had to perch on the plane's toilet to watch the screen. At once, ASV radar proved indispensable for hunting U-boats. The Leigh Light, used for U-boat hunting at night or at close range, was invented by an inquiring RAF officer named Humphrey de Verde Leigh. Leigh used the heavy-current generator of a Wellington bomber to power a standard naval searchlight 24 inches in diameter. The whole rig was housed in a retractable turret, lowered when the light was used. The Leigh Light wrote the end of many a startled U-boat.

By May 1941, the Royal Navy had attained a strength which began to approach fighting effectiveness. In Liverpool, Londonderry, and Belfast, Admiral Noble at Western Approaches Combined Headquarters had mounted a force of 127 vessels he could send out against the scatter of German U-boats, up from 111 the year before. The Mediterranean Fleet, vital to the Admiralty's strategy, had swelled by the score from eighteen warships in 1940 to eighty one year later. By contrast, the great, armor-belted Home Fleet, with its array of twenty-two tall, bristling capital ships and cruisers, which guarded home waters, had fallen from ninety-four ships the year before to fifty-six in 1941. That year, the Royal Navy had begun to reach fighting pitch.

By scope and design, the war was an escort war. The sturdy V and W Class destroyers dating from World War I, with their long, almost flat foredecks, square bridges, and angled 4-inch guns, and swift D Class and E Class types with their straight bows, tall, gently angled stacks, and top speed of 36 knots were crucial in bringing across the precious convoys. "Tribals" were more modern, fine, swept ships with rising forecastles, fast, streamlined silhouettes, and scythelike bows. They mounted eight big 4.7-inch guns, six AA guns, and four torpedo tubes.

These were the ships on which the transportation of the great Allied surge of supplies to fuel the war rested, thirty-eight separate classes of them. Inside, in their compartmented trim, they were neat, complex, bulkheaded machines of naval power, engines of fighting proficiency.

The functions, fighting array, and combat systems of a destroyer start forward, just before the mast, on the bridge. The bridge of HMS *Cavalier*, which served on the North Atlantic and also did time on the convoy run supplying North Russia, was open, like all Royal Navy bridges, with no roof, shelter, or enclosed structure. Here, exposed to the elements, the officers, lookouts, and seamen on duty stood watches. In the winter, crew and captain endured bitter cold and heaving sea. Men usually wore their uniform, two sweaters and oilskins, and scarves, or towels around their necks. The guts of the bridge, its equipment banks, instruments, and consoles, were located down and to the left, under a bulkhead, to the side of a platform at the center where the captain stood. Radar, navigational equipment, rudder angle indicator, and a flurry of other panels made up the array. From here battle was commanded—navigation, gunnery, speed, course, chase.

Belowdecks, the fighting components of *Cavalier*, a 363-foot stallion angled with purpose and speed, were laid out like a bunker at sea. In the gyro room was the gyrocompass, the guidance system for the ship, a great gray and glass pod four feet tall that corrected all compasses and looked futuristic, robotlike. On the starboard, right, side of the ship was the radio room. Ten banks of transmitting and receiving equipment lined the wall to the right, another four banks to the left. There were other consoles, as well as Huff-Duff receiver, telexes, and safes for codebooks. During battle, this room would be a winking, beeping beehive of activity, monitoring communications from other ships.

Forward of the radio room was Gunnery Control, dominated by a large targeting board with dials calibrating such functions as "Target Speed Knots," "Target Compass Bearing," "Relative Wind Speed," "GRU wander," and many more.

The heart of the destroyer, though, was her operations room—the CIC, or Combat Information Center, in the U.S. Navy; the AIC, or Action Information Center, in the Royal Navy. Thirty-five feet across, every foot of the destroyer's AIC was jammed with plotting boards, electronics, fire directors, banks of installations, screens, switches. The sonar position was forward, and prominent in the AIC were two plotting tables—tables where the scheme of action was drawn—and a transparent "Fleet Disposition Board." Twenty sailors worked in the operations room during *Cavalier*'s days at war, placing enemy contacts, keeping track of the lay of battle, training guns, wielding the defensive systems of the ship. In the thick of battle, this room was the nerve center of *Cavalier*, running, glowing, ticking, blinking, bustling with activity.

Two hundred fifty men ate, slept, and lived aboard this destroyer. Sixty hammocks hung in the forecastle during the war; they were well used. Very often one sailor would tumble out of laydown and go on watch just as another came in and dove into the same hammock. The canvas hammocks were strung everywhere possible, in the laundry area, in doorways, in machinery spaces.

Last compartment of all was the captain's cabin, with the only bath on the ship, located directly below the bridge; his day cabin, spacious, where he took his meals and worked or relaxed in off hours, was one deck below that. Naval custom again differs. On American ships, captain and officers ate together in the ward room; on British ships, the captain could eat in the ward room only on invitation of the senior officer, traditionally the ship's second in command. Captain's privileges reign; officers' customs, too, sometimes.

*Cavalier*, a lean, 1,710-ton warhorse, served until the end of the war. Her pennant number was D 73. She was one of the tough, fast, versatile destroyers that waged the Battle of the Atlantic. Today she is preserved as a museum in Chatham, on Britain's east coast.

But the real heroine of the war, the rust and bucket keel of the fleet, the ship for which the laurels of the champion must be reserved, is a celebrated, pocked, nimble midget—the stubby, little corvette.

The Flower Class corvette, the most numerous production type, measured 205 feet—roughly one half the length of a typical destroyer. It weighed in at 1,070 tons, only two-thirds the payload of a destroyer. Corvettes were pint sized; they were tiny, stout, indefatigable; they made up the lion's share of the North Atlantic escort squadrons. Captained by a senior officer of escort in a destroyer or sloop, these escort squadrons were filled out by stubby Flower Class corvettes and their sister classes. In the lift and yaw and plunge of the worst North Atlantic weather, with mountainous green seas and tops crested with white, the corvettes gave the ride of a roller coaster, plunging and tumbling, a testament to the crews who served dutifully in them. Mass-produced from 1940 on, corvettes were called "cheap and nasties" by Churchill. They were small; but they were powerfully armed, with one 4-inch gun, three antiaircraft guns, and depth charge racks and throwers. Stubby, blunt corvettes probably did more chasing, dogging, penning, cornering, bombing down of U-boats across the sea than any other class of ship in the king's lineup. They were the pit bulls of the fleet, ever mauling the subs.

Somewhere, along some stretch of shore in the Western world, a monument should be erected to the pugnacious little corvette. Today only one is preserved, His Majesty's Canadian Ship *Sackville*, at the Canadian Naval Memorial in Halifax. All the rest have vanished.

The ships of the Atlantic fleet were gray, light gray, streaked with rust, usually in need of paint. Men lived in these ships, and fought, and died, and wrote letters home, ate "scoff" (chow) in them. Shipboard life is lived in close quarters, crowded, almost always amicable, sometimes wet and woefully uncomfortable.

The food was abundant—stews, fish, bacon and eggs, soup. Sometimes, when a depth charge had disturbed a school of fish, the crew would go back and fish. When they were successful,

there was fresh seafare for dinner. Snacks and fillers were available in abundance—if you got to know the cook. "If you
wanted something in between [lunch and dinner], you could get
a ration of eggs and bacon and the cook would cook it up for
you," says Charles A. "Bungey" Edwards, a leading seaman, of
life onboard HMS *Hesperus* during the war.[1]

Bread went moldy quickly; even so a green crust of bread
was often a reward for bringing a bucket of coal down to the
galley, or doing some other chore.

Life, as much of it as you got off, was lived in the narrow
but ample spaces of the forecastle, always crowded but companionable, the forward angle of the bow. Here, men ate, slept,
talked, sometimes drew, wrote letters home. A table was set up at
mealtimes; during other hours, time was filled with chatter, stories, jokes, advice. When they had the time, men played games,
cards, bingo—sometimes draughts or poker. Bungey Edwards
recalls, "You're in a very confined space. Generally speaking,
everyone gets along with everybody else, simply because you
have to. You do your living, eating, and dhobying [laundry]
there." Even on the best, tranquil day, though, action was never
far away.

"Now and again there'd be a little enjoyment," Edwards
says. "Generally speaking, you had a lot, you had enough to do
to keep you busy. . . . You were 200 highly trained blokes. . . .
Each chap knew his job, when to do it, how to do it.

"We'd be in action on and off for sometimes forty-eight
hours with hardly any sleep," he recalls. "Then you'd go the
next two or three weeks with nothing, just the monotony of
back and forth in front of the convoy, waiting for someone to
pop up.

"Generally speaking, it was a very happy ship, well crewed,
well trained."

◆ ◆ ◆

Then the weather would come up, the wind would build, the seas would grow to hillocks, and life onboard was wet and miserable. Abovedecks, you were soaked; not even oilskins kept you dry. If it was cold, the wind seared hands, face. The weather would blow like a typhoon, the seas would mount, the ship would heave up, high, to the crest of the waves, then come expressing down into the shuddering, undulating troughs of gray below. In blows like these, the seas poured down the hatches, rushing belowdecks, soaking clothes, books, shoes, everything.

Sleeping in a hammock was almost a gymnastic feat. "The hammock remains absolutely stationary and follows the laws of gravity," recalls James Woodhead of HMS *Enchantress*. "But the ship doesn't."[2] So the ship would sway, roll, rock to one side—and your hammock stayed stationary. "Then the ship goes the other way. It's really frightening."

Abovedecks, the experience was hard. Woodhead recalls: "You'd go down into this water and you just knew a couple of tons of water would come over this bridge. You knew there was nothing you could do to stop it, you just did your best to accept it and get on with your job. . . . You knew how small you are. You knew you're in the hands of the Lord."

The cold was the worst. It whistled past, icy, razor-sharp.

"You'd just be soaking wet. And cold," recalls Roy Hemmings, a seaman-torpedoman onboard HMS *Walker*. "I saw a fellow up there one time—he was crying. He was up there on the bridge and he was actually crying. I had never seen a bloke crying [from the cold]."[3]

The cold blew; the ships struggled over the waves; the men swayed in their hammocks; in better times they enjoyed the hot meals, hung on rails in twos or threes, talking; some penned doggerel, thought up practical jokes, others wrote up notes of their battles. The OOD (officer of the deck) kept the ship on course, scanned the horizon, maintained speed, watched as always, for the U-boats. In 1941, there were signs that the U-boats were losing their edge, signs that the war was shifting, slowly, gradually, by the slightest increments, to the British hand.

The cumulative, meshing advances—technology, training, increased number of ships—all began to show results out at sea. Not that the war was in hand, but that fortune was sifting past, and the Battle of the Atlantic was on in earnest. By the end of 1941, one of every seven U-boats attacked by a surface ship was being sunk; one out of every three was being damaged.

And, by December, the Royal Canadian Navy had grown to line strength. The RCN was the Royal Navy's robust cousin in the British Commonwealth; its story was one of bravura, and almost incredible expansion. It had started the war with a fleet of only thirteen ships and a roster of 3,684 men; by the end of World War II, it had increased in one single convulsion of mobilization to a flotilla of 378 ships and 95,000 men. In six quick years, it had multiplied over thirty times. The RCN was big—it was also game and spirited; its ships—*Chilliwack, Kenogami, St. Laurent, Ottawa, Saguenay,* and *Smith Falls*—finally provided 47 percent of the escort hulls on the Atlantic throughout the war. The arrival of the RCN as a major fighting element was critical; its ships made up a major portion of virtually every North Atlantic escort squadron. Its size—about as big as the U.S. Navy today—provided the vast coverage required by a convoy system with roughly 125 ships at sea on any given day. The Royal Canadian Navy was the fiber, the timber of the escort squadrons. While its rapid expansion caused problems, particularly for the young, raw recruits who joined and had only brief and rudimentary training, the Canadians' contribution to the war was vital and outsized. The RCN was the cohort of the Royal Navy's resounding victory.

The Western Approaches, widening out in a fan from Land's End at the western jut of the British Isles to the open Atlantic—vast, chilly—flooded west toward Rockall Bank, the key approach forming the throat through which all the huge convoy tonnage converged into the North Channel. Immense, gray, the Western Approaches flowed smooth and quiet, a funnel of open ocean conducting the principal traffic lanes into Britain. That year they flowed with change. The British had marshaled their strength, their crews were honed by better training; the escort ranks had multiplied. That year the convoys were coming in over the top of Ireland, the escorts were hardened by almost two years of fighting, and there were signs, the barest signals, that the British offensive had begun to shunt ahead, begun to nudge, by the barest of measures, toward effectiveness. There were indications, the most tentative signs and bellwethers, that the gathering advance was slowly crystallizing, gradually, slowly, by the faintest of indices, taking shape. The battle was crossing, shifting in fortunes, but it was still a test of Britain's will, a trial by action and fire. The U-boats were ever waiting in the Western Approaches, lurking, hovering in the murk of the depths. They carried twelve torpedoes, the bigger ones fourteen; these covered three miles in just under two minutes; then the scene was the same: a freighter going up in flames, the crew scrambling into boats, then the ship slowly sliding beneath the surface of the waves. The convoys came in more regularly, but that year there were still bad battles. Convoy HX 121 lost four ships. Convoy SC 19 lost three ships. The Germans hit Convoy SC 26, but that was a tough convoy, a convoy from a nightmare.

# Merchant Ships Sunk by U-Boats in the North Atlantic

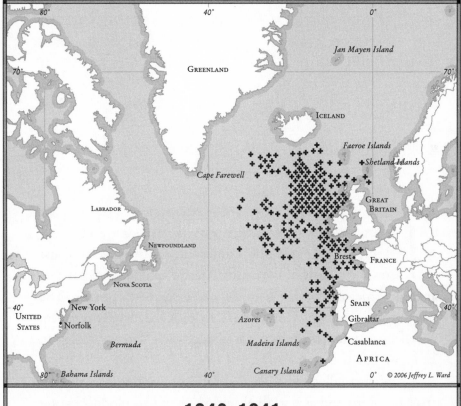

· **1940–1941** ·

# 8

THEY WERE OUT, FAR OUT WHERE THE WAVES FLOW IN long, green furrows, 417 miles due south of Iceland, lost on the middle of the empty ocean expanse, under an immense dome of sky that fell down to a sea just as blank. The twenty-two ships of Convoy SC 26 proceeded in formation, seven loose columns, most of three ships each. The sun had been brilliant, fair and clear all day.

Night had fallen. The black shroud of evening had slipped over the ships and as dark had settled, they had plodded along like a caravan of camels, one shuffling beast following the one before it. Now they lumbered along, hulking giants, hooded in the night, rolling slowly east.

Convoy SC 26 had an unusual escort, not the familiar screen of six to eight destroyers and corvettes, but, like Convoy HX 84, which included the *San Demetrio*, SC 26 was defended by an ocean liner fitted with guns, an armed merchant cruiser, this one HMS *Worcestershire*. The *Worcestershire* was studded with big cruiser guns, commanded by the senior officer escort, Captain J. Creswell. The ships drove on, lumbering back and forth to keep on station, heading due east, toward Cape Wrath, in northwestern Scotland.

The Admiralty U-boat disposition report for this day, April 2, 1941, would have had great interest to Captain Creswell and Convoy SC 26. The intelligence plot showed nine German U-boats to be operating in the area of the flotilla, north of 57 degrees north latitude, and west of 18 degrees west longitude. Just after dusk, the Admiralty had advised Convoy SC 26 in a signal that it was probably being shadowed by a U-boat. That signal reached *Worcestershire* at 9:25 P.M. The Admiralty's intelligence was very accurate.

Late that day, south of Iceland, *U-74*, commanded by Kptlt. Eitel-Friedrich Kentrat, had made contact with the formation and was now tracking it. Earlier that day Kentrat had entered into his log: "Convoy made out. Course east. Way [speed] ca. 7 knots. Sent reconnaissance report. Intent: To get ahead for a daylight attack at sunset, then pursue and [make] night surface attack."[1]

Kentrat's message had been picked up by BdU, which had reacted at once. On land, Dönitz had ordered Kentrat to hold off attack, but to shadow and send location reports so other boats could be brought to converge on the convoy. The other U-boats were summoned; Kentrat continued to shadow through the day; eight other subs were finally collected; these boats now began to arrive and slip into place, surrounding Convoy SC 26 in the late hours of April 2.

The convoy steamed along, a moon had come out. "It was a fine clear night with light clouds partially obscuring a moon in the first quarter and it was practically never dark," the convoy commodore, Vice Admiral G. T. C. Swabey, had noted in his log.[2] The freighters shoved along through the night, Swabey's flagship, *Magician*, in the lead at the head of the fifth column; the big British tanker *British Reliance*, 7,000 tons, just behind; the Greek *Taygetos*, 4,295 tons, carrying grain, second ship in the sixth column; the little Norwegian *Helle*, carrying steel and pulp, third ship in the third column, then the array of the other ships in SC 26 marching in order in their neat rows. The sea was dark all around. Not a sound bothered the flotilla. Smoke slipped behind from the funnels.

The moon was bright. The light on the waves was silvery. A slight gust blew. Now the wolves began to arrange themselves around the big, shuffling caravan. In the lee of the moonlight, each boat slipped into place around the edges of the convoy. Nine serpents waited in the dark. They were *U-46* (Obtlt. Engelbert Endrass), *U-69* (Kptlt. Jost Metzler), *U-73* (Kptlt. Helmut Rosenbaum), *U-74* (Kentrat, the shadowing boat), *U-76* (Kptlt. Friedrich von Hippel), *U-97* (Kptlt. Udo Heilmann), *U-98* (Kptlt. Robert Gysae), *U-101* (Kptlt. Ernst Mengersen), and *U-94* (Kptlt. Herbert Kuppisch). These subs formed the largest wolfpack assembled so far in the war.

SC 26 plodded along, following the ocean tracks east, toward Ireland, twenty-two freighters and tankers carrying gasoline, oil, wheat, flour, scrap metal, representing the many Allied nations fighting against the Germans. It was 12:30 in the morning.

All of a sudden, an explosion roared through the convoy from the second ship in the fifth column. The *British Reliance* had been hit sixty feet aft of her bow on the port side, sending a geyser of water shooting sixty feet into the air. Before the convoy could recover from this shock, thirty seconds later another torpedo slammed into the 7,000-ton giant, landing near the engine room and causing a thundering explosion. This shot had come from the port side, too. Debris splashed onto the water. The ship came to a stop. The *British Reliance* settled, then she rose slowly by the bow until she was perpendicular to the sky, then slowly slid below, stern first, enough time for the crew to abandon ship. Only five men were slightly injured.

The *British Reliance* was gone; leading off the attack, Obtlt. Engelbert Endrass in *U-46* had claimed the first victim of the night.

In the next four hours, the pack of jackals unleashed a savage barrage on the convoy which accounted for six ships between 12:35 and 4:43 in the morning. A debacle of havoc and destruction was played out; the subs struck everywhere among the darkened rows of the convoy; more than one fourth of the formation was torpedoed under the quicksilver light of the moon.

At 1:45 A.M., the night was split again by another roaring detonation coming from the first ship in the first column. This time the 4,313-ton British freighter *Alderpool* had been hit, again on the port side. Endrass in *U-46* had struck again, bagging his second catch of the night. Captain A. G. Phelps Mead, the master of the *Alderpool*, was on the bridge at the time of the hit and was knocked off his feet by the force of the blast. Captain Phelps Mead ordered "Abandon Ship"; all hands were picked up by another freighter, the *Thirlby*. Not much later, Captain Phelps Mead saw a second torpedo strike the *Alderpool*. Five minutes later, the ship went to her grave.

There was no letup by the U-boats. Two torpedoes now came streaking toward the *Thirlby*, with all the crew of the *Alderpool* now aboard. The crewmen watched dumbstruck as one torpedo missed, crossing just in front of the *Thirlby*'s bow, and the second torpedo went whizzing past, missing astern.

Next, at 4:06, another explosion rocked the convoy. This

time the 4,274-ton Greek freighter *Leonidas Z. Cambanis*, carrying wheat, had been struck. She was twenty-four years old, a long life for a ship, but she had made her last voyage. The *Cambanis* plunged below. Kentrat in *U-74*, who had shadowed the convoy all day, had struck this time.

For four minutes it was quiet. The convoy steamed on in the moist, windy night. Then, next, at 4:10, from the first ship in the fourth column, *Westpool*, a deafening roar sent a tower of water thirty feet into the air. The *Westpool*, 5,724 tons, British, carrying a deadweight of scrap metal, disappeared from the surface in less than twenty seconds. Thirty-seven men out of a crew of forty-three were lost. C. L. Robertson, a sailor on the *Westpool*, recalls, "I ran along to the boat deck, the starboard No. 1 Boat was blown away, No. 2 was badly damaged, and the ship started to sink rapidly, so I dived over the side into the water.

"I heard my friend call out that there was a raft not far off, so I called to him to swim to it, but he was injured and could not do so. I told him I would try and bring it over to him, but when I reached the raft, I was exhausted and not fully conscious. There were three coolies on the raft, the second cook, and myself. We remained on the raft until daylight. All around us ships were being torpedoed that night, but I do not know their names."[3]

The men on the raft were picked up by a British destroyer HMS *Havelock* the next afternoon.

Finally, at 4:15 A.M., five minutes after the *Westpool* had been hit, the 5,409-ton Belgian *Indier* was struck by a torpedo. She broke in half and went down immediately, taking forty-two of her forty-six crewmen with her and her load of steel and general cargo. Her call sign, used in radio traffic, was ONJA, Oscar, November, Juliet, Alpha. It would call no more. The four survivors, including her captain, were later picked up by a destroyer.

Now, in the cool, clear dark of the empty spring night, Creswell and Swabey conferred. In three hours and forty minutes, four of SC 26's ships had been torpedoed. In just under four hours, they had lost almost one fifth of the formation's complement. Swabey asked Creswell whether they should consider dispersing the convoy. It was a difficult decision; they considered it carefully. There were many factors involved.

They believed the bright shimmer of the night made conditions ideal for attack. The moon had set, but the Northern Lights still cast an ample glow across the sea. Captain Creswell believed further, based on the Admiralty's U-boat report, that even more subs might arrive. He also thought the present concentrated formation of ships afforded to the U-boats a better, clustered target.

"It seemed, therefore, that if the convoy was kept together every ship might be sunk by the morning—and even when day dawned there was to be no expectation of anti-submarine protection for another 24 hours and no hope of it for at least 12 hours," Captain Creswell later reported.[4]

Accordingly, under the ghostly sheen of the Northern Lights, Creswell and Swabey made the decision to disperse the convoy. At 4:21 in the morning, Swabey made the signal to scatter, and the seventeen ships remaining in SC 26 split up, separating in the dark. The decision left the ships on their own, defenseless; on the other hand it scattered them into an obscurity possibly far more advantageous than any convoy configuration. The remaining members of SC 26 began to leave the battle area, parting company.

Fourteen minutes after Swabey's order to scatter, at 4:35, Helmut Rosenbaum in *U-73*, who had dispatched *Westpool* twenty-five minutes earlier, sent a torpedo speeding into the 6,900-ton British tanker *British Viscount*, filled with volatile fuel oil. The ship erupted in a brilliant blaze. Swabey described the sight subsequently in a report. "[She] burnt with a vast blaze of light, illuminating every ship in the vicinity as in daylight. For two hours or more the reflection of the blaze was seen illuminating *Magician*'s forecastle bulkhead as she steamed away from the scene."[5]

Eight minutes passed. Then the unthinkable happened. Just as the ships began to make off in the night, before they had had the chance to absorb the last shock, Eitel-Friedrich Kentrat in *U-74* sent a torpedo straight into HMS *Worcestershire*. The torpedo struck behind the bow, flooding No. 1 and No. 2 Holds and starting a fire in the paint shop.

Kentrat gave a bridge-eye-view of the torpedoing in his log:

A rain squall provides fabulous attack conditions. Now I have the very big steamer in front of me. The first shot breaks the surface before reaching the target. Missed!

The last torpedo. I turn away for a stern shot. Steamer turns towards me somewhat . . . Fired. Steamer appears to continue turning towards me.

Hit approx 20 meters in front of bridge. Strong detonation and explosion. Steamer sinks somewhat toward the bow and starts to list. Is dead in the water and drifting in the vicinity of the burning tanker. Frustrated that I'm out of torpedoes! But the other boats are bound to see him.[6]

The armed cruiser *Worcestershire* now continued veering out of control, with the fire burning by her bow. Captain Creswell immediately determined that the ship's rudder was jammed hard-a-port and ordered the engines stopped. For the next hour, *Worcestershire*, stricken, sat on the surface, lit up by the blaze of the still burning *British Viscount*. By miraculous luck, no more submarines found the ship. The fire at the bow was quickly put out, and by six in the morning emergency steering had been rigged; the *Worcestershire* set out to get away from the battle area. Later the main steering was found to be workable, and could steer up to 20 degrees each way, port or starboard.

Now twilight spread its calm across the sea. The ships dispersed from the flaming wreck of the *British Viscount*, marking the battlefield. The dark was impenetrable and inky and full of wind and the sixteen remaining merchant ships scattered from the scene. For a time there was no more sound, and the heavy dark of the night cloaked the fleeing ships in an all-encompassing lull. The first round of battle was done; for the moment the U-boats relented.

By daylight, the scattered ships of the convoy were spread out over a wide patch of North Atlantic. To the east of the first battle, Admiral Swabey had come across a flock of stragglers, slightly to the north of the point where the *British Reliance* had been torpedoed. He gathered them together, then kept easterly, leading the small flock to a prearranged rendezvous 463 miles due south of Reykjanes, Iceland, where they would meet arriving destroyers. This formation, under Swabey, made off to the rendezvous, northeast.

Not far to the north, at 1:00 P.M., *Worcestershire* met the destroyer HMS *Hurricane*, which took the crippled cruiser under its guard, and stayed with her for four days, all the way back to Liverpool. Acting as escort, *Hurricane* steamed circles around the injured ship.

Gradually, through the day, destroyers, in twos and threes, began to show up to assist the survivors of SC 26.

At 2:30 P.M., to the south of both *Worcestershire* and

Swabey's formation, HMS *Havelock* and *Hesperus* arrived on the scene and spotted a burning tanker wreck. This proved to be the hulk of the *British Viscount*. *Havelock* stood by, picking up survivors from the *British Viscount*, from *Indier*, and from *Westpool*. *Hesperus* went about picking up survivors from the *Leonidas Z. Cambanis*. Leading Seaman Ron Smith, who was onboard *Hesperus* at the time of the battle of SC 26, still shows with emotion a page from a scrapbook bearing a note penned by a Greek sailor from the *Cambanis* who was plucked, jarred and exhausted, from the water that day. The note reads:

> "The English Nation it is the Butifoul [sic] Country of the World."
> —Nigos Aigira, SS *Leonidas Zanis Cambanis*[7]

*Hesperus* and *Havelock* stayed on station, combing the area for more survivors until 10:00 P.M.; then they set out north, searching for other stragglers from the ravaged convoy.

Elsewhere, earlier, at 4:00 P.M., Admiral Swabey's gaggle of ships had arrived at the prearranged rendezvous with the two destroyers, *Veteran* and *Wolverine*. Altogether, there were eight hulls; they took up a new formation, four columns, each two rows deep. Then they proceeded toward Britain, in order, eight ships: *Magician*, Commodore Swabey's ship; then *Harbledown, Empire Dew, Eelbeck, Editor, Taygetos, Daleby, Anacortes*, and the two destroyers in company.

Now evening descended. A deep purple and indigo spread out from the last glow of the sun, and the sea fell to a slate gray. The ships had traveled about 130 miles from the first scene of battle. Admiral Swabey led, watching his flock, the two destroyers in escort. The ships lumbered on, smoke slipping from their funnels.

The Germans had fresh plans for them, however.

Gradually the dusk passed to night, and full darkness set in. At the various points all across the ocean where the night found them, the straggling survivors of SC 26 made their way slowly home to Britain. One of them was the little Norwegian *Helle*, 2,467 tons, built in 1918. She was sailing all alone, steaming east, about seventy miles north-northeast of Swabey's formation. She did not know it, but one of the wolves, Robert Gysae in *U-98*, had her fixed in his sights. Gysae was patient. He followed the *Helle* for almost an hour. Then, choosing his moment, he slipped into position, set, and, at precisely 11:29 in the morning, he fired. Gysae's log captures the action:

> Shot from Tube 2. Hit fore of the bridge. It's the Norwegian steamer *Helle*, 2,467 tons, distance 1400 meters.
>
> Ship sinks slowly. . . . When the forward portion of the ship is completely under water and the stern is out of water with the screw, I leave the scene. Twenty minutes after the shot, the steamer's radio man reports "Now leaving." So it sank after all.[8]

The *Helle* had carried a cargo of steel and pulp. It would wind up on the ocean floor. The tireless, rusted freighter was the eighth ship torpedoed that night. But all her crew was saved. Her master, Karl G. Jorgensen, ordered "Abandon Ship" and her twenty-four men took to the lifeboats. They were later picked up by *Havelock*.

Gysae was not yet done. Two hours and sixteen minutes later, roughly twenty-three miles from the point where he had torpedoed the *Helle*, he ran across the British steamer *Welcombe*. Gysae trailed her for half an hour. Then he fired. The shot missed. He pursued for another twenty-nine minutes;

then, at 2:44, he fired again. This time the *Welcombe*, with her cargo of wheat, was not so lucky. Gysae's log again captures what followed:

> Fired at 800 meters. Hit, aft edge of stack, depth setting three meters.
>
> It's the English steamer *Welcombe*, 5,122 tons. Steamer sends SOS and position. Ship sinks after 15 minutes, stern first (boiler explosion). Reloaded torpedoes, then pursued toward east.[9]

Alone in the night, out in the middle of the wide sea, 650 miles west of Scotland, the *Welcombe* had succumbed. The ship's second officer, A. Croft, got as many of the crew into lifeboats as he could, then shipped away. "The ship took a roll to port and listed to starboard, about 25 to 30 degrees. There was only one explosion, at the after end of No. 4 Hatch, and the ship sank by the bow fifteen minutes after we left her," he later recalled.[10] Fifteen of the forty-one in the crew perished with the *Welcombe*, including her captain and all executive ranks except Croft.

Roughly eighty-seven gusty miles from the point where the *Welcombe* had gone down, Admiral Swabey's group lumbered on, in formation, shoving away to the east. The ocean was dark. There was not a sound in the sky. Only the faint wisps of smoke trailed from the funnels of the ships, and the wakes of the flotilla fell behind. The eight ships, still in four columns, two rows deep, plodded on under the shroud of the satiny black, rolling and yawing in the waves. Unbeknownst to them, another jackal was trailing them. This time it was Herbert Kuppisch in *U-94*.

He had picked up the group at 12:45 A.M. and had followed it for one hour. At 1:45 in the morning he had noted: "My bearing on enemy is 80°, 3 nautical miles away."[11]

The eight ships of the re-formed SC 26 steamed along. Not a sound stirred. The ships sailed on, leaving sashes of phosphorescent bow wave as they went.

Kuppisch now dogged the group until 2:27, and began his attack run. Then, at 2:41, he fired from a bow tube, twenty seconds later he fired a second torpedo, then, one minute and forty seconds later, fired a third in a fan at three large steamers spread out before him.

All at once, from the first ship in the third column, a thundering blast roared out through the flotilla. Two of Kuppisch's fish had struck the *Harbledown*, in Admiral Swabey's group, 5,414 tons, just abaft the No. 2 Hatch, the first one detonating ten feet below the waterline, the second one hitting the engine room and breaking the back of the ship. *Harbledown* was a proud, new ship, only eight years old. But she had seen her last journey. She went down one hour later; of her forty-one in crew plus two passengers, the two passengers, and one crewman, were lost.

For a time, quiet settled over the area again. Admiral Swabey's group continued steaming east, one ship smaller, accompanied by destroyers *Veteran* and *Wolverine*. The group was not hit again. The herd pushed slowly ahead, following *Magician* at the van of the convoy. Elsewhere, various ships assisted survivors of the convoy battle. The destroyers played floating tow trucks, ambulances.

*Hesperus* came across the straggler *Tenax* at 4:20 A.M., and, as she was in a dangerous area, took her in escort and guided the freighter back to England.

At 5:50 *Havelock* picked up twenty-four survivors from the

*Helle*, sunk by Gysae six hours and twenty minutes before, and several survivors from *Welcombe*, Gysae's second victim. Then she continued searching for survivors in the night; ultimately she rejoined the re-formed SC 26, led by Swabey in *Magician*.


Dawn broke bright on the morning of April 4, finding a wide litter of ships scattered across an immense 200-mile-wide field of ocean. Admiral Swabey's formation—seven hulls—was still together; the other five ships now remaining from SC 26 were dispersed across the area, sailing independent and alone. They were *Thirlby, Tennessee, Ethel Radcliffe, Athenic*, and *Nea*. These formed a small cluster of points, dusted across the North Atlantic in the rough area of the 60th parallel of latitude and the 20th meridian of longitude. Elsewhere, the various scenes of destroyers finding stragglers, chronicles of bits and pieces of the convoy, of men stranded in lifeboats, of assistance to surviving ships played themselves out. Noon passed, the afternoon wore on, dusk came. The Germans had one last move up their sleeve.

The convoy had been mauled by the pack; nine ships had been lost in a spectacle of devastation. One last round remained in the battle. The big British freighter *Athenic*, 5,351 tons, was one of the vessels sailing independently. She was well ahead of most of the other ships from SC 26, 174 miles northeast of the point where *Harbledown* had been sunk four hours and ten minutes before, one of Kuppisch's victims. At 6:30 on the evening of April 4, she was steaming along, making east toward England under the dying sun, unconscious of any immediate danger. Friedrich von Hippel in *U-76* had picked her up, however, and was moving in to take position.

The dim light of day was fading. Hippel closed, aimed, and at 6:56 in the evening fired a torpedo which slammed into the

*Athenic* just at the second hatch; then he went around the ship, fired a second fish into the other side of her. The *Athenic*, carrying a load of wheat, went down after about an hour. The crew, plus eleven men rescued from the steamer *Liguria* days before in a separate incident, were all picked up and there were no casualties. They were lucky sailors, especially the men from *Liguria*. Some of the *Liguria* men had been stranded on a raft, others in an open lifeboat, before being picked up. They were frostbitten from the knees down, their food had run out. The captain had had nothing to eat or drink in five days.

Before the battle of Convoy SC 26 was done, two other vessels from the convoy, *Thirlby* and *Eelbeck*, would be damaged in attacks, but not sunk.

Then the scene of battle went quiet, and the waves rolled on over the 30,000-square-mile area across which the great clash had taken place, where 52,000 tons of shipping had sunk, settled from the surface and gone down to the bottom of the sea. The sun set, the deep purple-blue of the evening spread across the region, and the waves rolled on, unknowing, unspeaking, quiet. But the battle of Convoy SC 26 had one last act left to play. Its title read revenge.

When last heard from, the seemingly unremarkable destroyer HMS *Wolverine*, an Admiralty Modified W Class destroyer built in 1919 by Samuel White at Cowes, England, had been escorting Admiral Swabey's group of seven ships back to England, somewhere about 280 miles east of the first battle area. In fact, *Wolverine*'s history had something of a luster to it. Her ship's motto was "Greedy of work, greedy of glory." She had had a considerable share of both, one month earlier sinking the celebrated ace Günther Prien in *U-47* after a five-hour chase.

Early on the morning of April 5, "greedy" *Wolverine* picked up a sonar contact from a U-boat forty-six miles north-

northwest of the point where Hippel had torpedoed the *Athenic*. The contact was the same boat, Hippel in *U-76*.

*Wolverine*, under the command of Lieutenant Commander James M. Rowland, the victor over Prien, began to track. She alerted two other escorts nearby, the corvette HMS *Arbutus* and the sloop *Scarborough*. Then she crept forward, closed on Hippel, and at 7:37 A.M. dropped a single depth charge on the sub. The salvo was so close that it smashed all the instruments in the U-boat's control room. *Wolverine* came around again. Fifteen minutes later, at 7:52, Rowland dropped a second depth charge, slamming the U-boat so hard a welded seam gave way, a stanchion bent, and all the lights were knocked out. At this point, an unexplained gremlin in her sonar forced *Wolverine* to abort her attack. However the sloop *Scarborough* had picked up Hippel clear and firm; she ran in, and, at 9:01, *Scarborough*, under the command of Lieutenant H. P. W. Northey, began to track. He closed for sixteen relentless minutes. Hippel's U-boat was on the receiving end now, and Northey's log recounts the agony of a writhing, cornered serpent. At 9:17, Northey closed up: "Increased to 13 knots. Target still drawing left. . . . Echo became very blurred. Extent of target 18°." [12]

Finally, three minutes later, *Scarborough* unleashed on the U-boat a pattern of eight depth charges—four set shallow to 150 feet, four set deep to 300 feet. The charges neatly straddled the submarine in a crumping vise of detonations. "Everything in the boat was shattered," Carl Becker, a steersmansmate onboard *U-76*, recalled. "The depth gauge moved like blazes. The boat assumed a vertical position and all was over. I had my escape apparatus and crawled up the ladder to the conning tower hatch. With the greatest difficulty, and using all the remaining air, we managed to bring the boat to the surface." [13]

The U-boat broke above the surface to a slash of machine

gun fire from one of the British ships. Becker and Hippel were on deck; the commander ordered "Abandon Ship." The crew plunged into the water one after the other in surrender, then started swimming toward the British escorts. *U-76* wallowed like a stricken whale in the seaway.

At this point, the commander of the corvette *Arbutus*, instantly aware of the intelligence value of capturing a German U-boat intact, now sent a boarding party in a small boat to the still floating submarine. The open boat came alongside, secured to the sub, and Lieutenant Geoffrey Angus, leading three other seamen, leaped aboard *U-76*—the first Allied officer in the war to board a German U-boat.

The rest clambered onboard; Angus's party raced to the conning tower, immediately going after the Enigma coding machine and secret papers onboard the sub. Other sailors tried to attach cables and a big hawser to the U-boat, to prevent her from sinking. The U-boat was going down fast, though; and at last, the doomed boat settled beneath the waves and plunged to the bottom of the sea. Lieutenant Angus and his crew jumped clear of the plunging submarine; they had failed to capture the prized Enigma machine.

*Wolverine* rescued Hippel and thirty-nine other struggling *U-76* sailors; *Scarborough* and *Arbutus* picked up one man each.

The team of escorts, *Wolverine*, *Scarborough*, and *Arbutus*, had tagged one sub. For *Arbutus*, as well as *Wolverine*, it was the second kill of their careers. The *Athenic* and the other ships had been partially avenged. *U-76* was the thirtieth U-boat sunk in the war. One "hearse" was dead.

Finally, the ships came in, the survivors, the stragglers, the weary, the scarred, and pocked of SC 26. Of the twenty-two original ships in the convoy, ten had been sunk, two had been damaged, and the escort *Worcestershire* had been damaged as well. Almost one half the convoy had been lost. Of the twenty-two hulls which had gone through the long ordeal from April 3 to April 5, three days and two nights, twelve finally came in. They brought 58,727 tons of cargo through the gauntlet—grain, wheat, flour, pulp, steel, trucks, gasoline, oil. In the middle of 1941, England needed every ton of that precious payload to fight the war the United States had yet to enter.

HMS *Worcestershire* hobbled safely into Liverpool in company of the destroyer *Hurricane* on April 8.

The *Thirlby*, British, came limping in to Loch Ewe on April 11.

The *Tennessee*, British, diverted when it picked up a signal from a telegraph in a lifeboat from *British Reliance* and went to pick up the crew. She then proceeded to 35 degrees west longitude, and put in safely at Iceland.

The *Ethel Radcliffe* and the *Tenax* arrived in the U.K. without further incident.

And Commodore Swabey's flock of seven ships, which had endured fifty-eight unbroken hours of trial after many days at sea, finally received permission to proceed to the North Channel, bypassing the Minches, at 8:30 in the morning on April 5, where they arrived at last on April 8 without further incident.

The *Worcestershire* was repaired and had a second life, converted to a Landing Ship Infantry in 1943.

The battle had passed, the day had ended, and the sea was clean. The sun set on a blank expanse of Atlantic older than history, and, for a moment, silent. Twelve ships had come through and ended their stories, for a beat, as all ships do when they sit, secured by a hawser, at a pier. These ships were in, as all ships are for a week now and again. One more convoy was home; scores of others would follow. Britain was marshaling its powers; the escorts were drilled to a new edge, the convoys came across the great circle route, across the wide, vast, unchanging ocean field, tank ships, general cargo ships, Liberty ships, rolling ahead in their neat, ordered columns, plunging, pitching, across U-boat country.

# 9

THE FAVORITE OF DÖNITZ'S MANY NICKNAMES AMONG his men was "Der Löwe"—The Lion. It was apt. In truth, his manner of operating was more akin to a ram. Tough, pugnacious, rigid, he combined unbending discipline with studied ferocity. He was impervious to a large degree, directed toward immediate goals to the exclusion of outside factors—in the end, this trait would fail him. Handpicked by Hitler to be the last führer, he would bear in on the steel and zeal in him, until, in his last days, he was obsessed, almost fanatic. Nonetheless, it is certain that Dönitz, too, felt the pressure of the British finesse. Dönitz's system of responses was finely tuned to the British, suspicious, astute.

As the winds blew across the gray, feathered tracts of the Bay of Biscay on the French Atlantic coast where the U-boats were based, in 1941, they brought to an end a year of contrasts, of mixed fortune. In November, the tiny staff at BdU had moved from Paris to Lorient; Dönitz had set up operations at the villa in Kerneval near his main base. There, amid the maps and sea charts and weather data on the walls, Captain Godt, the head of operations, and his staff of nine officers mapped the course of the U-boat war, plotting the fix of convoys at sea, digesting the reports of commanders in from patrol, amid a rapidly changing picture.

To begin, inexplicably, since summer, growing reports had begun returning from the front of continuing incidents in which U-boats had been suddenly jumped, caught unawares, pounced on by ships and aircraft speeding in out of the blue. As the conning tower of U-boats was low and so difficult to see, U-boats had almost always spotted the enemy first. Now the U-boats were being flushed out. Writes the German U-boat expert Jak P. Mallmann Showell: "The fact that these aggressors were reported to be bearing down on U-boats at great speed when they were first sighted suggested that they had detected the U-boat long before lookouts on the conning tower had seen the escort. Up to this time, the situation had usually been the other way around."[1]

There was more. All through the summer and fall of 1941, sinkings at sea of Allied merchant ships had fallen off, then dropped abruptly. From June 1941, during which sixty-eight Allied ships had been sunk, U-boat kills had plummeted: to twenty-three in July, twenty-five in August, down to ten by November. Dönitz's U-boats were scoring more and more dismally—even though there were more of them deployed than ever before. Dönitz began to probe the question of his U-boats' lackluster performance. What was to blame? Had the British developed radar? Had they possibly perfected radio direction finding (RDF)? They were known to have the ability to fix the location of a U-boat using its radio signals, but to counter this, the U-boats had been issued special short signal books, so they could avoid sending long signals. Dönitz suspected there might be informants within the German navy; spies at one of the U-boat bases in France. A rash of sabotage attempts had already occurred at the bases—water and sand in the U-boat lubricating oil; in one case the diesel exhaust system had been tampered with, resulting in the deaths of three crewmen. Dönitz pressed his investigation but nothing came to light, no spies, no informants, no clues. Why were his subs suddenly being caught unawares, and why were they hunting with such meager results?

One more possibility crossed his mind in the summer and fall of 1941: that the British had broken naval Enigma, the baffling, highly complex, secret military code by which the admiral talked to his U-boats at sea and they with each other. But his suspicions were allayed. He was assured by the German naval staff that a break-in to Enigma was impossible. The code, created by an electro-mechanical machine resembling a portable typewriter, was thought to be impossible to crack. Reassured, Dönitz never assumed that naval Enigma had been broken.

But it had been. Working at Bletchley Park, a country estate fifty miles northwest of London, teams of cryptographers recruited from every walk of British life had succeeded in the spring of 1941, after years of work, in breaking into the complex code. Once the messages passing between the U-boat admiral and his boats could be read, the Admiralty in London was able to reroute convoys around the wolfpacks. The effect of the break into Enigma was dramatic. Once Bletchley Park was reading the code, permitting the Admiralty to reroute convoys, the impact on ship sinkings was noticeable at once. Losses went from 320,000 tons in June, to 98,000 tons in July, to 84,000 tons in August. The effects had been immediate. The value of the breakthrough was enormous; it lasted only nine months. Then Dönitz, ever sensitive about the secret code, had added a new element of complexity to the Enigma machine which was used to encrypt messages. In February, Bletchley Park had been on the out once more.

The Germans, too, had had success at breaking British codes. The British system of naval codes relied on code books—far easier to crack than codes generated by the Enigma machine. Naval Cipher #3 had been the standard naval cipher since the 1930s. But during the Spanish Civil War the Germans had broken into the system; throughout 1940, the Germans held the decisive advantage in the intelligence war. B-dienst, the German naval code breaking arm, with 8,000 people working in its service, was deciphering 2,000 messages a month to and from the British convoys. From their offices in Kriegsmarine headquarters on Tirpitz-Ufer in Berlin, B-dienst would triage intercepted messages, separating the most urgent ones and sending them to BdU, so that Dönitz could move his U-boats accordingly.

The sudden decline in sinkings and the continuing detection of German U-boats represented the first problem confronting BdU that autumn. The almost total lack of aerial reconnaissance was just as serious. Dönitz had no eyes to find the Allied convoys, nothing but his subs, alone, on distant patrol. RAF Coastal Command had an entire force capable of winging far out across the ocean to hunt subs. Dönitz, too, vitally needed reconnaissance to scour the sea for convoys.

Almost since the start of hostilities, Dönitz had sought an independent naval air arm; he had ardently pressed for Luftwaffe coverage. Hermann Göring, the head of the Luftwaffe, however, had repeatedly refused to permit the creation of such a force. "Everything that flies belongs to me,"[2] Göring had once arrogantly insisted. From that dismal beginning, Dönitz's quest had proceeded, with mounting fervor.

In December 1940, the U-boat admiral, intensifying his bid to secure air reconnaissance, had written to the Naval High Command, stepping up his campaign. Naval air reconnaissance, he said, was a sine qua non for successful offensive submarine operations. The U-boat service needed, in his words, its own eyes.

"By means of long-range reconnaissance, the Air Force can obtain for us clear and accurate information with regard to the position and movement of enemy shipping at sea and thus give us the data upon which we can group our U-boats to the greatest advantage," he had written.[3]

Carrying his quest to the summit, Dönitz had finally brought his case before Grand Admiral Erich Raeder at the Navy Department in Berlin. That same day, January 2, Raeder had sent Dönitz to see General Alfred Jodl, the chief of the Operations Staff of the German armed forces. Jodl had been convinced. He accepted at once the need for naval air coverage. Five days later, on January 7, 1941, as a result of these meetings, Hitler himself had personally interceded and broken into Göring's fiefdom to order reconnaissance coverage for the U-boat service. In balance, it was hardly the grand triumph Dönitz had hoped for. For all his lobbying, Dönitz got but one squadron, Group 40 of the Luftwaffe, transferred to his command. It was a pitiful token of the broad, substantial wing he actually needed.

The air problems went on from there. Many pilots could not navigate well over the sea. There were reports of incorrect positions given for convoys. In other cases, pilots failed to establish correctly the direction in which convoys were traveling. What airplanes there were managed to pull off few attacks.

The overriding failure of Dönitz to win adequate air coverage marked one of the great, sweeping weaknesses of German strategy in the Atlantic battle. The British, by contrast, understood the vital role that aviation had to play in the war at sea, and incorporated RAF Coastal Command into their strategy. Coastal Command flew tens of thousands of hours of reconnaissance missions. It was vast—at its height it fielded a fleet of 793 aircraft in fifty-four squadrons. It served a multipurpose role—not only providing reconnaissance but also developing an attack function which was to prove one of the most important in the Battle of the Atlantic. The wing of air cover, immense and powerful and able to get hundreds of miles out to sea, was a factor the British understood early. The German High Command never understood it.

Thus, as the autumn winds scoured the wharves and basins of the harbor at Lorient, inside the bunker, where the graphs on the walls of the data room charted monthly Allied ship sinkings and the U-boat plots were drawn each day, there were problems. But there were signs, other bellwethers, suggesting that the offensive was far from dead.

The fleet, the long, bulbous Type IXs, smaller, tapered Type VIIs, had grown into an enormous, almost unrecognizable force more than four times its size in 1939. From a flotilla of fifty-seven subs, the U-boat arm had metastasized into a fleet numbering 233 boats. Thirty-five were operational at any one time, sixteen in the North Atlantic. All these numbers might seem low, but an enormous number of submarines was tied up in training. In addition, the standard calculation, again, was that roughly one third of a U-boat force was tied up in port reprovisioning and undergoing maintenance; one third was tied up in transit to and from the patrol areas, leaving one third for actual combat. Thus, the sixteen subs listed as in the Atlantic at sea represented a far bigger force, of perhaps fifty U-boats. The expanded fleet meant that more submarines were available for war on the Atlantic. More boats meant more wolfpacks. More wolfpacks meant more possibilities for shoving pieces around on the chessboard, setting traps for Allied convoys. Not only were there more wolfpacks, the packs—the *Markgraf* (Duke) group, *Seewolf* (Sea Wolf) group, *Paukenschlag* (Drum Beat) group— were larger than the packs of 1940. The metastasis had grown innumerable new cells, larger ones.

Production, too, had grown exponentially. Through 1940, German shipyards had rolled out submarines at the dismal rate of 4.1 boats per month. In 1941, the figure had skyrocketed to 16.3. Germany's shipyards were milling submarines like so many coins coming off a belt. Dönitz's pick for the best boat, given costs and combat effectiveness, was the Type VII C—220 feet long, carrying twelve torpedoes, with a cruising range of 6,500 nautical miles. These, he believed, were more economical and efficient than the large Type IX boats that were thirty-one feet longer and 400 tons bigger, because the Type VIIs were more cost-effective, carrying only two fewer torpedoes and performing just as well in an open ocean setting. The critical calculation in his choice: he could get three Type VIIs for the price of one Type IX.

In Berlin, where RAF raids in retaliation for the Luftwaffe strikes on London had by now damaged state buildings on Unter den Linden and food shortages and high prices were creating great anxiety among ordinary Germans, strategic decisions regarding other events on land also intervened, affecting the U-boat war.

In June 1941, German panzer divisions rolled across the border into Russia, launching Operation Barbarossa, the invasion of that country. With the ranks of infantry, mechanized infantry, armor, aircraft came the diversion of German assets and resources to the Eastern Front, away from other theaters. The factories, mills, and plants slowly began to devote their forges to Hitler's quest to subjugate Russia, further disappointing Dönitz's hopes that the rolling mills might be given over to U-boat production, now, with priority, with every available furnace. Dönitz looked on with continuing dismay.

And, too, the higher echelons impinged on an operational level, this time to take U-boats off the Atlantic, in support of other campaigns. At the end of 1941, Dönitz was ordered to transfer eight subs to the Baltic to face the Russians; another six were pulled off to the Arctic Ocean, again in support of Barbarossa. Three months later, the order came for the release of another fourteen boats to take part in subsidiary operations.

By November of 1941, these draw-offs had left BdU with no more than a dozen U-boats at sea at any one time to fight the Battle of the Atlantic. It was almost the lowest level fleet strength had reached during 1941. While for much of the year there had been an expanded force for operations, at the end of 1941, U-boat Command had but a pocketful of subs to fight the engagement it considered decisive.

Through all the confused developments and various evolutions, 1941 had brought to Dönitz and his men many gains. The fleet, on the whole, was larger; production had been stepped up. But the way, all too clearly, was falling off the U-boat offensive. The British had marshaled their assets, their ships, their gambit. By the winter, the year 1941 was, in final consideration, a year of British initiative. During the last six months of the year, only five of twenty-six SC convoys had been attacked, just one in the last two months of the year. Only two of thirty-one HX convoys had been hit in the last six months of 1941, three of forty-nine ON convoys—a growing percentage of formations were at last getting through unscathed. A total of 151 ships had been torpedoed on the North Atlantic through the last six months of 1941, a downturn from earlier periods. Ship sinkings per U-boat at sea, a critical index, had dropped from an average of 3.2 ships sunk per boat at sea in 1940, to 2.2 ships sunk per boat through 1941. The British "scrambling war" was finally beginning to slow the momentum of Dönitz's ravenous wolfpacks.

Then in May, just at the time Enigma was broken, the big German super-battleship *Bismarck* was sunk in a blaze of steel and fire several hundred miles off the coast of France, a milestone in the progress of the war.

The sinking of the *Bismarck* forever closed out the day of the heavy surface vessel on the North Atlantic. The end of the 51,000-ton juggernaut was spectacular, a cataclysm. After a massive five-day sea and air hunt for the fearsome warship and attacks from carrier aircraft and destroyers, the British battleships *King George V* and *Rodney* finally closed in around the hulking giant on the morning of May 27, supported by the cruisers HMS *Dorsetshire* and *Norfolk*. At 8:47, the final battle began, *Rodney* opening fire and commencing a whumping, crashing duel. It was the climactic engagement of the chase. Salvos flew back and forth, roaring and whining in the morning. Between 9:36 and 10:16, the great, devastated, smoldering 823-foot *Bismarck* took an indeterminate number of hits at point-blank range. Her forward turrets, "Anton" and "Bruno," were put out of action, her forward command post disabled. The crash and thump of volleys roared on. At 10:37, the cruiser *Dorsetshire* sent a last torpedo slamming into the hulk; it was the coup de grâce. At 10:40, blazing and listing, the huge, ruined, obliterated titan settled and sank to the bottom of the sea 475 miles off the Breton coast of France.

The loss of *Bismarck* signaled a new age in the Battle of the Atlantic. The sinking of the huge monolith marked the close of the heavy surface ship's central role in German strategy. Never again would a capital ship of the German navy venture out into the Atlantic. From May 1941 forward, the war passed entirely to the hands of the U-boats, and the blunt, dark raptors in which Dönitz had always believed saw the arrival of their hour.

The year 1941 was not entirely one of disappointments for the Germans. A new lineup of U-boat commanders was swelling the ranks of the submarine arm; new aces were emerging to populate the gallery of top guns. Highly capable, adept, they were figures like Korvettenkapitän Johann Mohr, twenty-five years old, who would go on to sink twenty-nine ships. On his first war patrol, Mohr had accounted for a considerable bag of six ships totaling 8,737 tons. Returning from the Americas one night, Mohr, a native of Hannover, had penned the following bit of doggerel: "The moon night is as black as ink/ Off Hatteras the tankers sink/ While sadly Roosevelt counts the score/ Some fifty thousand tons."

Kapitän zur See Wolfgang Lüth would go on to sink forty-seven ships and win the coveted Knight's Cross with Oak Leaves, Swords and Diamonds, the highest decoration a U-boat man could receive. Controversial, an ardent Nazi who gave Sunday lectures to his men on the history of the Reich, paternalistic and energetic in his concern for his crews, Lüth skippered five U-boats, serving in submarines from 1937 on. Albrecht Brandi, twenty-seven, would sink twelve ships; he, too, would go on to win the Knight's Cross with Oak Leaves, Swords and Diamonds. He commanded three submarines, completing nine war patrols.

These were the new virtuosos, the new stars, Mohr with his penchant for doggerel; Brandi, "always happy and gay . . . very popular," according to Rear Admiral Erich Topp; Lüth, the commander who arranged contests for his crews and strictly regulated the food, drinks, and cigarettes they brought onboard. They wielded the U-boats, driving by night, maintaining their crews at the highest pitch, then setting up attack, then, behind the glow of their binoculars, shooting. These commanders would play significant, substantial roles in the war at sea, which, so soon, would grow grim, then grave as the Germans summoned their might.

# 10

FRANKLIN ROOSEVELT WATCHED THE ADVANCE OF the war in Europe from Washington. His was the fencer's dilemma: he must fend off a still divided Congress, yet the parry of his own convictions insisted that America must move closer to engagement.

In March, the mechanisms of the huge, vital Lend-Lease program were passed by Congress; they were signed into law on the 11th of that month; eventually they would pump an enormous, accumulating flood of arms, supplies, and matériel to Britain. Ever mindful of stirring up opposition, inscrutable as always, Roosevelt conducted his guarded march toward involvement in the European war; his moves were subtle, variously aimed. In June he froze all German and Italian assets in the United States; he went on to close the German and Italian consulates. The measures were greeted with favor; the growing anti-German feeling in Congress could be glimpsed in its approval of both moves. Buoyed by these two scores, the president cheerfully cabled his friend Winston Churchill: "After freezing the German and Italian assets on Saturday, I closed the German consulates and agencies yesterday and the reaction here is, I should say, 90% favorable."[1]

In the summer, as the days lengthened, slanting more gently across the Atlantic, the American occupation of Iceland went ahead, bringing a swelling corps of 50,000 GIs and sailors to the island nation that sat so importantly sited, just over the convoy routes. The move extended the Neutrality Zone which the U.S. was bound to protect halfway across the ocean; American power now extended to within 500 miles of Britain.

Then in August, far in the north in Canada, Churchill and Roosevelt met secretly in the carved, gorged shelter of Placentia Bay in Argentia, Newfoundland, aboard the U.S. cruiser *Augusta* and the British battleship *Prince of Wales* for their first summit. The two conferred for three days—from the meeting came the historic Atlantic Charter, a declaration of Anglo-American war aims and commonality of interests. The president had inched forward one more notch toward support for Britain.

Finally, as the winds of fall brought their chill to the East Coast, two amendments to the Neutrality Act made it possible for merchant ships to arm themselves and enter war zones; and, at last, in September, the U.S. broke out the naval ensign and for the first time assigned American destroyers to escort Allied convoys through U-boat country, across to the CHOP line (Change of Operational Control), where they were handed off to Britain's Royal Navy. The assignment of U.S. destroyers was a positive force; it put American "tin cans" right on the front lines against the Atlantic engagement; the U.S., if not at war, had joined the battle for the civilized world. The North Atlantic duty gave American hulls responsibility for about one fourth of the convoy load trans-ocean; it would last ten months until they were pulled off in June 1942 for troop convoy duty in the South Atlantic in support of the North African landings, Operation Torch.

The American destroyers on picket duty that fall were raked, many modern, bigger than the British, with lines that every American sailor knew, cutter lines, fast, streamlined. Ships like the Bensons, with a tall, angled bow, a long, sloping foredeck; the Livermores with a shorter foredeck and trim lines, the Four Stackers, Porters, Sims—these were the ships that had built the U.S. Navy.

In fall of 1941, when they took up North Atlantic duty, the American destroyers were deployed to escort the fast HX series of convoys across 1,700 miles of the Atlantic; at the MOMP (Mid-Ocean Meeting Point), the geographic equivalent of the Chop Line, a date of actual operational transfer, formations were handed off to the Royal Navy. The Stars-and-Stripes were now everywhere across the vacant, trackless sea. American gobs fought shoulder to shoulder with their British and Canadian counterparts.

The line of gray, slender U.S. Navy destroyers rode herd on HX formations from the lee of Newfoundland all the way across to the MOMP; much of this duty would be during the frigid winter months when sailors faced another forbidding enemy: the weather. In winter, crewmen hacked deck ice off fairings, off guns and mounts; they stood watches on decks and stations swept by frigid waves. The USN stood watch for some forty-five convoy runs.

The first convoy to travel with "Mr. Roosevelt's Navy" was Convoy HX 150, departing Halifax, Nova Scotia, September

16, 1941. Nine days later, HX 150 was passed off to Royal Navy hands. On parting from his American defenders, the convoy commodore, Rear Admiral E. Manners, signaled to the American escort group leader, Captain Morton L. Deyo:

> Please accept my best congratulations on the brand of work and efficiencies of all your ships in looking after us so very well, and my grateful thanks for all your kindly advice and help. Wish you success with best of luck and good hunting. If you come across Admiral Nimitz, give him my love. We were great friends some years ago out in China.[2]

Captain Deyo made back:

> This being our first escort job your message is doubly appreciated. As in the last war I know our people afloat will see eye to eye. You have my admiration for handling such a varied assortment so effectively. Will give your message to Admiral Nimitz. I was in China later and knew Admiral Little and many of your people. I hope we shall meet again. Good luck.[3]

American destroyers were now riding shotgun on Allied convoys. The U.S. had moved to the point of belligerency, had cocked the trigger. The Germans, as it turned out, were the first to fire.

On September 4, 1941, the American destroyer USS *Greer* was proceeding toward Iceland alone, roughly 250 miles south of Reykjavik, under Lieutenant L. H. Frost. Shortly after noon that day, a U-boat, *U-652*, under Kptlt. Georg-Werner Fraatz, happened on the *Greer*, and attacked and fired a torpedo. The *Greer* saw the torpedo track in time to swerve out of the way and evade damage, then counterattacked. Fraatz immediately fired a second torpedo. It also missed. The incident marked the first time an American warship had been fired upon in World War II, despite Hitler's strict orders that neutral U.S. ships were not to be assaulted.

Next, less than forty-five days later, on the night of October 16–17, the Gleaves Class destroyer USS *Kearny* was clipping east, one of five American escorts called in to assist Convoy SC 48. That night, a long and heated battle broke out—ten submarines set upon SC 48. In the confusion of action, as the subs veered through the dark, at one point a corvette crossed the *Kearny*'s bow, and before she could resume speed, a German torpedo struck her on the starboard side about the turn of her bilge. Eleven sailors were killed and twenty-two others wounded. The *Kearny* herself survived and was later repaired.

Immediately on the heels of the *Kearny* torpedoing, just two weeks later, on October 31, USS *Reuben James*, DD-245, one of the destroyers defending HX convoys, in this case HX 156, was attacked 720 miles west of Cape Clear, Ireland, by *U-552*, far out on the sea.

The skipper of *U-552*, Erich Topp, who later rose to the rank of rear admiral in the post-war German navy and lived to ninety, recalled the attack on the *Reuben James*. "It was during the early morning, and I cannot say that it was very difficult to attack. . . . The convoy was secured by six destroyers."[4] Then, even for his age, Topp's eye turns cold and steely in the command of a U-boat ace's gaze, recalling the morning. "I was attacking from about 1,000 meters. With two torpedoes I was shooting and one was hitting into the American. It was an attack in the early morning; it was . . . dark. They were following me, but they had no chance to hurt me, to destroy me."

Topp's torpedo probably struck the *Reuben James*'s forward magazine—in any case it exploded so violently that the ship's forward end was blown off back to the fourth stack. The stern section sank within five minutes. One hundred fifteen men, including all officers, went down with the ship. She was the first American warship sunk in World War II.

The three incidents constituted an unwarranted provocation of the still neutral United States. Three U.S. Navy destroyers had been attacked; one had been sunk. Roosevelt, reserved, ever mindful of the need to avoid controversy within the still divided Congress, reacted with caution. But in the wake of the *Kearny* attack, as debate proceeded on lifting the last restrictions of the Neutrality Act, he did go so far as to say, "We have tried to avoid shooting. . . . But the shooting war has started. And history recorded who fired the first shot."[5]

American guns trained on the waves. The U.S. Navy was going to war, if not in name, in all other respects.

The fall of 1941 found Otto Kretschmer a prisoner of war in the northwest of England. On arrival at dockside in Liverpool in March, he and his crew had been mobbed by hundreds of angry women with husbands at sea, as they were marched off to Lime Street Station for the London train. In London, however, his interrogators found Kretschmer modest and courteous, "an officer and a gentleman," far from a fanatic Hitlerite. On his transfer to Grizedale Hall, POW Camp No. 1 in the northwest of England, Kretschmer was immediately appointed senior German officer commanding 100 naval and Luftwaffe prisoners. One would think that here, separated by prison walls and several hundred miles from his fellow commanders, his fortunes languished behind prison gates and barracks. But Kretschmer, sometimes rather intriguingly, continued accumulating notoriety.

Most tantalizing of all was Kretschmer's secret "Council of Honor," a covert body set up to try three prisoners accused by their fellow German inmates of cowardice. The proceedings unfolded in strictest confidence.

The curious story concerned the first and second lieutenants and chief engineer of *U-570*, the first German U-boat to be captured intact by the Allies. The three officers had arrived at Grizedale only to be shunned by their fellow prisoners; the German inmates challenged the men as cowards for surrendering their boat and permitting it to fall into enemy hands.

The Geneva Conventions prohibited prisoners from setting up courts-martial or courts of inquiry. Kretschmer, bound by such camp regulations and international law prohibiting prisoner trials, had nonetheless proceeded, within the secretive, shadowy underworld of prison life, to set up a highly unusual secret Council of Honor, with himself as head, to, in effect, try the three men.

The second lieutenant and chief engineer were acquitted. Then came the strange case of the first lieutenant. The council gave him every chance to clear himself, asking him carefully and repeatedly about his actions. But the man continued to testify that he felt he and his commander had been right in valuing their own safety over the consequences of allowing the capture of *U-570*. The inmates were astonished. The lieutenant was convicted. Kretschmer ruled that the officer was guilty; he was not to be allowed to participate in camp life or any activities. He was to be ostracized.

In a bizarre coda to the tale, the distraught officer—who had asked that he be permitted to commit suicide as an act of atonement—had finally been given a chance to restore his honor and place. *U-570* lay in the harbor of a town called Barrow-in-Furness. The first lieutenant was told that if he escaped, made his way to Barrow-in-Furness and managed to scuttle the U-boat, his position would be redeemed. The first lieutenant managed to get out of the camp, but was picked up by a patrol, and while trying to escape was shot. Finally, the officer was buried with full military honors, his dignity restored.

There the mournful story ended. Prison life resumed; the inmates passed the days; Kretschmer presided over his men. "Wise Otto" continued as the focal point of camp life, sitting behind the gates of Grizedale Hall, filling his time, reading, writing. He was pinioned, an eagle behind gates, but no less striking a figure in captivity than he had been when he had reigned as Germany's top ace.

To the south in England, gladder times came to Donald Macintyre. In November, at the Brompton Oratory in London, he wed the young woman who had captured his fancy, Monica Strickland, as love flowered in the midst of war. Their whirlwind courtship had been carried on in each port where Macintyre docked during his brief shore leaves—Dundee, Southampton, Liverpool. "Monica Strickland played quite a part in the life of the *Hesperus*. Much depended on whether [she] was on the jetty [when *Hesperus* came in at Liverpool]. If she was, he was in a good mood," recalls Captain Duncan Knight, then a junior officer under Macintyre.[6] The Macintyres' honeymoon in the New Forest was possible only with his ship in drydock; it ended when ship and company were ready for sea again.

And, in the rotation of rest that must come to all commanders in battle, new orders finally took Macintyre to the permafrost of Iceland, to relieve a destroyer of the Home Fleet protecting the capital ships at Hvalfjord. The British garrison on Iceland had permitted the escorts and aircraft to extend their range of protection over the convoy routes; now, in the summer of 1941 the Americans had taken over. In this barren volcanic landscape in the extreme north, Macintyre spent a mournful Christmas and New Year 1941–1942 lying at anchor in a harbor swept by gale force winds and lit by only five hours of winter daylight.

In Newport, Rhode Island, far to the west, Commander Paul R. Heineman, who had been lost amid the maze of corridors at the U.S. Navy's Bureau of Ships, was back at sea again, commanding the destroyer USS *Moffett*. That August, the *Moffett* had left her duty in the South Atlantic to take the cruiser *Augusta*, carrying President Roosevelt to his historic meeting with Churchill, to Placentia Bay in Newfoundland. There Heineman would have heard the bands of both flagships playing and seen the decks of the *Augusta* thronged with sailors cheering as the *Prince of Wales* pulled alongside and Churchill walked aboard the big American cruiser to greet FDR.

Heineman, back on a destroyer deck at sea, was one of the hundreds of young naval officers caught up in the eddies, freshets, and currents of war as the United States rolled up its sleeves and prepared for destiny.

# PART TWO

---

# AMERICA GOES TO WAR

# 11

O<small>N</small> D<small>ECEMBER</small> 7, 1941, A LONE J<small>APANESE</small> T<small>YPE</small> A midget sub attempted to follow the general stores issue ship *Antares* into the entrances to Pearl Harbor Naval Station and was sunk by the destroyer *Ward*. Word of the incident attracted little attention, though.

Shortly thereafter, the army radar station at Kahuku Point, Oahu, reported an unusually large blip approaching from the north. The operator was told to pay no attention to the blip, as a formation of U.S. Army Air Force B-17s was expected from the West Coast of the United States.

Then, "like a thunderclap from a clear sky," in the words of Admiral Matome Ugaki, Japanese carrier planes in both high-level bombing and torpedo roles, and bombers and fighters, a total of 353 aircraft from Vice Admiral Chuichi Nagumo's main striking force of six heavy aircraft carriers, roared in over Pearl

Harbor and commenced an attack on the base and nearby military installations and airfields.[1]

In their first wave, the diving planes hit and sank the battleships *Oklahoma* (BB 37) and *West Virginia* (BB 48). In the mayhem which broke out, the auxiliary (gunnery training/target ship) *Utah* also went down. Onboard *West Virginia*, her commanding officer, Captain Mervyn Bennion, led his ship's defense until felled and mortally wounded by a fragment from a bomb which hit the battleship *Tennessee* (BB 43), moored inboard of the *West Virginia*. Bennion was posthumously awarded the Congressional Medal of Honor, the nation's highest decoration.

Roaring on over the base, continuing their terrible attack, the Japanese aircraft also sank the battleship *Arizona* (BB 39), causing a devastating explosion of her forward magazine that took the life of Rear Admiral Isaac C. Kidd, commander, Battleship Division 1, thus making him the first flag rank officer to die in the war. Then, progressively, the Japanese planes hit the battleships *California* (BB 44), which sank, and *Nevada* (BB 36), which was heavily damaged and beached.

Speeding on, the attacking Japanese aircraft damaged the battleships *Pennsylvania* (BB 38), *Tennessee* (BB 43), and *Maryland* (BB 46), the light cruiser *Honolulu*, the cruisers *Raleigh* and *Helena*, and a whole series of other ships, including the destroyer *Shaw*, the heavy cruiser *New Orleans*, the destroyers *Helm* and *Hull*, and the repair ship *Rigel*.

The savage attack hit the Pearl Harbor Naval Station and Navy Yard, naval air stations at Ford Island and Kaneohe Bay, Ewa Mooring Mast Field, army airfields at Hickam, Wheeler, and Bellows, and Schofield Barracks in the brutal assault, which destroyed 188 aircraft. In all, 2,335 servicemen were killed in the strike, and 1,143 wounded, in addition to 103 civilian casualties.

By a chance of fate, the Pacific Fleet's three aircraft carriers were at sea and escaped damage, as did shore and oil storage facilities.

The Japanese were negotiating with the U.S. up to fifteen minutes before the attack on peace measures; Japan's declaration of war was received in Washington after word of the attack on Pearl Harbor had already arrived.

The Japanese strike was brilliant in the surprise it achieved, and, as an act of state, completely without honor. President Roosevelt, asking a joint session of Congress for a declaration of war against Japan, described December 7 as "a date which will live in infamy." The bold strike crippled the Pacific Fleet of the United States; it altered the map of global war instantly. On December 8, the United States declared war on Japan. On December 11, Germany and Italy declared war on the U.S. Later in the day, the U.S. declared war on those two nations.

The United States now rolled up its sleeves, picked up the rifle stock, and swiveled, trained, and sighted its huge arsenal, its vast industrial might, its fleets and regiments and air forces on Japan and the occupied territories of the Third Reich. It began to marshal its enormous resources, its navy of 252,276 men, its army of 1,455,565 troops, its forges, factories, and foundries for war on the Axis powers of Germany, Japan, and Italy. In the Pacific, American troops and navy tars moved out on the long, arduous campaign of "island hopping" that would lead to the momentous sea battle at Midway, which turned the course of the war in Asia, and then to the victories at Guadalcanal and New Guinea. On the other side of the globe, U.S. forces and their allies would start out on the torturous road marching through North Africa, Sicily, Salerno, and Anzio, then finally the decisive amphibious assault on the Normandy beaches on D-Day.

The United States fell in. From rolling mills and crucibles to army bases and fleet anchorages, the American giant stood, and stumbled forward. The navy broke out the big guns, and the army and the U.S. Army Air Force set out on a campaign that would march for almost four long years. The big automakers gave their plants over to war production, and factories across the U.S. manufacturing everything from washing machines to coffeepots retooled themselves for war. Along the four coasts of America, shipyards began a priority program of shipbuilding. Yet at mobilization, as the sleeping giant stirred and arose, for all its mass and industrial might, the situation for the U.S. and its Allies on the cold, jagged field of the sea went from bad to worse, then to twilight.

Hitler now loomed across a wide swath of Europe. He dominated most of the continent and Scandinavia. The Mediterranean was occupied by the Axis; Greece had fallen in May. In Russia, the first great counteroffensive, led by General Georgi Zhukov, had rolled forth as Zhukov broke out of the region south of Moscow. In North Africa, General Erwin Rommel's Afrika Korps, advancing in heavy fighting, was engaged in a bitter struggle with British armored units. North Africa was still contested. Germany now controlled a vast domain stretching in the west from the Atlantic coast of France to the frigid fields of western Russia in the east. Nazi Germany and the Axis rolled their Blitzkrieg ahead relentlessly. It was at this embattled juncture, with the U.S. declaration of war not one month old, that Hitler decided to send his submarines across the wide, gray reaches of the Atlantic—for a direct strike on America. The campaign, mapped out by Dönitz, was code-named Paukenschlag, Operation Drumroll.

The assault targeted the whole East Coast from Key West,

Florida, to Newfoundland; it got underway almost immediately. A first wave of nine Type IX U-boats sailed from their Biscay bases in early January 1942, in two groups, of five subs and four. Big, open ocean boats, the Type IXs carried fourteen torpedoes and 105mm deck guns, some of the heaviest armament mounted by German submarines. They drove across the wide Atlantic for ten days, faring west, traversing convoy country; they proceeded south and west across the wide, open stretches of the sea. The big Type IXs were 1,100-tonners; with their vast cruising radius they would be able to stay in U.S. waters for an extended period of time. The first attack was slated for January 12. When the nine boats reached the Eastern Seaboard, chaos broke out. Operation Paukenschlag exceeded Dönitz's wildest dreams; it rapidly deteriorated into a wholesale slaughter of Allied shipping along the East Coast.

The lead wave of submarines ran smack into an American defense which was, by any measure of judgment, entirely inadequate. The entire navy flotilla available for protection of merchant ships along the whole length of the East Coast consisted of three 110-foot wooden subchasers, two 173-foot patrol boats, a score of Eagle boats left over from World War I, and a few converted yachts, a handful of about twenty-five vessels. The Army Air Force had on hand for defensive air coverage no more than nine aircraft.

To make matters worse, the navy refused to institute the one system which had proved useful against submarines—armed convoys. All experience had shown that convoys dramatically reduced losses of merchant ships, but the navy adamantly stuck to its policy and refused to implement the practice. Admiral Ernest J. King, the commander-in-chief of the U.S. Fleet, an irascible, often arrogant, intemperate figure (who Roosevelt said, "shaved with a blow torch,"[2]) persisted in his opinion that convoys would be ineffective in the present scenario, refusing the offer of twenty-four British antisubmarine trawlers to help in establishing armed escort. In place of defense by escort warships, merchantmen were left to sail independently, without any shield.

The result was an open-ended shoot-'em-up with the lid off — a six-month spectacle of German raiding up and down the Eastern Sea Frontier.

The traffic lanes of the East Coast were an industrial alley crowded with ships running north and south — oil tankers bringing oil from refineries to the south, freighters carrying bauxite, raw material for the manufacture of aluminum, other ships and commodities. Like a sprawling eight-lane highway, the Eastern Seaboard ran with coastal traffic, a corridor of vital commerce.

Into this crucial flow of goods and industrial products came the nine subs of Paukenschlag. The action began immediately. On the 12th, the first day of raiding, Reinhard Hardegen in *U-123* took the first pelt, torpedoing the British freighter *Cyclops*, 9,076 tons, 300 miles east of Cape Cod. The gallery reeled with the plunder that followed. The next day, Ernst Kals in *U-130* got two more freighters. Two more ships were sunk on the 15th, including the 8,106-ton British oil tanker *Diala*, three ships were sunk on the 17th, three ships each on the 18th and 19th. Virtually every day German subs claimed their share of Allied hulls. The final tally for the month of January mounted to fifty-eight ships aggregating a whopping 307,059 tons — as good a box score as that for any month on the North Atlantic routes. And this was only the first month of the campaign.

The wanton marauding along the shore was made all the worse by seaside communities which brazenly kept their lights blazing, backlighting merchant ships for the Germans to see.

When the call came to darken the coasts, protests came back that the "tourist season would be ruined." The lights burned on; the Nazi vipers continued picking off coastal shipping by night. Finally, in April, the navy managed to douse waterfront lights and sky signs, and in May the army ordered a stringent curfew.

The great naval historian Samuel Eliot Morison wrote of Operation Paukenschlag: "No more perfect setup for rapid and ruthless destruction could have been offered the Nazi sea lords. 'The massacre enjoyed by the U-boats along our Atlantic coast in 1942 was as much a national disaster as if saboteurs had destroyed half a dozen of our biggest war plants,' " he quoted a military report as stating.[3]

All these sinkings encompassed the most grisly horrors, ships going down ablaze at night within sight of shore, flaming oil spread across the waters, men swimming through these pyres or diving underwater to avoid them, men in one case being machine-gunned to death.

Through month after month of full-field mayhem, the commander-in-chief of the U.S. Fleet, Admiral King, refused to institute convoys. King, one of the greatest admirals to rise through the U.S. Navy, would later go on to become chief of naval operations, the navy's highest post, and lead America to its stunning triumphs in the Pacific and Atlantic. But on Paukenschlag he blundered. Regardless of the evidence, he kept merchant ships sailing independently, without guard, rather than imposing convoy.

The chaos continued; the carnage went on, month after month. The second wave of attacks was set for February 16.

The day of the new attack, the 16th, a grand total of nine ships went down at the hands of the Nazis, Werner Hartenstein in *U-156* and Jürgen von Rosenstiel in *U-502* culling three victories apiece. Two ships were sunk on the 18th, five more on the

19th. Day after day, the slaughter went on, the U-boats raiding almost unrestrained. Eight ships were torpedoed on the 22nd, then five on February 23, then four more on the 28th, including the American destroyer USS *Jacob Jones* and the 7,017-ton American tanker *Oregon*.

Finally the free-for-all wound down. Admiral King and the navy woke up and instituted partial "Bucket Brigade" convoys along the coasts—taking convoys north in 120-mile lengths, then anchoring for the night; at last, in August, a complete interlocking convoy system between Guantánamo, Cuba, and Key West, Florida, and New York was instituted. The East Coast was now locked up defensively. Dönitz immediately cooled to operations there. Always, he favored dealing out his boats with minimum risk; now he shifted them south, to the Gulf of Mexico, where a lighter naval presence made hunting easier. His raiders chalked up numerous new victories in the Gulf, along the New Orleans–Tampa range. Paukenschlag finally fizzled out with Dönitz's wolves raiding in the Gulf and the Caribbean. Finally, "The Lion" pulled his boats completely from the Americas. The action had gotten too hot for him. U.S. Navy defenses were too tight.

Over seven swift months, Paukenschlag was a complete success. Between January and the end of March, German U-boats destroyed a total of 202 ships between the East Coast of America and the Western Approaches to Britain, with an aggregate tonnage of over 900,000. From April through July, Dönitz's subs claimed another eighty-three ships aggregating 416,657 tons. That made a total of 285 ships sent below—three fourths of what had been sunk in all of 1940—in only seven short months. In what was, to all intents and purposes, the first half of 1942, the oil flow to Europe had been interrupted; the Nazis had accounted for roughly 1.5 million tons of shipping.

Americans had only their poor preparation and response to blame.

On the North Atlantic, things went no better.


The autumn, then winter of 1942–43 encompassed the worst weather of the war. Gales swept the frigid North Atlantic, whipping it into a field of lifting hillocks and valleys, sending sheets of spray crashing over destroyers' bows, flying past bridge wings where officers peered into the maelstrom, hunting, pursuing, searching for the U-boats, which were never very distant. Meteorological data recorded sixty-three gales of Beaufort Force 7 or stronger in 1942, seventy-two in 1943, the highest numbers for the war to this point.

In the blustery, cold suspension of this winter, Admiral Dönitz now launched his winter offensive. Enigma was still blacked out; the Allies had no idea where the U-boats were. By autumn of 1942, U-boat strength stood at 382 boats. One hundred were at sea at any one time, roughly forty in the Atlantic, the greatest strength the Germans had yet mustered—the balance of the fleet being scattered in the Mediterranean, the Baltic, the Arctic, and elsewhere. The U-boat fleet, girded now with a substantial number of boats, tempered by years of battle, launched out on its most substantial bid yet to interdict the convoy web. The German initiative, targeting the region between Iceland and Greenland, struck convoys all along the Allied ocean lines. Submarines hit in the north; they hit in the mid-ocean void called the "Air Gap" where no air cover of Sunderlands, Catalinas, Hudsons could reach; they hit across the 500-mile stretch of the empty sea. They struck in concert, in the large, growing packs, and suddenly—in the hush of the months from September through to the spring—it seemed as if the whole shuddering, groaning convoy system might wobble and fall apart.

At the lip of this yawning, gaping pass stood one force alone—the Royal Navy, white cap, Black No. 5 dress, crisp stature, and its hearty cousin, the Royal Canadian Navy. The RN squadrons on the ocean were grouped into four or five convoys at sea at any one time; the U-boats roved in packs, these fielded 1,200 miles out from the Atlantic ports in France where they based. The Germans had about 40 subs at sea, always in their loose strings of patrol lines; the RN and RCN had about fifty ships at sea on the Atlantic at any one time; they had been stretched thin by draw-offs. Here, in the hesitation of this chill, whistling passage, the Battle of the Atlantic, and with it the fate of the entire war in Europe, came to hinge. To understand the precipice at which the Royal Navy now stood, it is necessary to understand not only what it faced, but what it was.

The Royal Navy was not simply the greatest navy in the world; it had been for three centuries, almost since the days of carracks and fireships. For almost 300 years, from its emergence between 1620 and 1660—until the ascendancy of the U.S. Navy during World War II—Britain's Royal Navy, with spar, topmast, rail, and line, had commanded the seas with virtual supremacy, through almost inconceivable shifts and transmogrifications of naval advance, the shift from rounded man o' war to ship of the line, the shift from sail to steam, the leap to steel warships, the development of: the revolving gun turret, the screw propeller, battleships—the list went on; Britain's Royal Navy had stood through all these ages as the dominating, towering master of war at sea.

In the course of a little less than three centuries, it had prevailed over the Dutch in the Third Dutch War (1672), disposed of the French in the Early French Wars (1692), bested the Spanish in the War of Succession (1701), shattered the French once again in the epochal Revolutionary and Napoleonic Wars (1797–1805), fought with Turkey and France against the Russians in the Crimean War (1853) and crushed the Germans in World War I (1914–1918). It was a glittering series of unbroken triumphs and prevalence.

The British navy had excelled, first, in gunnery. From the dusty days of the Three Days Battle (February 1653) down to the time of the Napoleonic wars, British ships and men had distinguished themselves in rapidity of loading, aim and steadiness of fire. There was no more lethal brand of gun duel than with the British.

As important in the frame of mastery that rose through the trunk of the RN was discipline—legendary, rigid, certain. By the dawn of the twentieth century, such draconian measures as flogging through the fleet (the whipping of a man aboard every ship in a fleet, from which few men emerged alive), and keel-hauling (in which a man was hauled under the barnacle encrusted bottom of a ship from one side to the other), had long since disappeared. But the discipline bracing every rating and officer on the gray destroyers and corvettes in the Second World War was no less crisp.

Last, above all in the sheaf of Royal Navy strengths which defined the corps of officers and enlisted men was that quicksilver, difficult to define quality one might call intrepidness. That combustible mixture of boldness and initiative had been passed down from decades and generations bygone of captains, lieutenants, boatswains, and foretopmen to the crews which rose and rolled across the seas in 1942. No champion out of British naval history shone more brilliantly, displayed more prominently this quality of rake, or blade, than England's best-loved hero, Vice-Admiral Sir Horatio Nelson. By the age of nineteen, he had taken his first prize, seized ship; he had led boarding parties onto two Spanish enemies and, with the 69th Regiment, seized them both, in hand-to-hand combat, by the age of thirty-nine. At forty-seven, Nelson had obliterated a combined Spanish-French fleet off Cape Trafalgar, staving off the possibility of French invasion, saving the King and country to which his loyalty was so absolute.

These three qualities—gunnery, discipline, intrepidness—wound like strands through every sailor on the gun mounts and quarterdecks of the weatherbeaten, tough escorts which pitched and tossed over the Atlantic, taking the convoys through U-boat country. Depth charge crews on the best ships could be ready in thirty seconds. Shiphandling, the aiming, training, firing of guns, depth charges in the heaving, yawing seas of the North Atlantic was the exact science—and the job—of RN crews. Macintyre once said he would charge a man back from an improper shore jaunt with desertion of his post of duty in time of war. This was the Royal Navy—superb in performance, capable to the highest pitch of tuning, cracking like a pennant in the wind. It had been as taut and tried for almost 300 years.

Thus, in 1939, at war's outset, the British navy stood with a corps of officers and men—also the Royal Navy Reserve and Royal Navy Voluntary Reserve—and a fleet, which were formed by these brilliant traditions. These three grooves, by the start of World War II, had honed and turned the fleet into a peerless, winding fighting machine. The Royal Navy in 1939 was the arbiter of seapower, with a heritage among its armor-belted battleships, its towering cruisers, its raked frigates and sloops that included an unequaled record in war. If it could hold, then so would the war. If it could not, then civilization stood at the abyss.

One of the crisp, schooled figures who exemplified this long Royal Navy tradition of polish and esprit was Commander Donald Macintyre, the victor over Schepke and Kretschmer, commander of Escort Group 5. From Iceland, Macintyre, nerves frayed from the strain of two years of continuous North Atlantic duty in small ships, was posted to a shore assignment as the British representative to the new American naval base at Argentia. There, where Roosevelt and Churchill had met the previous year, the Americans were carving out of the Canadian wilds the forward base for their new Support Force, which oversaw the American role in the Battle of the Atlantic and acted as a layover installation for British and Allied escort groups between convoys. Winter passed; Macintyre enjoyed the pleasures of Argentia; soon, as the days grew warm and the sun returned to the sea again, summer brought Macintyre round once more to sea duty.

In June, he finally left his shore postings. Macintyre opened his orders; the Admiralty had assigned him to take command of HMS *Hesperus* again. By autumn of 1942, he was back on the bounding ocean, once more in the habitat which suited him most truly, stalking U-boats in the wind and the spray. Macintyre was back on a pitching bridge, one of many officers carrying forward the ancient cutlass of the Royal Navy as it faced a reckoning that was, slowly, everywhere, unmistakably, gathering all across the Atlantic.

Thousands of miles across the ocean, on the Canadian mainland, Otto Kretschmer found himself in new surroundings. Like most U-boat POWs captured by the British, Kretschmer was transferred to a Canadian prison camp at Bowmanville near Lake Ontario. There, the Germans found a bleak life in limbo inside the camp barbed wire. As the new senior German officer,

Kretschmer soon transformed it. Under his direction, sports fields, tennis courts, a swimming pool, even vegetable gardens were laid out; sports leagues and camp concerts were set up for recreation, and courses in navigation were organized for midshipmen. Here, in the wilderness of Canada, Kretschmer continued his steady, often curious, rise to celebrity with a defiant melée. In August 1942, Kretschmer led a full blown prison rebellion.

The incident began over the matter of shackling prisoners. Far away, in Europe, after the Dieppe reconnaissance raid, 100 British prisoners of war had been taken in chains to Germany. Now, indignant and abrupt, British military officials had insisted that 100 prisoners at Bowmanville be shackled in turn, as a response to the German move. Kretschmer was duly summoned to the camp commandant's office. The commandant, one Colonel Bull, announced the news. Kretschmer quietly but firmly responded that German prisoners would resist the shackling measure with force. Bull offered that he was sorry for the breakdown in the cordiality of relations.

Kretschmer now withdrew. He consulted with fellow officers, then at once set about organizing the resistance. A defense headquarters was readied in a large, brick-walled kitchen; another redoubt was set up in a brick hut nearby. Officers and men barricaded themselves inside the structures, armed with iron bars and sticks. At 2:00 P.M. on a Saturday, the donnybrook commenced.

Three times, the guards stormed the German prisoners' defenses, as well as other small huts where the inmates had massed. Axes flew to break down doors, clubs swung, sticks whacked, not entirely in total seriousness. The guards were driven back again and again. At 6:00 P.M. all was quiet. The prisoners stood down from their stations.

Colonel Bull now decided to send for regular army troops.

The next morning, as Bull had planned, a battalion of Canadian Army troops marched into Bowmanville with hoses, clubs, and fixed bayonets. Kretschmer's irregular army of ragtag warriors, brandishing hockey sticks, fire axes, and stones, stood across the main gate of the camp. Behind were other rows of prisoners, still other inmate-defenders to either side of the main group. The army troops marched in, the clubs flew. All day long, a pitched battle raged, both sides by now almost enjoying the spirited melée; by dusk, the army troops had prevailed.

Both sides withdrew; an emergency first-aid station was organized by Canadian and German doctors to treat the injured of both sides; in time order returned, darkness fell. Later that night, the entire camp assembled in the open grounds of the facility as 100 German inmates were shackled and led out of the camp. Bowmanville returned to order and peace; prison life resumed. Kretschmer was rapidly becoming as legendary as he had been as the Golden Ace. To his status as senior German officer, he had added the mantle of Hero of the Bowmanville Rebellion. Camp life picked up; the days went on; the guards watched their prisoner-charges, perhaps with more of an edge. Summer waned to autumn.

And at latitude unspecified, a thousand miles away, under the clear sun and chill winds at sea, Captain Paul Heineman—he had been promoted—once lost in the maze of corridors at the U.S. Navy's Bureau of Ships, then commanding officer of the destroyer USS *Moffett*, had a new hat. He was now an escort group leader, skipper of the A-3 Escort Group. That fall, there were eleven Allied Escort Groups on the North Atlantic: six British (B), four Canadian (C), and one American (A). The A-3 group would be the lone American escort on the Atlantic during the difficult fall and winter of 1942–43. The Germans were moving. In the chill as the sky turned cold, scouring the slate stretches of the vacant sea, Admiral Dönitz launched his winter offensive. His submarines were almost at the peak of their wartime strength. On the charts, as the neat lines of longitude and latitude scored off the expanses of the Atlantic in quadrants, he planned to send his subs west, far west—to a remote stretch between Greenland and Iceland, the zone called the "Air Gap," where no Allied air cover could reach. He would send big open-ocean boats; he would send Type VIIs; he would send them in greater mass than ever before. Here, in the Air Gap, he hoped, his wolfpacks might at last be able to score decisively to cut the Allies' ocean lifelines. A reckoning awaited, a yawning, plunging pass over which lay the mantle of victory, or the pall of defeat. The Royal Navy faced the ocean pit the Nazis called "The Devil's Gorge." The Royal Canadian Navy faced it, too. One of the first through the pit that autumn was Captain Heineman. He was a "tin can" skipper, a destroyerman. Of Americans, Heineman was the best.

# 12

H E WAS LEANING INTO THE FORWARD BRIDGE BULK-
head as she took the waves, looking with his glasses
out the round portholes of the *Spencer*, quiet, studied,
looking grim; but his face had a certain hardness in it which always made him look grim, but for his smile. He was an American, trim, tall, angular, and he was looking at the distance, at
nothing in particular. But then you never knew what to look for,
the tiny pod of a periscope, a conning tower, an exhaust trail.
There were hours like this, scanning, hunting, peering at the ruffled, gray field.

It had already begun; the U-boats were out there. Earlier he
had encountered two, and attacked, with inconclusive results.
Then it had been quiet the rest of the day. They were out there,
though; he had seen them, all morning long the signals had come

in and he had passed them on to the other ships in the escort group.

At 9:20 in the morning: "S/M [submarine] sighted 0916Z [9:16 Zulu, i.e., GMT] 19th."

At 11:05: "SC 100 submarine sighted 1105Z 19th."

At 8:12 in the evening: "From Cominch [commander-in-chief, U.S. Fleet] To U.S.S. *Spencer*: U-Boat Warning. U/B estimated in your vicinity by D/F has made sighting report of convoy or important unit at 2012Z/ 19th."[1] It was September 19, 1942.

Captain Paul R. Heineman, U.S. Navy, formerly a desk jockey, was now on a broad sea, leading the American A-3 team. Later, he would accumulate a reputation in this role as one of the crack Senior Officers, Escort, on the North Atlantic. He would go on to be awarded the Legion of Merit, with Combat Distinguishing Device V, then a Gold Star in lieu of a second Legion of Merit with Combat V and eleven additional decorations. He would command a cruiser in the Pacific; his group on the North Atlantic would become legendary, known as "Heineman's Harriers." Today he was a forty-five-year-old escort leader in command of a squadron of nine escort ships, based on Argentia, Newfoundland. On the 12th of September, they had picked up at Halifax the twenty-four merchant ships of Convoy SC 100 for the long transocean crossing to the U.K.

"He was five feet, ten inches, relatively stocky, a nice-looking man," recalls Mike Hall, a Coast Guard captain who was onboard the *Spencer* at the time of the battle of Convoy SC 100. "He was probably the epitome of a naval officer in those days in his attitude toward whatever you encountered. He was very aggressive. When he came aboard, he used to send individual escorts to search around (away from the convoy to hunt

U-boats). We had never done that before under another escort commander."[2]

Roughly 150 miles away, on the dusky ocean, they slipped into place, silent, unseen, waiting. Nine U-boats of the *Lohs* (Lohs is the name of a World War I U-boat commander) wolfpack arrived on station on September 8, 400 miles northeast of Cape Race, Newfoundland, and formed a patrol line, lying in wait as the packs always did for whatever happened along. For nine days they had lurked, hovering in their line along the slate, rolling sea, a long, tedious vigil.

Then, a breakthrough. On September 17, German intelligence had decrypted information giving the position of an eastbound convoy as of noon, September 16. It placed the formation 150 miles southeast of Cape Race. This was Convoy SC 100. BdU reacted at once. In March 1942, the tiny staff had moved back up to Paris. Now in their headquarters in a modern apartment block on the Avenue Marechal Manoury, they began to assemble a wolfpack. The boats of the nearby *Pfeil* (Arrow) wolfpack were gathered. They were ordered to join the *Lohs* group. The pack collected. There was now a sobering total of twenty-one U-boats in the vicinity of Heineman and his convoy. Enigma was still blacked out. Heineman could not know this. Finally, on September 18, *U-599*, one of the *Lohs* boats, found the convoy. He immediately radioed the location of SC 100 back to BdU; the wolves converged on the fix. The trap was set.

It was September 19. Heineman watched the field. All evening it was quiet. The sun set on the Atlantic as it does, so quickly it seems the last indigo light of the horizon and the black furrows of the waves plunge into darkness in the same dive, almost in minutes. Heineman had made contact earlier in the day with individual submarines, because of this, despite the loss of Enigma, both the hunted and the hunters by now knew of each other's presence. The convoy slipped ahead over the ocean, a caravan of mammoths, blacked out, shuffling through the moist sea night. The weather was fair, a light breeze blew; a moderate swell stirred the immense, dark sea.

The next morning broke so fast they were tumbling over each other to try to keep the subs down as the jackals hit at once.

At 8:55, while sweeping on the starboard flank eleven miles from the convoy, the 205-foot Canadian corvette *Bittersweet* sighted a U-boat off her starboard side, six miles distant. She lunged ahead at full speed; she at once saw smoke and a conning tower just to the right; this was a second U-boat. She surged, opening fire with her 4-inch gun. On she drove, firing away, but the subs were drawing ahead and outrunning her. Heineman ordered the 327-foot sister ship of the *Spencer*, USS *Campbell*— both were coast guard cutters, manned by coast guard crews—to take over the chase. The *Campbell* leapt off her position and ran on the attack.

Then, in the next ninety minutes, the battle unfolded.

At 9:55, the Canadian corvette *Lunenberg*, on the starboard side of the convoy, sighted another U-boat five miles distant, almost off her right flank, and went on the attack, to no avail.

At 11:11, the Canadian *Rosthern*, on the port bow of the convoy, picked up a sonar contact dead ahead at 1,200 yards. At almost the same instant, two torpedoes went streaking past her no more than twenty-five yards away, aimed at her or the convoy. Heineman later stated in his log, "They were apparently electric [powered by lead/acid accumulators as opposed to compressed air], running very shallow, heads and parts of body clearly discernible, with no wake, but often surfacing in the troughs."[3] The U-boat submerged, but *Rosthern* made contact and attacked with a five-depth-charge pattern which she thought hit the sub.

Now Convoy SC 100 made an evasive 45 degree turn to the right; and just as it did, a deafening explosion tore through the convoy ranks, roaring through the pack, as the British freighter *Empire Hartebeeste*, first ship in the seventh column, blew sky-high in a column of debris. She had been hit between Nos. 4 and 5 Holds; the detonation had blown a load of trucks on her decks high into the air.

First victory had gone to Gunter Jahn in *U-596*. "Shot at freighter of 6,000 tons. Distance 2,000 meters. Hit. Detonation heard after two minutes, 18 seconds," his log reads.[4] One of the other U-boat skippers nearby, Kptlt. Paul-Karl Loeser in *U-373*, recorded: "Some time later, the characteristic crumbling of the bulkheads of a sinking steamer was heard."[5] These were the death throes of the *Hartebeeste* breaking up.

The crew of the *Hartebeeste* abandoned ship in the three salvageable lifeboats and "all the boats had just cleared the vessel as she sank vertically by the stern within five minutes of being struck, finally disappearing at [11:30 A.M.]," Captain J. F. Travis, master of the *Hartebeeste*, reported.[6] There were no casualties, but the *Hartebeeste*, 5,676 tons, and her general cargo plunged below. She was an old dog, built in 1918. Another Allied ship had fallen to the Nazi raiders. The shooting went on without a pause.

At 11:18 the *Spencer* jumped into action. She was one of the most illustrious ships of World War II, participating in more battles than any other Coast Guard warship to serve in the war, and the most highly decorated Coast Guard vessel of the war. Now she took off like a jaguar after a kill. Heineman here saw another torpedo track running 2,000 yards ahead of the convoy.

He lunged ahead, racing off in hot pursuit. The action, and the loose torpedoes, had just begun. Bedlam broke out as the pack hit.

The *Lunenberg* picked up a sonar contact off the right rear of the convoy and attacked with a seven-depth-charge pattern.

Between 11:31 and 12:45 P.M., the *Spencer* and the Canadian corvettes *Bittersweet, Mayflower, Lunenberg, Rosthern,* and *Trillium* loosed eight attacks on solid contacts, the *Rosthern* attacking a sub repeatedly at 12:29, 12:34, 12:40, and 12:44. When she let up, oil appeared on the surface and an oily smell was detected. Sonar echoes of the area showed no more contacts, signs of a probable sinking. *Rosthern* stood down and passed on.

Then the action faded. As quickly as it had come up, the fury of battle died away. The shooting stopped, the sonar contacts disappeared, the guns and depth charge racks fell silent. The U-boats seemed to let up. From 12:44, all day and night, the lull following combat set in. Sailors drooped over their guns, depth charge crews stood down, the convoy escorts once more took up station in place around the formation. Convoy SC 100 had only begun to face the ordeal it would experience 790 miles south of Kiahnek, Greenland, out far in the immense void of the Atlantic expanse. Tomorrow would bring surprises.


When September 21 dawned, the wind was whining and shrieking a 65-to-70-knot blow, a full hurricane. All across the tilting, yawing face of the sea, the huge, mountainous green walls of water built up into bluffs and rose far overhead. The wind moaned like a ghost and tore the tops off the waves in sheets of spray. The ships, laboring in the agonized seaway, bobbed to the tops of the waves, plunged into the troughs; then they buried their noses into the seas and lifted up, tons and tons of white water spilling off their bows. As far as the eye could see, the heaving face of the ocean was a mountain range of gray, tormented peaks.

"The *Spencer*, when it got real rough weather, you would shudder to the top of the wave and then it would come down— WHAM. You knew it. There's some enormous waves up there," says Harold Rogers, the baker onboard the *Spencer* at the time of the battle of Convoy SC 100, of the North Atlantic.[7]

"The worst seas I had ever encountered were in September of 1942 and I was concerned we weren't going to get over these mountainous seas," says Mike Hall. "We were down here and those seas were going up and up. I spent several years on weather patrol. There were some seas as bad."[8]

Early in the morning on the 21st the situation became untenable on the tossing, heaving ocean field. Heineman ordered the convoy hove to, brought to a halt in place to ride out the hurricane. He now tried to head the flotilla up into the wind, pointing straight into it, the best heading for riding out a storm. But because of the heavy load of deck cargoes, automobiles, trucks, airplanes, tractors, lumber, only some of the ships managed to make the heading. An entire convoy, twenty-four merchant ships, was halted, brought to a complete standstill in the middle of a convoy battle by a raging, howling hurricane. The terrible strength of the storm tore through the ships. Havoc swept the sea. At 6:15, the British corvette *Nasturtium* lost its steering. "My steering gear jammed hard-a-starboard and we found ourselves going round in circles in one of the worst gales I've ever experienced. The position was most unattractive," the commanding officer of *Nasturtium*, Lieutenant C. D. Smith, later wrote in a masterpiece of understatement.[9] The gale howled and shook across the sea. The entire battlefield was a cauldron of whipping weather. The U-boats had problems of their own.

At 8:00 A.M., the antennas of *U-221* were ripped off by the force of the hurricane. The sealed openings and covers to the boat's pressure hull were sprung by the storm.

Later, in the raging gusts, a seaman on board *U-432*, one Weinhold, had both his arms broken when he was knocked down while trying to secure the conning tower hatch while tethered only by his safety belt.

Still later, across the heaving sea, *U-258*, under Kptlt. Wilhelm von Mässenhausen, would lose its navigator when he was swept overboard.

Back in Paris, sobered by reports of the storm, Dönitz now canceled the pack operation on the 22nd due to the weather. He was unaware that several boats were still in contact with the convoy.

The hurricane blew all day on the 22nd, but the winds were quieting. The seas moderated a bit; Heineman now began looking for his ships, not knowing whether the U-boats would hit first, or the storm would pick up again. Captain Heineman, an officer who always displayed pronounced concern for his men, set out to round up his flock; on his shoulders fell responsibility not just for the 285 men on his ship, but for the entire convoy. "He exhibited great interest in the crew," says Hall. "He paid more attention to whether we were happy, the crew, generally speaking, than the captain did. He was outgoing." Abroad, in the slop of the afternoon, the corvette *Nasturtium*, back in the running, found eight of the flock, including the commodore N. H. Gale's flagship, *Athelsultan*, and got them on course. *Spencer* and *Nasturtium* finally managed to gather twelve of the merchant ships and several escorts. The formation now got underway again in the diminishing gusts.

So Heineman continued, driving through the pitiless rage and the howl of the winds. Daylight passed. Evening fell. The sun set, and now it was dark on the white-capped, tumbling face of the ocean. The convoy pounded east. For another twenty-four hours, the ships lurched on, swaying and rolling in the quieting seaway. They pushed ahead, bucking the swells into the night of the 22nd. Unbeknownst to them, another intruder had arrived. He trailed them from a distance, shadowing the convoy. This was Kapitänleutnant Albrecht Brandi, age 28, commanding *U-617* on his maiden patrol. He had found the armada in the confusion of the storm.

Kptlt. Brandi observed the convoy for a time. He dogged the formation like a bloodhound, stalking his quarry. Then, at 8:50 P.M., he started laying out an attack.

The convoy lumbered on, twenty-three ships plunging across the dark sea, unaware. At the time, convoy Commodore N. H. Gale was having tea with Captain J. D. Donovan, the master of his flagship, the tanker *Athelsultan*. Nothing disturbed them.

All of a sudden, roaring through the herd, an explosion ripped the night apart; then another, louder one. Two eels from Brandi had found their mark. The *Athelsultan* had been hit in her engine room on the starboard side. A big British ship of 8,882 tons carrying molasses and alcohol, she would never make it to England.

Brandi recorded: "Hit on the tanker. Crash dive. Second detonation can be heard in the boat, followed by a number of explosions (boilers). With the naked ear one can hear unmistakably the sinking of the tanker." [10]

Donovan rushed out onto the bridge of the stricken vessel to find the boat deck awash for thirty feet aft. Soon water was coming aboard everywhere; the ship was sinking. The scene became one of fast action as the men took to the boats. Donovan went to look for the radio operator, who had flashed out an emergency signal, but could not find him. "On trying to return, I was washed down from the bridge to the deck below where I found a sailor, whom I told to jump over the side as the ship was sinking fast, but he said he was not strong enough to swim. I left him behind and jumped overboard myself. As soon as I touched the water I noticed the ship was tearing past me, she was sliding under stern first and sank at approximately [8:30 P.M.]." [11]

Captain Donovan "seemed to be submerged a very long time." [12] On surfacing, he found some white doors to which he tried to hang on, but without success. He finally found two pieces of wood to support him. Men were all about, hanging on to rafts and in the water. In all, they were swimming for about one and a half hours. Donovan and one other man were at last picked up by HMCS *Weyburn*. Feeling through the night and the wreckage, the British corvette HMS *Nasturtium* found one other survivor on one raft, six more on another.

Commodore Gale was never seen again. In all, fifty-one of fifty-nine in crew were lost in the torpedoing of the *Athelsultan*.

The *Athelsultan*, 475 feet long, registered in Liverpool, was only thirteen years old. She had been the flagship of the convoy, first ship in the middle column, proud. Now she and her cargo were gone.

The convoy picked up, and labored on. The ships pitched ahead for almost an hour and a half. The wind had died to Beaufort Force 8, gusting to 40 knots. The sea was State 7, moderately high waves with the edges breaking into spray. All around the sea was a range of swells, windblown. For a long time it was quiet. The ships drove on, blacked out, lifting and falling in the night as the spray lashed in sheets. Heineman was out front, ahead of the convoy. The wind flew past, the waves phosphorescent in the night.

Then, out of nowhere, at 9:40, a second detonation roared

through the convoy and a huge column of black smoke and water erupted as the British freighter *Tennessee* was hit. The torpedo struck amidships, in the engine room. The *Tennessee*, 302 feet long, had made it through the long ordeal of Convoy SC 26 eighteen months before, surviving the hard way, but now her life was ending. One of Brandi's torpedoes had hit her on the port side.

Brandi's log coldly records her death: "[9:21 P.M.]: At 130 degrees true a steamer straggling at the end of the convoy comes into sight. [9:32]: Attack, shots from tubes III and IV. Misses, because [target] speed set too high. Turn away for attack with stern tube [9:42]: Shot from tube 5 is observed as hit midships. Steamer starts to list and sinks rapidly after 11 minutes with a boiler explosion. Estimate 5,500 tons."[13]

Kptlt. Brandi's guess was way off. The little *Tennessee* was just 2,342 tons; her call sign was Oscar, X-Ray, Papa, Charlie, OXPC. She had been built in Copenhagen, Denmark, in 1921 by A/S Baltica Vaerftet. But Brandi's torpedo had hit its mark, and she and her cargo of grain were finished.

Onboard the sinking ship, the after-starboard lifeboat lowered away with twelve men in it. As Able Seaman H. K. Neilsin climbed with four other men onto a raft stowed on the ship "the vessel turned over onto her port side, and sank by the stern within three minutes of being struck, our raft floating clear as she foundered."[14] Two other rafts with crewmen also floated clear.

Three other men, including the second mate and the cook, finally made it to Neilsin's float. The eight men would spend four days adrift on the raft. "It was terribly cold ... blowing half a gale most of the time, with huge seas, the water was bitterly cold," Neilsin later stated in a report.

They had water and tinned food, including biscuits, pemmi-

can, some chocolate and some milk tablets. The second mate, a
Dane named Jensen, took charge on the raft and they were allotted three meals a day of pemmican, two biscuits, three or four
pieces of chocolate, and the milk tablets. "I did not much care
for the pemmican, but I ate it," Neilsin said. They had three
large dippers of water each, about nine ounces, for the first two
days, then they shortened the ration, not knowing how long
they would be adrift. They spent four days in the float. They
were thirsty constantly. Water was always shipping into the raft.
They lashed themselves to it in the heaving seas so they would
not be swept away. They were desolate, frozen by the cold
water. They massaged each other's feet with oil, which helped
their discomfort. All the time they were in the raft, the sea
stayed stormy, blowing gale force. One day they saw a ship;
they lit a smoke float and threw it into the water, but the ship
did not see it.

Then, on the 26th of September, they sighted another vessel;
this time they attached a smoke float to a bamboo pole, and the
ship saw the smoke. Upon the open roll of the wide ocean, the
huge white hull of a U.S. Coast Guard cutter drew up. It was
USCGC *Ingham*, a sister ship of the *Spencer*. They were pulled
off the raft and taken aboard; the *Ingham* sailed to Reykjavik.
There they all arrived on the 2nd of October. Neilsin later learned
that the boat he had seen lowered from the *Tennessee* at the time
of the attack had been picked up within one hour by a corvette.

Sixteen men of a crew of thirty-six perished with the *Tennessee*, including the captain, the chief officer, the third officer,
and the chief and second engineers.


In the area of the battle of SC 100, on the 23rd of September, the
weather finally relented. The wind died further, blowing out of

the north-northwest at Beaufort Force 4–5. The storm had died substantially, diminishing in wind and force, blowing itself out. Convoy SC 100 lumbered east, rolling more easily through the gentler swells now. Captain Alex Mitchell, master of the British tanker *Empire Opal*, was appointed the new convoy commodore. The *Empire Opal* now led the herd as the first ship in the third, or center, column. The seaway pitched along.

Elsewhere, eight other ships not with the main body of the convoy were scattered like hay, blown across a vast area of the sea. Some ships were out ahead, far out in front of SC 100; some were behind, straggling, dispersed by the three-day blow to a flurry of points on the field. One of the stragglers far behind the convoy was the American freighter *Pennmar*, rocking slowly across the last hours of the passing storm alone. She was a breakbulk freighter, no more than an anonymous workhorse of the oceans, no less than any other dog that sailed in convoys on the North Atlantic.

Built in 1920 in Kobe, Japan, the *Pennmar* was aging. She was 385 feet, 3 inches long, big at 5,868 tons. She had a squarish, sturdy bridge; in her holds she carried general cargo, an assortment of just about everything under the sun. She was an American ship; her owners were the Calmar Steamship Corp.; she was registered in New York.

The commander of *U-432*, Kptlt. Heinz-Otto Schultze, could not know all this about the *Pennmar*; all he knew was that he had stumbled onto a steamer straggling from Convoy SC 100. It took him four minutes to send the loyal *Pennmar* below.

At precisely 9:44 P.M. on the night of the 23rd, he fired three torpedoes at the ship.

His log reads: "Spread of three from tubes I, III and IV. After running time of four minutes, one hit forward." Then Schultze, in a moment of the coldness which comes in war, picked up the

*Pennmar*'s distress call; she was calling for the last time: "Torpedoed position 58° 12 North, 35° 35 West. KUNF [the ship's call sign]."[15] Her life was finished; the freighter was sinking. The *Pennmar* slowly settled in the water, began to founder, then she slid beneath the waves.

The *Pennmar* was the fourth ship in the convoy torpedoed. The formation passed on, now composed of nineteen ships. SC 100 was now about 1,000 miles due west of Scotland, still far out on the Atlantic. The main body, eleven ships, and the scattered stragglers—the ships sailing alone—made their way at their differing speeds, on their various tracks, eastward across the ocean. They were dispersed over some 150 miles, like chips strewn across a vast table.

September 24 dawned gray, the sky socked in, but the weather calm. The sky was pale, overcast; a light drizzle fell, otherwise the sea was quiet. The ships dogged along; the way seemed favorable. Kptlt. Brandi had not gone home yet, however. He had one last trick up his sleeve.

The *Roumanie*, a 3,568-ton Belgian freighter, was one of the ships sailing alone, separated by the terrible blow of the hurricane. A breakbulker, she had high masts and derricks forward and aft; she was 341 feet, 7 inches long, built by the Flensburg Shipbuilding Co. in Flensburg, Germany, in better times, 1906.

At precisely 9:58 on the morning of the 24th, Brandi in *U-617* lined her up in his sights. This is what she looked like through the periscope: "Dived for submerged attack. Steamer has a cannon astern and machine gun emplacements on the bridge, at both masts and in the bow superstructure." Then Brandi pumped two fish into her.

"Two hits. Only a large cloud of smoke visible . . . Steamer sank rapidly. Only rafts and barrels are floating at the point of sinking," Brandi recorded in his log. He stopped to pick up the chief engineer, who was drifting on a raft. "I take the Chief Engineer. . . . This person said under interrogation that the sunk steamer was the *Roumanie* (3,600 tons)." [16]

The *Roumanie*'s good life was done. Her call sign—Oscar, Romeo, Yankee, Alpha, ORYA—would never call again. The little ship plunged to the bottom with her cargo of foodstuffs, butter, autos, and gasoline. She was the last ship lost from the convoy. The battle of Convoy SC 100 was over.

The sea flowed on. The waves flooded east, gentle now in the mild weather that had broken at last. The wind blew, flying away across the blue surface of the ocean, tame and fresh as it went. The convoy had covered about 135 miles in four days, since the torpedoing of the first ship. The field of battle now stretched across almost 70,000 square miles.

On the 24th, the convoy was finally within range of shore-based aircraft; air cover came out. The gorgeous drone of Allied airpower arriving overhead spilled through the sky. All day long, the aircraft, assisted by escorts from Heineman's team, worked in coordinated air/sea attacks on the U-boats, trying to sink them with depth charges, at least keep them down. HMCS *Rosthern*, working with a plane, depth-charged a U-boat at 12:54 which gave up an oil slick, signs of a sinking. The U.S. Coast Guard cutter *Campbell* engaged in two depth charge attacks on contacts. The aircraft in the vicinity sighted submarines seven times, attacked twice, scoring one direct hit. All over the sea, the cover of planes, one a B-24 Liberator, one a Sunderland, welcomed the ships of SC 100 from their ordeal.

On September 24, two more stragglers found the main formation. Two more linked up on the 26th, and another two on the 27th. At last, the main body of the convoy pulled into Belfast in Northern Ireland on September 29.

Of the original twenty-four ships comprising SC 100, a total of eighteen finally made port. Five had been torpedoed, one, the *Empire Soldier*, had sunk on September 15 in an accident. Eighteen of the twenty-four ships steamed in under Heineman's guard, bringing their valuable cargoes of steel, lumber, sugar, iron ore, tobacco, benzene, paraffin, oil to the docksides where ships finally tie up and discharge their indispensable, priceless loads. The longshoremen came aboard; the hatches were cracked; the derricks turned.

SC 100 was home. For its sailors, Belfast—and the other ports to which the ships dispersed—meant sleeping more comfortably than in short spells crammed in between four hour watches. But there was little joy in the darkened streets, and little to buy. The west coast ports—Liverpool, Bristol, Belfast—had all been damaged by aerial bombing the year before. Nylon stockings and cosmetics were practically nonexistent, pubs were empty of spirits and short of beer, and rationed food supplies to restaurants and tea shops were severely restricted; only one course could be served. Across the sea at Halifax, other convoys were setting out from North America, starting the long, perilous voyage across the Atlantic and U-boat country. In autumn 1942 and on into the winter and 1943, it was a very costly passage. The Germans were driving full force. They were driving with more strength than they had ever gathered before.

And then for six frozen months in the winter, as the Germans thrusted, the entire convoy system, groaning and sagging under the onslaught, almost came apart.

# Merchant Ships Sunk by U-Boats in the North Atlantic

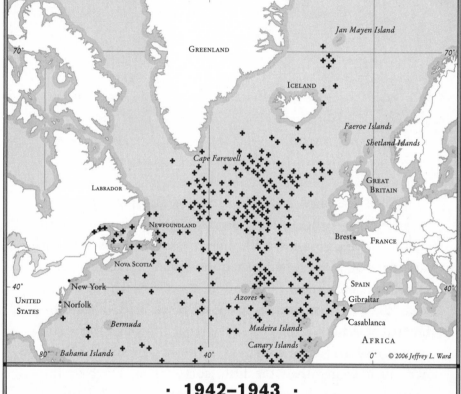

· **1942–1943** ·

# 13

THE U-BOATS THRUST OUT FROM LA PALLICE, BOR-
deaux, sortieing in tubular, black groups, running to the
hunting grounds, 1,500 miles away. The boats had a surface speed of 17 knots and an endurance range of 6,500 nautical
miles, so it took them three to four days to reach the combat
areas. Low, gray, so dark as to appear black, with raked bows,
blunted at the lip of the nose, they ranged through the waters,
pirates, looking for the convoys. The boats were small, 220 feet,
not much bigger than the little corvettes at 205 feet; they
coursed through the seas, tough wolves, stubby, 761 tons of
driven, overcharged Nazi attack power, armed with twelve G7e
torpedoes, one 88mm deck gun, and one 20mm antiaircraft gun.
An 88mm deck gun is as big as a Volkswagen, terribly complex,
and looks like a dark device conceived by Moloch, so great and
menacing is it. By December of 1942, there were 382 of them in

commission, 100 at sea at any one time, forty on the Atlantic. The actual figure for total U-boats committed to the North Atlantic was far higher, but, again, requirements of maintenance and transit to and from combat areas drew from the fleet at sea, now representing more offensive power than BdU had ever wielded before.

In winter, the Germans moved out. Finished at last with Paukenschlag, his campaign in the Americas, Dönitz threw everything he had into the Air Gap, that isolated zone between Iceland and Greenland beyond the reach of Allied air cover. In the deep freeze of this winter, the Germans now mounted their most intensive thrust. An increasing percentage of convoys crossing to England fell into the German ambushes. In the thirty-five weeks of the cold season, thirty-one convoys were attacked. British imports fell to 34 million tons—one third less than the 1939 levels. As the winter held its breath, the entire, enormous convoy system groaned, sagged, creaked—and threatened to give way.

Shipping now suddenly became the formula on which the entire war was posited. In the year 1942, a staggering total of 1,006 ships aggregating 5,471,222 tons had been lost, the worst figures for the entire war. British shipyards had a bulging backlog of 2.5 million tons of repair work. It became plausible to wonder whether the entire convoy system itself, feeding the war effort in Europe, could hold up. And if the convoys no longer came through, what strategy could the Allies turn to to bring their supplies across the Atlantic and support the citadel of Europe? What would happen to war planning?

Admiral Dönitz had calculated he needed to sink 700,000 tons of Allied shipping per month to cripple the Allies' convoy chain. Actually, the figure was lower; the Admiralty had put the number at 600,000 tons per month. But the margin of safety was growing far too thin. Through all 1942, the Germans averaged sinkings of 456,000 tons a month—alarmingly close to the limit. For five months out of the year, sinkings exceeded 500,000 tons. Dönitz's fists were landing hard.

The bulge of mounting numbers and urgent estimates was the backdrop against which, in the whistling cold months, the Germans advanced. The U-boats clipped out to the empty waters of the Air Gap, growing colder as the seasons swept ahead; they lay in wait or stalked the seas for the convoys German intelligence had located, then the packs collected. The spotting boat would pick up one of the huge, lumbering formations, wire back to BdU, then Admiral Dönitz would choreograph his dark ballet, bringing in his wolves. The packs would collect. Radio silence would hold—absolute silence had to be maintained during attack so the U-boats would not be detected—and then the savaging would begin. The U-boats lunged, the destroyers and corvettes veered off in pursuit, and the terrible battles would break.

Convoy SC 104 was hit the night of October 12–13 by five boats of the *Wotan* pack (*Wotan* is the name of a Teutonic god). Seven ships were lost from the convoy. Convoy HX 212, under Captain Paul Heineman was next across. Five ships were torpedoed between October 27 and 29. Three days later, Convoy SC 107, guarded by the Canadian C-4 Escort Group, was hit by no fewer than fourteen U-boats of the *Veilchen* (Violet) pack and lost fifteen merchant ships as corvettes peeled off in the dark dropping depth charges, starshells bursting in the windy black, and flaming ships lit up the sea.

The escort groups were the guards, the defenders who shielded the convoys against German torpedoes, German guns; they were the scutarius fighting the ferocious, raging battle against the U-boats that winter. On the watch, commanding the escort squadrons, were the RN best, the able, quick lieutenants, commanders, and sub-lieutenants of the Royal Navy, the RN Reserve and Voluntary Reserve, all descended from 18th-century First Rates, trim, capable, competent above all in seamanship; these were the almost remote figures on duty at the pass that winter as the Germans tried to rush through.

Commander Richard C. Boyle, leading the British B-5 Escort Group in HMS *Havelock*, was one of the many faces at the brink that year. Boyle was forty years old, an expert horseman, had entered the Royal Navy at age fourteen, and liked to shoot. An early fitness report had said of him: "Should make a good officer . . . quiet disposition, even temperament and not easily upset. Capable of making a decision and sticking to it."[1] Boyle would later play a leading role in one of the greatest clashes of the entire Battle of the Atlantic, involving two whole convoys, totaling eighty-nine merchant ships, pitted against thirty-eight U-boats.

Another face in the watch crew that winter and fall as the Germans pressed to win at sea, and so turn the course of the war, was Commander E. C. L. Day. Day led the B-4 Escort Group. Day's ship was the powerful destroyer HMS *Highlander*, built by Thorneycroft, a sister ship of HMS *Havelock*. Edward Campbell Lacy Day's first fitness reports had assessed him as a "capital leader, very good influence . . . exceptional ability and promise; marked qualities of leadership and command. . . . Personal magnetism to a marked degree."[2] Day was thirty-seven years old.

Commander A. A. "Harry" Tait was an ace; he would go on to sink three German subs; Tait was an inveterate drinker of gin (liquor was permitted on all RN ships); he was careful, the son of a preacher, zealous in style and tenacious. He had been commissioned as an acting Sub-Lieutenant at the age of twenty.

Lieutenant Commander Peter W. Gretton was another ace. Gretton, SOE of the crack B-7 Escort Group, a trim figure with an angular face, taut but bright, had served in three destroyers before taking over HMS *Wolverine*, the victor over both Günther Prien in *U-47* and von Hippel in *U-76*. Gretton would go on to become a Lord Commissioner of the Admiralty, Deputy Chief of Naval Staff and 5th Sea Lord after the war. In 1942, he was thirty years old.

One of Gretton's crewmen, Jack Raikes, a Welshman, recalled Gretton's high-performance, ceaseless drilling. "It was all sessions. He was telling us where we were going, what we were going to do," said Raikes. "He was fearless. I would go anywhere with him." Raikes never left behind the intensity and shock of battle and convoy action. "You'd be [at your station] ten hours. They'd bring your food to you. You were muffled up in clothing, two thick jumpers, a duffle coat, oilskins, and boots. Sometimes you'd get wet. One minute you'd be looking at the water, the next minute you'd be looking at the sky. There was no shelter, only the clothes you had on." [3]

These were the hands on the watch, rough, weatherbeaten, rugged; wound, too, in the 300-year-old mesh of RN fife-rail seamanship. The ratings were sturdy, knew their jobs, were stout, trained to a pitch. These crewmen and officers stood at the divide which stretched across the green, streaked, yawing wastes of the North Atlantic that winter.

The ships they wielded were tough, fast, modern shafts, carrying the ever advancing weaponry of war. O (Obdurate) Class destroyers, *Offa, Oribi, Obedient, Obdurate*, had raked, powerful lines with a high, peaked forecastle head, low, deadly bridges. They were powerful, packing four main 4.7-inch guns, four 2-pounder antiaircraft guns, three 40mm AA guns, and eight torpedo tubes. Os carried the RN's salute to U-boats, too:

an armory of seventy depth charges. *Havelock* and *Highlander* were ex-Brazilian H Class destroyers like HMS *Hesperus*, mounting three main 4.7-inch guns. There were older dogs, still ferocious from their World War I service, Thorneycroft V and W Class, Admiralty Large Design, with five main 4.7-inch guns, Thorneycroft Modified W Class, with stolid, stately lines, Admiralty S Class, A Class destroyers.

These ships, and the mates along their rails, gunwales, mounts, and bulkheads, stood at the gates as the Germans drove home, trying to sever the critical trans-ocean supply lines. In the autumn the U-boats sortied; they raced across the gray, chilly, jagged wastes, they fanned out across the ocean, they hunted. The weather was growing cold, and the skies would bring rain, snow, blizzards. The U-boats launched out to stalk the lumbering convoys. They roved in the greatest numbers which BdU had managed to mount, striking in the black of the night, as they so liked.

Convoy HX 209 lost one ship, with one damaged, to a wolfpack on October 2. In November, two ships from SC 109 were torpedoed. Convoy ON 144 lost five more ships on November 17 and 18. Week after week the losses piled up, tonnage crumped at intolerable levels. In all, seven out of twenty-seven SC convoys were hit with a loss of ships between September 1942 and April 1943. Eleven out of twenty-nine HX convoys, more than one third, lost ships to wolfpack attacks in the cold months; eight of thirty ON convoys.

Now a crucial argument closed about the Battle of the Atlantic. Since summer, a bitter argument had divided the British military staff on the question of allocation of VLR Liberator bombers, heavy long-range bombers. The Admiralty's first sea lord, Admiral of the Fleet Sir A. Dudley P. R. Pound, vehemently insisted that the losses in the Air Gap could not continue at their present levels. He urgently pleaded his case before the Battle of the Atlantic Committee: release more VLR Liberators to close the Gap. But Air Marshal Sir Charles Portal insisted that Britain's main bombing campaign striking at factories, mills, heavy German industry was more important and must take precedence. Portal was backed by the legendary chief of Bomber Command, Sir Arthur Harris, who had once remarked that his sole ambition was to "bomb Germany back to the stone age."

To use bombers at sea for reconnaissance and attack was like trying to "sever each capillary vein one by one," Harris insisted, whereas the main bombing campaign against the U-boat pens and construction yards would "cut the artery." Despite the imperviousness of the massive U-boat pens to bombing, and later evidence that shipyard raids had had little effect, Churchill sided with Bomber Command and Portal. The "Bomber Row" would flare for months. Harris, supported by the prime minister, would continue to assign all VLR Liberators to the main campaign against industry, despite the fact that only two dozen or so would have closed the Air Gap. It would be many months before the Air Gap was closed. The Nazi offensive in the northern tract beyond air coverage went on without letup.

"To the British Admiralty it was plain that the Battle of the Convoy Routes was still to be decided, that the enemy had greater strength than ever before, and that the crisis in the long-drawn struggle was near," Captain S. W. Roskill wrote in the official British history of the war at sea.[4]

It was at this obscure, uncertain moment of the engagement that the Germans decided to rush into development a new weapon of extraordinary futuristic design which could completely reshape the Battle of the Atlantic. The project centered around an advanced submarine called the "Walter boat," after its inventor, Hellmuth Walter. The chief attribute of the sub was its outlandish underwater speed, a stunning 18 knots. With the drive to develop the Walter boat, the German offensive at sea took on a new, sophisticated element of possibility.

Eerily streamlined, with a pared-down design, the Walter U-boat looked like no other submarine—subtly curved and spartan in appearance. The ship was based on an extremely complex chemical engine designed by Walter in 1935. With its speed, the Walter U-boat could outrun any corvette, do twice the speed of any merchant ship, and sail circles around a convoy. Walter's engine proved difficult to control, however; there were too many problems to bring it to production, Dönitz realized. He nonetheless adapted Walter's super-streamlined hull design for use with massive 100-ton batteries and electric engines. The Walter boats, the Type XXI and Type XXIII, would still be capable of whooshing along underwater at their extraordinary 18 knots.

In September 1942, Dönitz met with Hitler to discuss the innovation. The führer granted immediate approval for production of the Walter boats as soon as design was complete. Dönitz put into motion the development of the sub. In the shipyards and design shops, work began, and in autumn 1942, the drive for the Walter boat was on.

The German offensive in the Air Gap proceeded relentlessly. As the convoys came through the bare ocean pass, they were hit with mounting force by the U-boats. The U-boats sortied and lay their ambushes in the frost-cold zone between Greenland and Iceland.

In November 1942, two ships were lost from Convoy HX 217. Fourteen days later, Convoy ON 153 lost three ships, with one damaged to a wolfpack in ferocious, howling weather. Next came Convoy ON 154; thirteen of its merchant ships were sent below. The sinkings continued. The question now posed itself: how much longer could such an assault be sustained without cutting into the grain of war planning? Supplies dwindled. The tonnage gap—the gap between what was needed and what was making it through—kept narrowing.

Roskill summarized the mood: "Grave anxiety was felt that future offensive plans might be delayed or even frustrated for lack of shipping. In particular, fuel stocks had fallen to a very low figure. In mid-December there were only 300,000 tons of commercial bunker fuel [for ships] in Britain, and consumption was running at about 130,000 tons a month."[5]

The strategy for the war in Europe had come to rest on the war at sea.

In November 1942, the gladius of command at Western Approaches passed into new hands. Admiral Sir Percy Noble, C-in-C since 1941, went to Washington as head of the British Naval Mission in the United States; in his place, one of the most experienced and capable flag rank officers in the Royal Navy was appointed commander-in-chief, Western Approaches— Admiral Sir Max Kennedy Horton, awarded the Distinguished Service Cross on three occasions. No more supremely qualified individual for the post existed in the Royal Navy. He arrived at a grim moment in the ever changing war at sea.

Horton, with a fiery reputation, colorful, tough, irascible, was a lifelong submariner with experience dating back to 1914. He had commanded a submarine in World War I, compiling an outstanding record; since 1940 he had served as vice-admiral submarines, in charge of all home-based boats. Now, with his hands-on knowledge of submarine warfare, Horton would take charge of planning and direction. He would have oversight of all operations and strategy, would take over the scheme, extent, and conduct of daily battle in the Atlantic.

"He possessed a deep grasp of all the intricate human and technical problems involved in submarine warfare," wrote Roskill. "There was no living officer who better understood the U-boat commander's mind, nor could more surely anticipate what his reactions to our countermeasures would be." [6]

Appointing Horton to head the Western Approaches Command was, it was said, "like setting a thief to catch a thief."

Horton, with his demanding insistence on performance, his quick grasp of detail, his sober growl, now took over conduct of the war on the gray, heaving Atlantic described by the vast map on the wall of the Operations Room at Western Approaches. By day, this man of maddening habits would insist on his golf game in the afternoon and his rubber of bridge in the evening. At night, however, when the convoy battles broke out, he would burst into the "Plot" in his pajamas to direct the action at sea with uncanny insight. Out there, on the sea frontier, the destroyers, the tough little corvettes, the sloops and frigates, still fought a war that was running and sliding, on the long, gray swells, to the German hand.

The U-boat war on the Atlantic was now at a crucial, decisive stage. Dönitz's U-boats ran across a wide swath of North Atlantic, stretching from Brest in the east all the way to Cape Farewell at the bottom of Greenland in the west. Dönitz's predators were piling up an impressive number of victories. The convoys, arcing out, up over the great circle route, were now on an extended schedule, with longer periods between sailings, to make up for a shortage of escorts. From Cape Farewell to Rock-all Bank, 270 miles west of Loch Ewe, Scotland, the ocean was a running, blank field. This was U-boat country, the endless monotony of lookout duty, the work of scanning an unending and barren field, straining the eyes and the muscles of the mind. The distances to be searched were vast. They had no distinguishing features. Your eyes played tricks on you and you thought you saw dots, specks, only to have them disappear. Hours and empty leagues of nothing were the steady diet of the lookouts. But the U-boats infested these tracts, roving in big, ravenous packs, combing the waves for the herds of merchant ships crossing from America. Then the battles broke out.

A red rocket would go up, an "SSS" would be flashed, sometimes no more formal warning than an explosion in the black of night and the livid fires crackling up from a stricken ship would signal the presence of a wolfpack. In December 1942, there was no more dangerous run in the world. The ocean was blank for endless periods, then, all at once, the night would be alive with the horror that only a convoy battle could entail, ships scurrying in the dark, signal lamps flashing, explosions, destroyers veering in on attack.

The worst sight, the one that no one forgot, was the men in the water, the men it was impossible—because of battle, because of weather, because it was too risky, for one reason or another—to pick up. The memory of men in the water sticks in countless minds.

"My clearest memory of the war," recalls Roy Hemmings, then a twenty-three-year-old seaman-torpedoman on HMS *Walker*, "was . . . when you see the lads floating by and you can't pick them up, because of weather or action. That I shall never forget."[7]

"It was a difficult decision for the captain . . . to make, to see these ships sunk," recalls Captain Duncan Knight, then a lieutenant onboard HMS *Hesperus*. "Then you've got a problem as to whether to go back and pick up survivors. That's a very difficult decision. It's not one that involves a lieutenant, I'm glad to say." [8]

Harold Rogers, the baker onboard USS *Spencer*, recalls, "I saw plenty [of ships] on fire and sinking. It would light up the sky like a city on fire sometimes. You'd get up on deck, and the men in the water had little red lights on their life jackets, and you could see the red lights, see them bobbing all around, and hear the fellows hollering. It was a lot of just plain hell, a lot of rough weather, a lot of subs. If the weather didn't get you, the subs were trying to get you." [9]

The thick of action was never the same twice; each battle had its own face, its own memories, sometimes inspiring, sometimes stunning. Combat brought the stirring, and it brought the almost incomprehensible.

Ron Smith, a twenty-two-year-old leading seaman aboard HMS *Hesperus*, recalls escorting Convoy OB (Outward Bound from Britain) 298 south to Gibraltar when aircraft suddenly attacked an ammunition ship in the convoy, the *Benvorlich*, of the Blue Funnel Line. "She was carrying mines for Singapore and hand grenades, and a Focke-Wulf went straight for [her]. I think they must have known she was carrying ammunition, because they opened fire with incendiary bombs." [10]

The *Benvorlich* detonated in one immense blast, vaporized instantly. "She went straight up, a tremendous explosion," says Smith. When the water and debris settled, the surface of the water was covered, strangely, with cigarette packs.

Smith was one of the small-boat party that went to look for survivors. "I think we picked up three Chinese, an Arab donkeyman, and the Scottish engineer. One of them [the Chinese]

was more dead than alive, but I said, 'Bring him in anyway.' "
These were the only survivors of the *Benvorlich*. The man in the
poorest condition subsequently died.

"We took the other two [Chinese] to the deck," Smith re-
lates. "I can see it in my mind's eye. One of the two was trem-
bling, just like that," Smith says, extending his hand and letting
it shake. A crewman then offered the man some tea. "The chap
turned to give him a cup of tea, and [the Chinese] dropped." The
man was dead. The shock of having the *Benvorlich* detonated
under him had so traumatized the sailor that he had keeled over.
"He was dead. And his cigarette was still burning in his hand,"
Smith recalls.

"The other chap saw his friend die and said, 'Me makey
die.' " The crewman put his hands beside his head like a pillow,
keeled over, and said again, "Me makey die." At this point another *Hesperus* crewman said sharply, " 'You no die, John.' He
gave him a shot of rum. It saved him."

German crews, too, faced fates that were equally sober on the
face of the sea, tests that were just as summary. When a sub was
destroyed underwater, in the chill, dark gloom of the deep, it
sailed down to 300 feet, 400, 500, to 660 feet, the "crush depth"
of the sub, the point at which the boat could no longer with-
stand the enormous water pressure. Then the sub finally im-
ploded, blowing in in one abrupt spasm.

Depth charge attacks were ordeals which brought white
knuckles and wide eyes to even the most experienced U-boat
hands. Sitting still for each concussion in the dim, cryptlike catacombs of a sub hull for each hammer blow was a harrowing experience. Kretschmer, early on in the war, once sustained a
marathon depth charge attack that went on for eighteen straight

hours, involving the dropping of 107 depth charges. Few attacks were as epic. Werner Hirschmann, the chief engineer of *U-190*, recalls the effects of a depth bombing on the North Atlantic as jarring, almost paralyzing.

"The boat does not move a fraction of an inch. You experience a feeling as when a giant sledgehammer hits an immovable object. This mass of 1,000 tons, the submarine, is surrounded by an almost solid medium."[11] There are shouts—for wrenches, spare parts, to fix broken equipment.

"You hear the splash of a depth charge entering the water. Twenty seconds from now, you know you may no longer be alive if that depth charge hits you. Then the explosion happens and you hear the next one coming and the whole process starts again. I would call any man who isn't afraid for his life a liar. One requirement inside the boat is quiet or they will find the boat. Anyone who sneezes is called a traitor."

There were German men stranded in the water, too, when crewmen abandoned a sinking sub. Whether they were picked up or not was a life-or-death question. Kptlt. Horst Elfe, the commander of *U-93*, who had been Kretschmer's second watch officer, recalls the night in January 1942 when he lost his boat northeast of Madeira to one of the top British escort group leaders, Commander A. A. "Harry" Tait.

Tait, then commanding *Hesperus*, picked up Elfe's boat on radar, and lunged forth in pursuit in the black of night. Kptlt. Elfe tried to outrun *Hesperus*, but Tait overtook him and finally rammed *U-93*. Now the two ships sat side by side on the dark water and Tait opened fire with his guns. Elfe ordered the conning tower crew to abandon ship and jump in the water. A depth charge exploded under the boat and water began rushing into the shattered sub. At this point, saltwater threatened to mix with the acid in the batteries and form deadly chlorine gas. Elfe ordered the rest of his men to abandon ship at once. They were bobbing in the icy waters of the Atlantic in the impenetrable black of the night. There they could very well be left to drown. Tait, a gentleman by any standard and in every situation, decided to pick them up. He brought *Hesperus* to a halt and began to recover the German crewmen struggling in the water. One by one, the *U-93* men were pulled out of the drink and brought onboard *Hesperus*. Once onboard, Elfe was immediately identified as the commander of the U-boat and given a cup of rum by a sailor. Elfe recounts that the sailor said to him: " 'You take it easy, sir.' Not, 'You bloody German.' 'Sir.' "[12] In due course, Tait sent down a clean shirt, trousers, and sweater for his prisoner.

In the morning, Commander Tait summoned Elfe to the bridge. "There he stood," recalls Elfe, "the prototype of the Royal Navy, white shirt, white cap, like if he waited [for] a visit by the first lord of the Admiralty." The following exchange ensued:

Tait held out his hand and said, "I'm sorry for you, sir."

Tears came into Elfe's eyes. He said back: "Sir, I was just trying to torpedo you."

"Yes, I know," said Tait. "We have the highest respect for you."

"Sir, this compliment I am giving back to you. We also for you."

"I had you seven hours in my new device, radar," Tait said. "You had no chance. I knew exactly where you were."

Thus was Elfe, a captured German commander, received on the bridge by the great Harry Tait, his men rescued, with the highest respects of his captor.

Tait was responsible for two U-boat kills; he assisted in sinking a third. He was one of the top Allied aces of the war. An enthusiastic drinker, Tait nonetheless lived with finesse and care; he cut a striking figure in the Royal Navy. An evaluation had assessed him as having "notably high mental caliber . . . good command of men . . . pleasing personality . . . intelligence promising . . . high opinion of professional ability, capable and relaxed." Among the idiosyncrasies of his command was his famous relationship with his steward, George Wills.

Every night at 2:00 A.M. Wills would take cocoa up to Tait. At the end of every convoy escort job, tied up in Canada, Tait would summon Wills to his quarters and reward them both with a good, stiff drink. Recalls Ron Smith: "He'd take a bottle of gin and two glasses and then he'd say, 'Well, that's a good job, Wills. Have a drink.' And he'd be drinking with his servant."

The currents that year flowed to the Air Gap and to a German tide. That winter Dönitz's U-boats operated in a saturation, all kinds of boats—thirty-four types developed during the war. Type IXs, Type XIVs, Type Xs, Type IIs, especially the most common production types, the Type IX, of which 236 were built, and the Type VII, of which 709 were built. These were the spears of the Nazi onslaught; they were spartan, smaller than American subs, stripped down, everything reduced for function. German submarines were cramped tubes of instruments and equipment; they barely had room to move about. Inside, a Type IX C U-boat was a tightly fitted fighting machine full of devastating efficiency.

The brain center of the U-boat was its Control Room, in the middle of the hull. A jam-packed warren of pipes and dials, all the functions for battle and operation were lodged here. To the left in the Control Room, looking forward, was a navigating table, small but sufficient. Above the chart table were a depth finder, valve wheels for flooding the negative buoyancy tanks, which gave the boat weight, allowing it to dive, a gyrocompass, and a helm indicator. To the left of the chart table was a clock always set to German Central Time.

On the right of the Control Room were diving plane controls—the planes were big fins which directed the U-boat up or down—and trim tank controls for keeping the bow and stern level, or tipping them. The critical piece of equipment, the periscope housing, was located in the center of the Control Room. All the basic machinery and gear necessary for a commander to operate the sub, and carry out an attack—diving controls, periscope, trim, flood tanks, depth meter, much more—was at his fingertips in the Control Room.

Ahead of the Control Room were bunks on either side, in the various compartments assigned to different ranks. First came the commander's bunk; he had the luxury of a green curtain he could draw across his berth for privacy, and a cabinet for his belongings; across from the captain's space was the radio room. Then, going forward, were officers' bunks, a tiny galley which served out three meals a day to the crew of about fifty, petty officers' and chiefs' bunks and crew bunks, the crew bunks wedged into the equipment in the forward torpedo room.

Behind the Control Room were the diesel engine room, the electric motor room, and more crew quarters stuffed into the after torpedo room. All of this was crammed into a 252-foot cylinder; not a foot of spare space was left over; sausages, hams, bread hung from overhead, boxes of vegetables lined the sides of the narrow space between the bunks.

U-boat life was demanding; even under the best conditions, existence aboard was arduous, uncomfortable, fraught with difficulties and beset by adversity.

The German navy's medical service listed the following conditions as being detrimental to a U-boatman's health, according to U-boat expert Jak P. Mallmann Showell: "humidity; stale air; smells from paint, oil, fuel, bilge, galley, lavatory, wet clothing, sweat, dirty bodies and rotting food; sea sickness; short periods for recreation and lack of sleep; shallow depth of sleep . . . unhygienic eating conditions and poor food preparation facilities; lack of vitamins; extremes in air pressure; being subject to constant vibrations and wave action; having to breathe through personal ventilators to remove carbon dioxide from the air; living in cramped conditions; and the psychological pressures of being scared and not knowing what was happening back at home."[13]

U-boatmen had a special slang name for the mixture of frayed nerves, weariness, and excessive stress that service in a sub could entail: they called it *Blechkoller*, literally "tin can disease."

Sub crews had all the perquisites of an elite service, the best provisions, as many decorations as Dönitz could push for, recognition at home as heroes. They put up with a life which, by any standard, was hard. Politics was seldom discussed aboard U-boats, the crews ran the gamut from distaste for the Nazis to open enthusiasm for them and Hitler. Fate in late 1942 all too often favored these hunters.

In December, with Western Approaches' 108 escort ships fighting the sea and the Germans, Commander Donald Macintyre, the victor over Kretschmer, brought one more score home. Macintyre had been back at sea just six months. At this time, astride the bridge of *Hesperus* once again, pursuing the ping of a U-boat contact, he was still, to a degree, unknown. This anonymity would not last for long. Macintyre would go on to become the second highest scoring Allied U-boat killer, one of the leading commanders of World War II, sinking a total of seven German subs.

He scored his third kill on December 26, 1942, Boxing Day, a British holiday. In the afternoon, he made contact with *U-357*. Macintyre's own memoirs suggest the thrill and elation a hunt could sometimes entail:

> It was a sparkling winter day with a calm sea, except for the long Atlantic swell into which we were soon burying our nose, scooping green water up on to our forecastle and even on to the bridge. Only that morning, David [Mottistone], the horsey member of the wardroom, had remarked that it was a perfect day for the usual Boxing Day meet. Now we were off on a more exciting and deadly hunt.[14]

Macintyre sped off with the destroyer *Vanessa*, one of his squadron, assisting. They pursued the sub across the bounding waves, the sub eluding every maneuver. Once *Vanessa* tried to ram; *U-357* evaded. Now *U-357* turned and twisted, with *Hesperus* in hot pursuit. Macintyre stayed on the sub's heels—until the skipper, Kptlt. Adolf Kellner, made a false move. Macintyre swung his ship, *Hesperus* barreled in, and as the British destroyer hurtled toward the submarine, Macintyre rammed the boat directly perpendicular, and sent her below.

"A straggling cheer came up to the bridge from all parts of the ship," Macintyre wrote. "On the bridge, the reaction after the desperate excitement of the chase was terrific. Handshakes and congratulations all round were the order of the day."[15]

It was a classic Macintyre kill, half divining and half ship-handling. Charles A. Edwards, then a leading seaman on board

*Hesperus*, remembers of Macintyre: "He could smell a U-boat. We always said he could smell a U-boat. He had a nose for them. He had a nose for where the U-boats were."

Commander Macintyre had given the Royal Navy a superb Boxing Day present, one U-boat bagged. Captain Johnnie Walker, the top Allied ace, organized a grand reception for *Hesperus* when she came into Gladstone Dock in Liverpool, and Admiral Sir Max Horton, C-in-C, Western Approaches, came down to greet the ship on her return. Macintyre had added another hide to his pelt.

"Every time we went into action, we were [certain] he could get us out," continues Edwards. "Obviously we cursed him at times, on inspection, but generally he was well respected and liked. If you would speak to any of the crew, they'd tell you Macintyre was the boy." [16]

# 14

IN DECEMBER 1942, A BRITISH INTELLIGENCE BREAK-through of unparalleled and invaluable dimension took place, with far-reaching ramifications for every aspect of the Atlantic battle. Working at Bletchley Park, fifty miles north-west of London, British cryptanalysts once again broke Germany's Enigma code. In May 1941, they had broken the se-cret military code, only to be blacked out in February 1942. Now, in December, Enigma was compromised conclusively, yielding up its secrets to the naval intelligence staff at Western Approaches and the Admiralty's Submarine Tracking Room. From December 1942, except for one gap lasting but weeks, the British team was able to read Enigma, often within hours of a transmission, giving naval commands access to vital informa-tion on German submarines.

Now, with renewed access to U-boat radio messages, the Admiralty could once again determine their location and reroute convoys around them. Through the war, no effort was more urgent, highly prioritized, or critical to the Allied cause than the race to crack Enigma.

Invented in 1918, Enigma worked through a keyboard device that looked something like a portable typewriter. When one entered a letter on the keyboard, three rotors and a system of electrical contacts translated the letter into a completely different one. The words "made contact" might come out in completely different, unreadable form. Yet because not only the rotors but also the wiring of the Enigma machine could be configured in an endless number of ways, the possibilities for encrypting a letter were almost unlimited. The possibility of breaking Enigma—without a machine and the daily settings for starting it—was estimated at roughly 150 million million million to one.

The teams which finally broke Enigma worked in the estate at Bletchley Park and in its outbuildings but soon grew to a preposterous population filling wooden huts built to accommodate the growing numbers. By the middle of the war, a community of 10,000–12,000 people worked on cracking the top secret German cipher; they were housed in inns, boardinghouses, and private homes in every town and village within a twenty-mile radius of Bletchley. These experts—cryptanalysts, mathematicians, engineers, classicists, linguists, college students recruited from Oxford and Cambridge, even crossword experts and chess players, all selected for their problem-solving skills— applied their sharpest wits to the task of deciphering the baffling, complex code of naval Enigma, which, of the eighty variations that existed for different branches of the German military, was the most sophisticated. The code-breakers worked around the clock in three shifts, often bicycling in from their billets on blacked-out roads. The race to crack Enigma used manpower as an army uses troops.

First mesh of contact were the Y stations along the British coasts, which actually intercepted the U-boat signals. Thousands of telegraphists, mostly women, sat for countless chilly hours, listening intently through headphones, to pick out of the air the German radio signals in Morse code. These signals were then passed to Bletchley Park, converted into alphabet, and the battle of wits was on.

Messages were decoded by hand, using a collection of ingenious approaches with such outlandish names as "Banburisms," "rodding," and "cillis." Advanced mathematical formulas were employed in the race to decipher signals, the experts picking apart the encoded messages. Primitive electro-mechanical computers called "bombes," invented by the brilliant mathematician Alan Turing, were employed. The bombes could race through millions of letter combinations quickly, saving untold hours of manual checking. The bombes—as tall as a large bank safe—were highly sensitive and frequently overheated or disabled by dust; whole companies of Wrens (Women's Royal Naval Service) were employed to fan and dust the complex machines.

Deciphered messages went straight to a horseshoe-shaped desk called "The Watch" for translation into English and interpretation. Voluminous card files and a library of old messages assisted the Watch in interpreting traffic.

The value of the decoded Enigma traffic to the Admiralty was inestimable. So crucial were the deciphered signals that decrypts had a security classification even above top secret. Enigma decrypts were slugged "Ultra."

The signals were an intelligence gold mine. Decoded messages were sent at once via teleprinter to the Submarine Tracking Room in the Admiralty's Operational Intelligence Center, or OIC, in London. There, in a bomb-proof underground complex, Captain Rodger Winn, a former barrister, and his staff would assemble the messages together with information from interrogations and press reports to form a picture of U-boat operations at sea. Sometimes Winn and his crew knew information detailed enough to be able to reroute convoys around a patrol line of U-boats, but even in the absence of such precise information, the accumulation of signals allowed Winn and his group to develop a reasonably detailed estimate of what the U-boats might do.

With his analysis complete, at 9:00 A.M., Winn would get on the scrambler for a conference call with the commander-in-chief, Western Approaches, RAF Coastal Command, and the Admiralty Trade Division Convoy Plot, which had up-to-date information on the location of every convoy at sea. Based on the picture as assembled by the Submarine Tracking Room, the C-in-C Western Approaches, sitting in his glass-fronted office overlooking the huge wall plot of the Atlantic, would make his decisions on how to move convoys, how to deploy escort forces and air patrols. The importance of the Ultra intelligence was obvious immediately. Once the code-breakers at Bletchley first broke naval Enigma in May 1941, ship sinkings had dropped abruptly. Although for the rest of the year there were many days when Enigma could not be read, even with irregular access to U-boat signals, the Admiralty could often outsmart the Germans throughout the rest of 1941.

Then, in February 1942, the Germans had drastically shaken up the whole picture. They had added a fourth rotor wheel to the Enigma machine, providing for an even more complex array.

Bletchley Park was completely blacked out. For ten months, the code-breakers had been blinded, cut off. The new cipher was beyond all decrypting methods. The wizards were stumped.

The new four-rotor cipher had been code-named "Shark." To decrypt it, Turing's team calculated it would need bombes twenty-six times as fast to break the code in the same amount of time. The teams of experts lodged in wooden huts all over the 300 acres of Bletchley Park began work at once. In Huts No. 4 and 8, where the staff working on naval Enigma was housed, the race was on. The laborious, intricate process of breaking Shark began as soon as the team figured out what had happened.

At last, in December, with the help of many of the new bombes to crack the daily rotor settings and much brilliant guesswork, the experts pulled it off. From December of 1942 to the end of the war, with the exception of a few weeks in March 1943, the deciphering teams were reading Shark "currently"—within hours—and knew the kind of message being transmitted even if its full content could not be read. The British had access to all radio traffic of the German navy.

The break back into Enigma was not the only breakthrough during the harsh winter of 1942–43. Far on the other side of the Atlantic, across the ocean, where American workmen were rolling up their sleeves and the industrial might of the United States was turning its forges to the war in Europe, President Roosevelt initiated a bold new program which would dramatically alter the shape of the Battle of the Atlantic.

Announced on February 19, 1942, at a top-level conference held in FDR's bedroom at the White House, the program, FDR advised, would amount to "the greatest shipbuilding program in world history." The "Ships for Victory" program would be headed by Admiral Emory S. Land of the U.S. Maritime Commission. It would entail a massive merchant shipbuilding initiative that would restack the odds on the Atlantic, the kind only the "Arsenal of Democracy" had the muscle to undertake.

Though crash production of ships had already started in 1941, under Ships for Victory, American industry was to erect no fewer than forty new major shipyards on its coasts, boosting capacity from ten such yards to a whopping fifty by 1945. The basic product of the new program would be the Liberty ship. Ungainly starlets, Liberty ships were mass-produced, standardized freighters stamped out in no time at all. From California, under the program, clear across to Maryland, derricks would turn, mills would roll, tool shops would rattle, and American shipyard workers, many of them women, would hammer, weld, and turn out a crop of Liberties which was nothing short of prodigious.

Everything about the Liberties and Ships for Victory was eye-opening, monumental. Delivery times rapidly dove to phenomenal brevity. At the start of the program, it had taken four and a half to six months to build a Liberty ship; by August 1942, Henry Kaiser, the famous industrialist, who was new to shipbuilding, had erected a complete ship in his Portland, Oregon, yard in only thirty-one days; his Richmond, California, yard built the *Joseph N. Teal* in sixteen days. Then, in November 1942, breaking all precedents and stunning planners, the Richmond yard, on San Francisco Bay, turned out the *Robert E. Peary*, an entire Liberty ship, in just four days, fifteen hours. The huge yard had completed the building of an entire seagoing freighter, with 250,000 different parts, from keel to masthead, in just under five days. It was the fastest production time of the war.

The Liberties were practically innumerable. American shipyards turned out no fewer than 2,708 of the vessels during the war—a fleet almost the size of the entire British Merchant Navy, the largest in the world, in 1937. Although FDR had dubbed them the "ugly ducklings," the Liberties were handsome, with a fine, gentle sheer on the foredeck and solid lines. They were versatile, rugged, with three holds forward, two aft; a single ship could carry a volume equal to that of 300 railroad cars. A Liberty ship had space for 2,840 jeeps, 440 light tanks, 230 million rounds of rifle ammunition, or 3,440,000 C rations.

With thousands of ships to name, the U.S. Maritime Commission became a spigot for ship names. Competitions were held in schools urging children to come up with names; the commission reverted to mind-numbing means to generate the scores of name boards required by Ships for Victory. Eventually, some sixty name lists honoring figures suitable for the ugly ducklings were developed, including authors, athletes, abolitionists, painters, historians, political and social reformers, Indians, pioneers, merchant mariners, and many more. Liberty ships bore the names *Betsy Ross, Abner Doubleday, Daniel Webster, Sun Yat-Sen, Johnny Appleseed, F. Scott Fitzgerald*, and *Zane Grey*. One ship was even named the *Pocahontas*.

Liberties were workhorses, pack mules; they served in every theater of the war, making up a substantial share of the convoys by 1945. They were standardized completely; every Liberty was indistinguishable from her hundreds of sister ships—but for the slight difference in tonnage necessitated by the distinct specificities of various shipyards. They were based on an 1879 British tramp ship design. The Liberties were designated EC2, E for Emergency, C for Cargo, 2 for large capacity. They were fine to look at, with big, raked hulls, three sets of cargo masts, and a central deckhouse which included the bridge. Liberties were powered by a reciprocating steam engine which delivered 11 knots. The crew of a Liberty ship numbered about forty-five.

To crew and man the bulging crop of Liberties, the War Shipping Administration established schools for ordinary seamen in Sheepshead Bay, New York, St. Petersburg, Florida, and Avalon, California. Schools for officers were set up at Fort Trumbull, Connecticut and Alameda, California. The schools for unlicensed seamen turned out a huge population of 155,000 sailors—enough to crew 4,000 Liberties and other ships. The U.S. Merchant Marine Academy and the state maritime academies educated a body of officers no less impressive, a pool of 10,000 ready, capable mates and engineers. There was a dire shortage of radio operators; schools prepared some 7,500 of them.

The scale of the Ships for Victory program was epic; it is probable that a similar feat of wartime production will never be seen again. Through 1942, American yards sent forth 746 Liberties totaling 8,089,732 tons; in 1943, they put out 1,896 ships aggregating a staggering 19,238,646 tons, more than 1,200 of them Liberties. These ships went to other nations, as well as the U.S. To suggest the magnitude of this output, the British Merchant Navy, again the largest in the world, had comprised 20.4 million tons in 1937. In 1943, U.S. yards turned out a fleet almost the size of the largest merchant navy in the world at the start of the war, in one year alone.

By the fall of 1944, ship operators for the War Shipping Administration were supervising more than 3,500 ships and dispatching loaded ships from U.S. ports at an average of one every thirty minutes. Such a traffic of American hulls did the convoy effort demand.

The Ships for Victory strategy was simple: America would produce ships at a rate faster than the Germans could sink them. The Royal Navy was primarily responsible for knocking out the U-boats, but Admiral Land, Henry Kaiser, and Ships for

Victory tipped the scales with more shipping produced than the Germans could dispose of.

Liberty ships by the score took to the seas, restacking the odds in favor of the Allies by vastly expanding the shipping reserves. The Liberties went up, they shipped out, they joined the convoy lanes and altered the entire cast of the war, unglamorous, plebeian as they were, by their numbers. They simply saturated the Atlantic Ocean.

# 15

OF THE BLEAK RUNS TRUDGED IN UNRELIEVED DESO-
lation by the convoys during that pitiless winter; of the
cold, unforgiving routes they traveled on the forsaken
leagues of the seas, no run was bleaker than the Murmansk Run,
to north Russia. Plagued by ice so bad it would close over guns
and depth charge throwers, beset with whistling cold so frigid
that those above on watch limited their exposure to one hour,
maybe two, constantly buffeted by ice and snow, the Murmansk
Run went into the north Russian ports of Murmansk and
Archangel. The convoys, designated PQ, QP, JW, RA, departed
Iceland or Scotland, then climbed up into the icy, slush-covered
frontier of the Arctic Ocean, cut east through the Barents Sea,
finally passing into the Kola Inlet, guarded by the imposing
fortress of the North Cape. The subarctic weather was the
worst of any sea frontier. Stricken ships were sometimes ma-

rooned in ice. Survivors of torpedoings faced grim, harrowing stakes in the bid to survive.

With no second front in the west to reinforce the Russians, struggling to push back Hitler's assault, the Allies realized the critical importance of opening up a supply run to stoke and support Moscow's defense. The Russian convoys, loaded with trucks, bombs, general cargo, ammunition, tanks, detonation caps, dynamite, weapons, and more, brought and delivered vital ordnance and matériel, without which Russia could not have held off the Germans. The Murmansk Run was as important to Russia's survival and the final expulsion of the Nazis as any other Allied support. But the North Russia run was hell on ice.

In the bitter north, the convoys were subjected to an almost unimaginable array of German armament. Running north along the coasts of Norway and Russia, the flotillas passed within range of land-based Luftwaffe squadrons. Air attacks punished and ravaged the herds of merchant ships. The ever present U-boat attacks were a given; in this northern stretch a third weapon could be sent against the convoys—surface ships based out of Narvik and Altenfjord in Norway. Conditions in north Russia were altogether different. U-boats were painted polar white for camouflage. During the long arctic summer, darkness never descended; a constant daylight burned in the sky. The Murmansk Run was the center of some of the heaviest fighting in the Battle of the Atlantic; from its beginning in August 1941 the shuttle immediately developed a reputation as the shell corridor of the North Cape, at the northern tip of Norway.

Convoy PQ 13, bound northeast for Murmansk, ran smack into a barrage of the infamous German crossfire. The armada left Reykjavik March 20, 1942, ran into foul weather, then a full gale out in the frigid arctic wastes. German commanders sent destroyers to intercept the formation; the battle for the convoy broke out on March 28; it lasted three days. The Germans hurled high-level bombers, dive-bombers, and U-boats at PQ 13. On the 28th alone, one American merchant ship, one British, and two Panamanian cargo ships were sent below. A second attack was mounted the next day, but failed in the howl of the storms. PQ 13 arrived in Murmansk on March 31.

Convoy PQ 16 left Reykjavik May 20, 1942; five days later it ran into a Nazi execution squad. The battle of Convoy PQ 16 lasted six days, until the flotilla reached Murmansk. No fewer than ten separate attacks were loosed on the convoy by Luftwaffe bombers and torpedo planes, in addition to U-boats; the American freighter *Michigan* was the target of at least six separate assaults on the 27th alone. The *Michigan* survived and made it to port. In all, seven of the convoy's thirty-six ships were sent below.

But the grimmest convoy of the Russian run, the convoy which endured an ordeal beyond all limit and proportion, a trial which became a grave marker on the ledger of the war, was Convoy PQ 17, "The Convoy from Hell."

In June 1942, Hitler and his admirals, increasingly gratified by the damage German air and sea assaults had inflicted on the PQ convoys, decided to prepare a decisive blow, a defeat so punishing it would convince the Allies to give up the Murmansk Run. If Allied supply lines to Russia could be cut, such a move would have a devastating effect, vastly increasing chances for success on the Eastern Front. The operation was code-named Rösselsprung, or Knight's Gambit.

Luftwaffe squadrons were put on alert. A force of U-boats with the code name *Eisteufel* (Ice Devil) was sent to form an intercepting line at sea. Four of the most feared German surface ships, the super-battleship *Tirpitz*, the pocket battleship *Scheer*, and the heavy cruisers *Hipper* and *Lützow*, were sent out to form the final element in the ambush.

All of this arsenal was arrayed against Convoy PQ 17.

PQ 17 left Reykjavik on June 27 with an escort force which was nothing short of daunting, far greater than the ordinary guard. The force was composed of sixty-two warships; it numbered twenty-one escort class vessels, a seven-ship cruiser covering force, and a distant covering force composed of the aircraft carrier *Victorious*, the battleship *Duke of York*, the heavy cruisers *Nigeria* and *Cumberland*, twelve supporting destroyers, the U.S. Navy battleship *Washington*, and two modern American destroyers. Fifteen submarines were deployed ahead of this vast armada.

PQ 17 ventured out into the Norwegian Sea, then headed into the open range of the Arctic Ocean. Its senior officers had no way of knowing what awaited the convoy; the thirty-eight ships of the fleet proceeded in tight formation. Then, on July 1, the flotilla was picked up by *U-456*, commanded by Kptlt. Max-Martin Teichert, one of the *Eisteufel* boats. Teichert immediately sent back an establishing fix on PQ 17; the other *Eisteufel* boats converged on July 2, at about the time PQ 17 passed the returning QP 13 from Murmansk.

That day, the first air attack was launched against the convoy. Eight torpedo planes jumped the formation; one was shot down.

The surface force was now sent out to stage itself in waters to the north near Narvik and Altenfjord. At the same time, six *Eisteufel* boats plus four others converged on PQ 17 in a sea of glassy calm covered with ice slush. The first U-boat attacks failed to inflict any damage; a second air attack also failed. On the 4th, two air attacks sank one cargo ship and hit three others.

At this point, a dramatic and perhaps foolhardy decision was taken, of which there are many versions and opinions. But what is established fact is that the Admiralty, on learning that the German surface force had put to sea, now concerned that the combined German air and naval units could devastate its force of warships, withdrew the entire escort cover for PQ 17. The seven-ship cruiser flotilla was ordered to retreat to the southwest and withdraw; in the confusion of the maneuvers and orders, the six destroyers in the close escort force withdrew as well, though not specifically so ordered, and the remaining fifteen close escort warships, also beset by confusion, fell out of formation and departed. The ships of PQ 17, now stripped of defense and thus completely exposed, were told to scatter.

In the forbidding chill of the northern wilderness, the air and sea forces of the Nazi bear trap now snapped shut on the defenseless ships of the convoy. The Luftwaffe, screaming overhead, swooped in, bombing, strafing, and attacking the ships in the rising sea smoke and haze. The U-boats soon pounced. The British freighters *Empire Byron* and *River Afton* were sunk by *U-703*. Kptlt. Heino Bohmann in *U-88* bagged the American freighters *Carlton* and *Daniel Morgan*. All the while, the Luftwaffe unleashed its fury from the skies.

The American SS *Washington* and two British freighters were sunk by nine attacking JU-88s on July 5. The crew of the *Washington* set out on a forbidding saga of survival. They abandoned ship in two lifeboats and rowed through the frigid, desolate sea for three days. On July 8, they ran into a six-hour snowstorm. The next day, another snowstorm swirled. On July 11, they neared the ice-locked coast of Novaya Zemlya, and landed there on the 12th, near starved and bitten by exposure. Ensign Charles M. Ulrich, in charge of the Naval Armed Guard detachment of the *Washington*, killed a seagull while other men managed to snare eight goslings, and the survivors made soup

Admiral Sir Max Kennedy Horton, left, with Admiral Sir John Tovey,
commander-in-chief of the Home Fleet. Horton served as commander-in-chief,
Western Approaches, during the crucial years when the Allies turned the
tide of the war on the Atlantic and swept to victory, from November 19, 1942,
to August 15, 1945. (Imperial War Museum)

taken, of which there are many versions and opinions. But what is established fact is that the Admiralty, on learning that the German surface force had put to sea, now concerned that the combined German air and naval units could devastate its force of warships, withdrew the entire escort cover for PQ 17. The seven-ship cruiser flotilla was ordered to retreat to the southwest and withdraw; in the confusion of the maneuvers and orders, the six destroyers in the close escort force withdrew as well, though not specifically so ordered, and the remaining fifteen close escort warships, also beset by confusion, fell out of formation and departed. The ships of PQ 17, now stripped of defense and thus completely exposed, were told to scatter.

In the forbidding chill of the northern wilderness, the air and sea forces of the Nazi bear trap now snapped shut on the defenseless ships of the convoy. The Luftwaffe, screaming overhead, swooped in, bombing, strafing, and attacking the ships in the rising sea smoke and haze. The U-boats soon pounced. The British freighters *Empire Byron* and *River Afton* were sunk by *U-703*. Kptlt. Heino Bohmann in *U-88* bagged the American freighters *Carlton* and *Daniel Morgan*. All the while, the Luftwaffe unleashed its fury from the skies.

The American SS *Washington* and two British freighters were sunk by nine attacking JU-88s on July 5. The crew of the *Washington* set out on a forbidding saga of survival. They abandoned ship in two lifeboats and rowed through the frigid, desolate sea for three days. On July 8, they ran into a six-hour snowstorm. The next day, another snowstorm swirled. On July 11, they neared the ice-locked coast of Novaya Zemlya, and landed there on the 12th, near starved and bitten by exposure. Ensign Charles M. Ulrich, in charge of the Naval Armed Guard detachment of the *Washington*, killed a seagull while other men managed to snare eight goslings, and the survivors made soup for the half-frozen men. Then they took to their boats once more, hoping to find a settlement of natives.

They rowed on through the freeze and slush; after two more days, they met the survivors of the SS *Paulus Potter* marooned in four lifeboats. All these battered, frozen sailors pulled up in their boats on Novaya Zemlya, and, on the permafrost of the island, they captured more than 100 helldiver ducks and together prepared soup for some 100 hands, one third of whom were unable to walk due to frostbite. On July 15, they set out in their boats again. They finally ran across the grounded freighter SS *Winston-Salem*, which took them aboard; on the *Winston-Salem*, they had rest and real food—their first in ten days! They transferred to a British merchant ship; all finally arrived in Archangel on July 25.

The rest of Convoy PQ 17 was easy prey for the German forces. The heavy surface ships were withdrawn, but in the moaning cold and the floating ice of the Arctic floes, over the next five days, from July 5 to July 10, air and sea attacks decimated the formation. On July 10, the freighters *Hoosier* and *El Capitan* were sunk in heavy air raids. The British freighter *Earlston* was lost to U-boat attacks. Teichert in *U-456* sent below the 7,000-ton American freighter *Honomu*. The Germans picked off one merchant ship after another; no mercy was given to the convoy in the barren, icy expanses of the sea. The battle continued, with both aircraft and U-boats sending the merchant ships below over the course of the five-day slaughter.

Only fourteen of the original thirty-eight merchant ships of Convoy PQ 17 finally pulled into Russian ports. Twenty-four ships, almost two thirds of the convoy, had been lost in the bitter, frigid wastes of the Arctic Ocean and the Barents Sea. Convoy PQ 17 had come as close to total destruction as any convoy

An aerial photograph of a convoy spread out across the sea, this one Convoy KMF 1, one of the largest troop convoys of the war, en route to the invasion of North Africa in November 1942. (Author's Collection)

Another convoy on the North Atlantic, this one slogging through heavy weather in 1945, carrying reinforcements and war supplies for the Allied armies breaking into Germany. (Official U.S. Coast Guard Photo)

A valiant ship: M/V *San Demetrio*, shown with buckled upperworks
after the attack on Convoy HX 84. The sixteen *San Demetrio* survivors
managed to reboard the blazing hulk and sail her back to England
with no navigational equipment. (Imperial War Museum)

Another victim of German torpedoes: this one burning five miles off
the Atlantic coast of America. (Hulton-Deutsch Collection/Corbis)

Admiral Sir Percy L. H. Noble served as commander-in-chief, Western Approaches, the command which oversaw the Battle of the Atlantic, through the difficult early years of the war, from February 17, 1941, when he assumed command, to November 19, 1942. (Imperial War Museum)

Admiral Karl Dönitz was commander, U-boats, until he became commander-in-chief of the entire German navy on January 30, 1943. Here shown reviewing a U-boat crew. (U-Boot-Archiv)

Admiral Sir Max Kennedy Horton, left, with Admiral Sir John Tovey,
commander-in-chief of the Home Fleet. Horton served as commander-in-chief,
Western Approaches, during the crucial years when the Allies turned the
tide of the war on the Atlantic and swept to victory, from November 19, 1942,
to August 15, 1945. (Imperial War Museum)

Cpt. Donald G. F. W. Macintyre RN, DSO with two Bars, DSC, the crisp, rulebook officer who could sense where the U-boats were and became the second highest scoring Allied U-boat killer of the war. (Imperial War Museum)

HMS *Walker*, an Admiralty W Class destroyer, entered service during World War I. One of Cpt. Donald Macintyre's early commands, she plucked a substantial prize from the sea when she sank *U-99*, capturing top German ace Otto Kretschmer and his crew. (Author's Collection)

HMS *Hesperus*, the ship that Cpt. Macintyre said he "knew I could lose
my heart to," here shown returning to a cheering crowd with her bow crumpled
after ramming and sinking *U-357* on December 26, 1942. Macintyre scored
three of his kills while commanding the ship. (Imperial War Museum)

Kapitänleutnant Otto Kretschmer was the top German U-boat ace,
scoring forty-four ships sunk through his career. Cool to the Nazis,
reserved, he was nicknamed "Silent Otto." (Bundesarchiv)

Kptlt. Horst Elfe was second watch officer on Kretschmer's *U-99*, then commanded *U-139* and *U-93*, until it was sunk and its crew captured by Cdr. A. A. "Harry" Tait aboard *Hesperus* in January 1942. (U-Boot-Archiv)

The crew of the *U-99* posed for a formal photograph. Kretschmer is second from right, lower group. (Author's Collection)

Vice Admiral Sir Alan K. Scott-Moncrieff RN, KCB, CBE, DSO and Bar, right in white cap, rose to commander-in-chief, Far East. As a forty-year-old commander, he led the battle of Convoy SC 11 onboard his HMS *Enchantress*. (Imperial War Museum)

HMS *Enchantress*, a Bittern Class sloop, was Cdr. Alan K. Scott-Moncrieff's escort leader and led the battle of Convoy SC 11. (Author's Collection)

HMS *Worcestershire*, an armed merchant cruiser, led the battle of
Convoy SC 26. She took a torpedo in the terrible fight but was later
repaired and converted to a Landing Ship Infantry in 1943.
(Author's Collection)

Cpt. Paul R. Heineman, USN, left, the much decorated senior officer, escort, who led the battle of Convoy SC 100, with Cdr. Harold S. Berdine, the skipper of U.S. Coast Guard Cutter *Spencer*, Heineman's escort leader. (Official U.S. Coast Guard Photo)

One of the 327-foot Treasury Class cutters, USCGC *Spencer* led the battle of Convoy SC 100. "It's the best escort on the North Atlantic," Cpt. Paul R. Heineman said of the ship. (Author's Collection)

Torpedoed: The American tanker *Dixie Arrow*, her back broken, crumbling amidships under heat of fire, settles toward the bottom of the ocean on March 26, 1942, after being hit off the American coast during Operation Paukenschlag. (Official U.S. Navy Photo)

Three British seamen clinging to a raft following the sinking of a merchant ship. Merchant seamen faced ordeals lasting days and weeks in open lifeboats and on rafts such as this. (Official U.S. Coast Guard Photo)

A Type VII U-boat, the most numerous production class built by the Germans in World War II. (Imperial War Museum)

One of the larger Type IX U-boats, also one of the biggest production runs. (U-Boot-Archiv)

The tiny corvettes were the mainstay of the North Atlantic escort squadrons, filling out many groups. This one is MS *Gardenia*, a Flower Class, the most numerous type. She participated in the battles of HX 55 and HX 96 in 1940, before being lost due to a collision in November of 1942. Churchill dubbed these powerful little ships "cheap and nasties." They sank more than their share of submarines. (Author's Collection)

A U-boat under aerial attack. Minutes after the photograph was taken, the U-boat was sunk. (Bettmann/Corbis)

Charles A. "Bungey" Edwards, foreground, who found life onboard ship companionable, but remembers "you had enough to do to keep you busy. . . . We'd be in action on and off for sometimes forty-eight hours with hardly any sleep." Here enjoying a moment of relaxation with a mate.
(Author's Collection)

B-24 Liberators proved one of the most successful U-boat hunters. These, belonging to RAF 120 Squadron, are shown at their base in Northern Ireland. (Author's Collection)

A Sunderland flying boat, one of the RAF's most successful ASW (antisubmarine warfare) aircraft. (Imperial War Museum)

of the war. The Admiralty suspended all further sailings to Murmansk for the rest of the summer, until the long Arctic winter gave the protection of darkness against Luftwaffe attacks.

The North Atlantic—and the great circle route climbing up, east, out past Newfoundland, then crossing under Greenland and Iceland—was always Dönitz's primary concern. No other route held half the importance the Atlantic did, with its millions of convoy tons and its strategic place in the war effort. On the North Atlantic, with its invaluable North American convoys, the winter offensive went on, hurtling into the new months of 1943. The U-boats hustled west from the Bay of Biscay; they shuttled back and forth from the Air Gap; they struck in packs, hitting at night, generally on the surface. They came back in when their fuel or torpedoes had run out, or they developed mechanical problems, or they sustained battle damage too serious for further action.

The weather for the first months of the year was the worst the Atlantic had seen in fifty years. Storms prevailed for 116 days of 140 that winter. The convoys labored up the heaving seas, struggling up to the tops of the waves, then careened into the yawning canyons below. The swells were massive, shuddering hillocks of gray, crested with white.

Against the backdrop of this bitter weather, Dönitz pressed on with the winter initiative to break apart the Allied cross-ocean chain. German U-boat strength had nearly reached the zenith of its wartime levels. Shipyards were rolling out new subs at the remarkable rate of twenty-four every month. With a total fleet complement of 416 U-boats, 110 at sea at any time and fully fifty on the Atlantic—this combat force representing a much larger total fleet—the U-boat admiral at last believed he had reached the critical quotient of strength he needed to thrust decisively at the Allies. Dönitz carried forth his bid.

Convoy HX 222, thirty-four ships out of New York, lost one whale factory ship. Convoy SC 118, under Lieutenant Commander Francis B. Proudfoot, lost eleven ships in February to the *Pfeil* (Arrow) group. Captain Paul Heineman's Convoy ON 166, forty-eight merchant ships under the A-3 Escort Group, had a rough, costly crossing, with eleven ships lost and one damaged between February 11 and March 3. The jaws of the Nazi wolf were snapping. In February, he had sharp teeth.

ON 167 lost two ships on February 21. Convoys ON 176 and ON 178 lost one ship apiece on April 12 and 26. Then, in one of the decisive clashes of the war, Peter Gretton's B-7 Escort Group—he had been promoted to commander—guarding the westward-bound ONS 5, fought a nine-day battle against some forty U-boats. Eleven merchant ships were sent down, but Gretton claimed six subs in return with two more damaged. The Germans hit everywhere along the convoy routes with the jump of a field howitzer.

The North Atlantic that winter was a vacant, slate gray wilderness, streaked with foam, on which too many ships were lost. Alongside the RN and the RCN, the U.S. Navy and Coast Guard stood watch on the heaving green waves through to spring. They were escorting small troop convoys across to England for the buildup there. The U-boats hit these convoys, too, usually in the middle of the night, on the surface, as they preferred to do. The U-boats were not the only peril.

Convoy TA (Troop American) 18 suffered a calamitous fire aboard the transport *Wakefield* which ravaged the ship for hours. Hundreds of men were trapped in the forward part of the ship, cut off by flames. Rescue efforts were undertaken by the cruiser USS *Brooklyn* and the destroyer *Mayo*; these ships performed heroic assistance work, taking all 1,500 civilian workers and crewmen off the stricken transport. The *Wakefield* was later repaired and returned to service. Two tugs took the *Wakefield* under tow and brought her back to port in Halifax.

Convoy SG 6, a six-ship formation leaving Sydney, Cape Breton, August 25, 1942, ran into the wolves on August 27. On that night, the army transport *Chatham* was torpedoed twenty or thirty miles off the coast of Canada; half an hour later she went to the bottom. The U.S. Coast Guard Cutter *Mojave* searched the area for subs for two hours but found nothing; she then commenced rescue response. Of more than 560 crewmen and American and Canadian soldiers aboard, almost all were saved.

But the greatest disaster to befall the troop convoys, the most harrowing tragedy of that winter, was the loss of the steamer *Dorchester*. The *Dorchester* was a 5,252-ton army transport carrying 1,000 tons of cargo, 751 American troops, and 130 crewmen. At 3:55 on the night of February 3, 1943, she was torpedoed 614 miles east of Labrador and forty-six miles south of Greenland by *U-456*. No distress signal could be sent out, as the power onboard had been knocked out; no flares were sent up; and in the inky dark of the sea at night, the rest of the convoy remained unaware of the *Dorchester*'s fate until she had sunk.

At 3:58, three minutes after the torpedoing, the captain ordered "Abandon Ship." Chaos ensued. Life rafts released from the transport hit men struggling in the water. The port lifeboats could not be released; others capsized from poor handling or overcrowding. The decks ran with frightened, disoriented soldiers trying to abandon the sinking vessel, others refusing to leave. In the confusion, four courageous, loyal navy chaplains quickly took over, trying to calm the frightened soldiers, tending to the wounded and leading men to life rafts. They passed out life jackets, and when the life jackets ran out, the four chaplains took off their own life jackets and gave them away, knowing they would go down with the ship. The Reverend David Poling, a cousin of one of the chaplains—Lieutenants C. V. Poling and G. L. Fox, Protestant ministers, Lt. A. D. Goode, a rabbi, and Lt. J. P. Washington, a Catholic priest—later said the action of the four was a shining illustration of Jesus' charge, "Greater love hath no man than this, that he lay down his life for his friend."

As the ship went down, the men in life rafts saw the four chaplains, arms linked, braced against the slanting decks. One survivor said: "It was the finest thing I have seen or hope to see this side of heaven."[1]

Below was a scene of bedlam. Soldiers and crewmen, some injured, some succumbing to the cold, filled the frigid water. Men clambered to get aboard lifeboats or rafts. Others drifted, dazed, held up by their life jackets. The water temperature was 34 degrees Fahrenheit; the air 36 degrees.

Six hundred seventy-seven men lost their lives in the icy waters that night as a result of *U-456*'s torpedo. One of them was a twenty-eight-year-old crewman named Thomas Corrales. On the bridge of a containership crossing the dark ocean fathoms in the windy black of the night in 2002, where sixty years before U-boats roved, the son of Thomas Corrales, Tom Jr., is standing lookout. He chats as he looks across the sea. He recalls his father:

"I remember . . . one time I was in my grandfather's house and I ran to him [my father]. But I really can't say I remember him. I was only five years old. . . . He was a merchant seaman and he was gone much of the time," Tom Jr. says in an interview.[2]

Thomas Corrales was a good-looking man, about five feet, eight inches tall, stocky, no fat on him. After his death, Mrs. Corrales received a letter on War Shipping Administration letterhead. It said:

Dear Mrs. Corrales:

By authority of the Congress of the United States, it is my honor to present to you, the wife of Thomas Corrales, the Mariner's Medal in commemoration of the greatest service anyone can render cause or country . . . [Mr. Corrales] was one of those men who today are so gallantly upholding the traditions of those hearty mariners who defied anyone to stop the American flag from sailing the seas in the early days of this republic. He was one of those men upon whom the Nation now depends to keep our ships afloat upon the perilous seas—to transport our troops across those seas; and to carry to them the vitally needed materiel to keep them fighting until victory is certain and liberty secure.

Nothing I can do or say will, in any sense, requite the loss of your loved one. He has gone, but he has gone in honor and in the goodly company of patriots. Let me, in this expression of the country's deep sympathy, also express to you its gratitude for his devotion and sacrifice.

/s/
E. S. Land
Administrator[3]

Thomas Corrales left an only son and a wife. In time Mrs. Corrales remarried.

By and large, the troop convoys passed across to the U.K. with little incident. They were taken across by the U.S. Navy and Coast Guard, zig-zagging across the plunging Atlantic and U-boat country, dodging the U-boats and the 23.5-foot *"aale"* or "eels" (torpedoes) of the blunt, tapered Type VIIs and the bigger Type IXs. Ultimately the troop convoys were given over to the big, fast "superliners"—the *Queen Mary*, the *Queen Elizabeth*, the *Isle de France*, the *Pasteur*, the *Aquitania*, the *Nieuw Amsterdam*, high speed crack liners. The big fast superliners were so fast they could outrun any U-boat they met. Not one was caught by a submarine through the whole series of the "Monster" Convoys, as the express shuttles were oddly named. The queens of France and Britain showed their heels to The Hun.

In January 1943, a series of events took place in the military High Command in Berlin which were to affect every element of the U-boat war from that moment forward. Hitler, increasingly dismayed by the continuing failure of heavy German surface units to inflict more serious punishment on the north Russia convoys, finally reached a peak of disenchantment. In December 1942, the trim British escort of Russian Convoy JW 51 B had convincingly bested the cruisers *Lützow* and *Hipper*, and the *Hipper* had been badly damaged. Operation Regenbogen (Rainbow), as it was called, was the second significant operation using heavy surface ships, following Rösselsprung, which had decimated Convoy PQ 17.

In the humiliating aftermath of the failure of Regenbogen, Hitler had summoned Grand Admiral Erich Raeder, sixty-nine years old, to appear before him. Face-to-face, without any sug-arcoating, Hitler had decreed that the day of the surface ship was done; the big ships were to be scrapped. Both Hitler and Hermann Göring believed the steel could be better used to produce tanks for the Eastern Front.

Raeder, the head of the navy since 1928, a champion of surface action and no friend of the Nazi party, objected that this would be tantamount to a victory for the Allies—and one that had cost them no effort. Hitler was unmoved. Raeder, the first officer to hold the title of grand admiral since Alfred von Tirpitz, realized he must resign. He did so, recommending Admirals Rolf Carls and Dönitz as possible replacements. Hitler settled on Dönitz.

On January 30, 1943, Karl Dönitz, fifty-two years old, the proponent of the submarine and *Rudeltaktik* (Wolfpacks), was duly installed as C-in-C of the German navy, commander of all sea forces of the Thousand Year Reich. With his new appointment came a move to Berlin and a stately home on generous grounds, surrounded by other ranking Nazi leaders. Here he enjoyed the perks of Nazi power, an SS escort, Mercedes staff car, private plane and private train with restaurant and sleeping coach. The U-boat headquarters was moved to Berlin, where it was housed five minutes from navy Headquarters in the Hotel Am Steinplatz in Charlottenburg.

Dönitz's ascendancy instantly converted the role of the U-boat in naval warfare. With Dönitz as grand admiral, the submarine weapon he had long advocated broke into the vanguard of German strategy at sea. The U-boat arm took center stage in the "war against shipping." Ironically, Dönitz finally convinced Hitler not to scrap the heavy surface ships.

As a result of his new access to Hitler, Dönitz was immediately able to carry out certain measures reordering the affairs of the navy. He set out on a housecleaning at the Naval High Command, getting rid of many old-guard admirals, replacing them with figures more to his liking. The U-boat campaign became the navy's highest priority, with all personnel involved in U-boat production exempted from military service. Dönitz won assurances from Reichs Armament Minister Albert Speer for the supply of the steel necessary to boost submarine production even higher.

But as important as the free hand he inherited with his new post, Dönitz also achieved an unprecedented intimacy with the führer, which was to work for him in many other ways. He recounts in his memoirs how the intrusions of Göring, Hitler's darling, into naval affairs were summarily dealt with in one meeting:

> The most violent, but also the last, of these [denunciations by Göring] happened at a large conference into which Göring marched and announced that German E-boats [patrol boats] had suffered heavy losses during an air raid on one of the Channel ports and that the Navy was to blame because the E-boats, instead of being dispersed and camouflaged, had been lying conveniently together in a little group. "I refuse to tolerate these criticisms of the Navy, Herr Reichsmarschall," I retorted swiftly. "You would be better advised to look to your own Luftwaffe, where there is ample scope for your activities."
>
> The complete silence which ensued was first broken by Hitler's quiet request that the officer submitting his report should please continue; and when the conference ended, Hitler, as on the previous occasion, took leave of Göring with a shake of the hand and ostentatiously pressed me to stay to breakfast with him.

After that incident, Göring indulged in no more criticisms of the Navy.[4]

Dönitz had arrived at the inner circle of Hitler's court. He could now advance his arguments and proposals as a chieftain on the inside. He was to use his new access with skill to advance the U-boat war, learning to "present my proposals in bold lines on a broad canvas, in such a way as would excite Hitler's vivid powers of imagination instead of 'merely tickling him.' "[5] So, the German side of the vast war at sea, ever changing, ever swinging, passed entirely to the hands of Dönitz.

At sea, where the U-boats raced across the plunging, folding swells of gray, their long, low hulls sluicing across the surface, the German offensive followed through, hurtling on into the new year without missing a beat. The U-boats hiked out to the Air Gap, where they formed into packs, hovering just below Iceland, just within Cape Farewell; these packs expertly shifted about the field of the sea like mobile hit squads by BdU. The German initiative followed through with the jump of a Mannlicher rifle, the U-boats accumulating a series of victories which seemed ever to grow. In early February, HX 224 lost two ships. Three weeks later, SC 121 lost seven cargo ships. In March, Convoy HX 228 lost four in convoy actions; in April HX 231 and 232 gave up three ships each to German raiders.

Then, as the headlong German thrust carried through, Harry Tait, who had stopped to rescue the crew of *U-93* and had so enjoyed drinking with his steward, George Wills, was lost with his destroyer, *Harvester. Harvester* went below when she rammed a sub in battle, damaging the U-boat, but leaving herself disabled; she was then torpedoed. Tait, disconsolate over the loss of life, chose to go down with the ship.

In March, Dönitz carried on with the heft and range of his

expanded fleet. The U-boats struck singly, they struck in packs. Through March 1943 there were enough U-boats to form a total of thirteen wolfpacks, exactly the number BdU had mustered three years before during the *full* year 1940. The U-boats carried G7e's, electric torpedoes, and G7a's, powered by compressed air; these traveled at about 30 miles an hour just under the surface of the water, and had a range of about 6,000 to 9,000 yards. By 1943, the Germans were producing 1,700 of these torpedoes a month. That winter, the convoys still followed the northernmost route, climbing up to Rockall Bank; the wolfpacks sat in the middle of the ocean like dangling necklaces of black pearls, lurking in wait for the first convoy to come along.

Captain S. W. Roskill wrote in the official British history of the war at sea about the offensive of early 1943: "In its intensity, and in the certainty that its outcome would decide the issue of the war, the battle may be compared to the Battle of Britain of 1940. Just as Göring then tried with all the forces of the Luftwaffe to gain command of the skies over Britain, so now did Dönitz seek to gain command of the Atlantic with his U-boats."[6]

At new year, Britain was implacable, implacable but weary and dug in. The homes and neighborhoods of London, whether low, red-brick, or white-painted and stately, were pocked by bombing and soot-grimed. "The public buildings of the city were also showing signs of fatigue and depression, as their facades became more grimy and decayed," writes the award-winning British author Peter Ackroyd.[7] Britons had abided through war, fire, flood, and with dismal news coming in from the Atlantic, Londoners endured. Along the sandbagged government buildings of Whitehall, the war in 1943 lay in the shipping statistics, worsening to ever growing dismay. Fuel stocks were at a low. The Admiralty, staid in its concern, advised that there were neither enough ships nor enough escorts to continue the supply of Britain, and the all-important buildup of the U.S. Army in the British Isles.

Soon, naval Enigma would be finally and definitively broken. But now, in March, with a temporary "Ultra" blackout, the Germans kept setting their dangling patrol lines like traps, then coalescing into the big wolfpacks which would strike.

Against this gray pall of perseverance and hardship, FDR and Churchill met at the Casablanca summit in January 1943, in the Hotel Anfa, overlooking the palm trees of the old city in Morocco. There, the British military staff put it to the Americans squarely: unless additional escorts, escort carriers, and as many B-24 VLR Liberator bombers as possible were provided by the U.S., the Atlantic supply line could not be kept going at a level sufficient to support the Allied strategy. The Germans had latched on to the key weakness in the Allied link: the inability of air cover to reach the Air Gap; still heavier U-boat attacks were expected. In the face of these warnings, D-Day was postponed from 1943 to 1944. At mid-war, the British believed the task was very much up to American supply and reinforcement.

The magnificent halls of Westminster and Parliament, hit many times by bombs, were stolid in concern. Elizabeth Bowen, the great Anglo-Irish novelist, described Londoners as living in "the lightless middle of the tunnel."[8] Rationing was in force; an individual was allotted two ounces of butter per week, three pints of milk, one egg; restaurant meals were limited to five shillings, about $1.25.

"There were no street lights, very few buses or trains. You didn't go visiting your chums except in the summer," recalls

Arnold Hague, a naval expert and author, who was then thirteen years old. "I remember being cold. I remember one very cold winter when we had no heating in the schools."⁹ Britain endured, abiding in its homes, and its churches, and its tea shops and factories.

In February and March, with the German advance following through at full pitch, all the flotillas and fleets of the Western Approaches command worked intensively to counter the U-boat thrust on the gray, marbled, rolling sea. New escort efficiencies meant that Admiral Sir Max Horton could reassign ships to his new Support Groups, free ranging, independent battle squadrons that crossed the seas as needed. Two new escort carriers were expected to beef up the command; later in the year MAC ships, freighters converted to small aircraft carriers, would come into service. Admiral Horton kept his escort forces, reinforcements, air adjuncts working at high pitch in the face of the German press on the void, vacant, cold, shifting sea.

And then in March came the climactic battle of the Atlantic engagement, Dönitz's master stroke, this one involving two entire convoys and three separate wolfpacks totaling thirty-eight U-boats. The battle, the summoning of cohorts, began, as it did so often that winter, in bad weather.

The battle of Convoys HX 229 and SC 122 was viewed by the Germans as involving one massive formation; it actually involved two. SC 122 was the first to enter the German lair.

Convoy SC 122 left New York March 5, fifty-one ships under the shield of Lieutenant Commander Richard Boyle, RN, and the British B-5 Escort Group. Two days out, the convoy ran into heavy weather, massive, building seas, winds mounting to near gale force, a gray, gathering seaway.

Then bad luck. On March 12, B-dienst, the German decoding unit, deciphered a signal rerouting SC 122 to the south to avoid a waiting wolfpack, the *Raubgraf* (Robber Baron) group. Two other wolfpacks were at sea, far out, roughly 1,100 miles south-southwest of Iceland, the *Stürmer* (Stormer) and *Dränger* (Pusher) groups. Neither Western Approaches nor any other Allied command knew of their presence; on March 8, the brief blackout of Enigma had occurred.

BdU, in Paris, now tipped off to the approach of the formation, began to shift its assets.

Three days after SC 122 left New York, a second convoy set out on its tail, fast convoy HX 229, thirty-eight merchant ships under the command of Lieutenant Commander Gordon J. Luther, RN, and the British B-4 Escort Group. HX 229 traveled at almost twice the speed of SC 122; there were now two entire convoys proceeding into the open sea along the same track. Together these formations totaled over eighty merchant ships, laboring on through the mounting seaway, into the German plot.

For the next twenty-four hours, HX 229 plunged on, unsuspecting of what lay ahead. Luther tended his flock, shepherd in the blowy weather. The formation plodded along, nosing ahead through the swells overnight, into the next day. Then, on the night of the 16th, U-boats from two of the packs, the *Raubgraf* and *Stürmer* groups, struck the formation for the first time, attacking in tandem. They fired a volley of steel fish at the darkened rows of ships; four were hit and sent below, including two sturdy EC2s, American Liberty ships, the *James Oglethorpe* and the *William Eustis*.

Approximately two and a half hours later, perhaps 100 miles across the sea, at 2:01 A.M., the assault on SC 122 began. *Stürmer* boats delivered their first attacks on this flotilla. Abysmal weather now prevailed, strong winds, high seas plunging away into shuddering canyons of cold.

SC 122 shoved ahead to the east through the black rumble of the wind. The ships were darkened. Lieutenant Commander Boyle, forty years old, was watching out ahead, minding his charge of fifty-one merchantmen. "An exceptionally capable officer, well liked, very tactful and good personality . . . quiet," [10] his superiors had said of him as a young officer. Boyle was watching the road. The night was silent. The convoy tumbled along. Then the calm of the early hours was blasted apart.

One of the *Stürmer* boats, *U-338*, under Kptlt. Manfred Kinzel, penetrated the screen of escorts and fired a spread of torpedoes into the blacked-out rows of ships. Four were struck by Kinzel's salvos and ultimately sunk, including the British *King Gruffydd* and the Dutch *Alderamin*. The escort ships now jumped to life. Boyle's team lunged ahead, going on the counterattack, chasing down contacts. Starshells illuminated the night. The convoy ran with men hurrying to action stations.

By 2:30 in the morning on March 17, on the wide, vacant face of the sea, across a vast expanse of windy, black ocean, two sites of battle had formed covering some 230 miles of longitude. The first, 1,185 miles due west of Cape Clear, Ireland, was the area where HX 229 was under attack. The second, roughly 250 miles east, further in toward Ireland, was the site where SC 122 was under assault. Counting U-boats, escorts, and merchantmen, almost 130 ships were involved in the massive imbroglio, plunk out in the middle stretches of the Atlantic.

At almost the same time as Kinzel dove into the midst of SC 122 on the night of March 17, *Stürmer* and *Dränger* boats returned, carrying out fresh strikes on HX 229. Over the next eight hours, between 4:56 A.M. and 1:05 P.M., they torpedoed and sank six more ships, including the British Liberty *Coracero* and the Dutch freighter *Terkoelei*. Luther's escorts were busy. Two submarines were sighted running on the surface and driven away into the night. The escorts lunged through the dark, chasing contacts. The night was full of shadows, the dim silhouettes of ships, U-boats.

Back at the site of the battle of Convoy SC 122, on the night of the 17th, *Stürmer* boats came back at that formation to raid once more. Hitting Boyle's convoy in the dark as it steamed on in the inky black of the sea, they scored three more victories, including the British *Port Auckland* and the 4,300-ton *Zouave*. The *Stürmer* boats then quit the scene. Then a lull as the clamor of combat fell away. The thick, velour curtain of night descended. The battle was almost done.

On the 18th, *Stürmer* and *Dränger* boats hit HX 229 one last time. They got off spreads which claimed three more ships, including the American Liberty *Walter O. Gresham* and the British freighter *Canadian Star*. Finally, on the 18th, the subs still in contact with SC 122 spread across the convoy's battle area 250 miles to the east, picking off two more Allied hulls. The last two vessels lost on the last day of fighting were the Greek freighter *Carras*, built in 1918, and the 5,800-ton British freighter *Clarissa Radcliffe*, which was probably sunk. The great sea battle was done. The ships continued on, the escorts stood down, the night was calm and windy and quiet. The U-boats fell off, turned for home or further patrol.

The graves of more than twenty ships littered the sea. As the convoys had kept steaming, the battle had proceeded along a line stretching for more than 600 miles, roughly the distance from Boston to Cleveland. The field of battle on which the enormous struggle had been fought covered an area 156,000 square miles in size.

The aftermath of the battle was sobering for the Allies. Fully twenty-two ships had been lost, aggregating a total of 147,000 tons. Roughly one fourth of the combined fleets of two whole convoys had been torpedoed. A priceless payload of ships, cargoes, and lives had been lost.

On the heels of battle, BdU proclaimed the victory "the greatest success yet achieved against a convoy.

"After the extraordinarily successful surprise blow on the first night, tough and energetic pursuit despite strong air and surface defense brought splendid successes to the submarines in their attacks both by day and night," BdU boasted.[11] News of the victory made a propaganda sensation for Nazi Germany.

In the winter, the convoys came in battered, weary, unbowed. They had crossed the ravine of the Devil's Gorge; they had survived the gauntlet of torpedoes and fire. The war at sea had come to a reckoning. In February, in March, the war seemed to sway on its mast. Samuel Eliot Morison wrote of this juncture:

> The enemy never came so near to disrupting communications between the New World and the Old as in the first twenty days of March, 1943. Clearly we could not go on losing ships and men at that rate. When convoy after convoy came in with six to a dozen ships missing, the morale of seamen who had to make the next voyage was impaired. The patriotism, the energy and the sheer guts that kept these men of the merchant service, and of the three escorting Navies, to their allotted task is beyond all praise.[12]

Captain S. W. Roskill, writing in his *The War at Sea*, the official history of the Royal Navy in World War II, remarks:

Whether final victory would have come sooner had our forces been differently allocated at an earlier date is likely to be a subject of dispute. For what it is worth this writer's view is that in the early spring of 1943 we had a very narrow escape from defeat in the Atlantic; and that, had we suffered such a defeat, history would have judged that the main cause had been the lack of two more squadrons of very long range aircraft [VLR Liberators] for convoy escort duties.[13]

The gap between defeat and victory may have been thinner than that. How thin it was could be related by any of the sailors who knew the convoy routes that winter, or by Admiral Sir Max Horton or any flag rank officer who had aegis over the ships at that cold, precipitate edge. The men and officers on the ships, officers like G. J. Luther, R. C. Boyle, the quiet commander "capable of making a decision and sticking to it," Macintyre with his polish, Scott-Moncrieff with his bravura, scores of officers and men on the tossing ships of the Royal Navy, the Royal Canadian Navy, and U.S. Navy pulled the effort through.

It was exactly these RN qualities of slash, rake, and esprit on which the Admiralty depended in the chill winter that year. One naval expert, Arnold Hague, the analyst who once worked at the British Ministry of Defence, portrays the atmosphere at the Admiralty at this time:

Everybody in the Admiralty says we cannot sustain losses like this. The system has broken down. And a lot of senior officers and Churchill himself [are] experiencing this view. Yes, it was the crunch time. It very nearly broke the will of the Admiralty and the politicians. It very nearly broke the escort force.

There was one exception. Horton wasn't tired. He was

not despondent. He did not think the system was breaking down. He wasn't despondent and I think it shows the general feelings at the moment. I think Dönitz must have been under the same pressure. Certainly his U-boats were.[14]

The long, 2,500-mile trans-ocean convoy system shuddered. On it rested the supplies fueling the war in Europe. The convoy feeder belt had reached its limit.

PART THREE

THE TIDE TURNS

# Merchant Ships Sunk by U-Boats in the North Atlantic

80°    40°    0°

*Jan Mayen Island*

70°    GREENLAND    70°

ICELAND

*Faeroe Islands*

*Shetland Islands*

*Cape Farewell*

GREAT BRITAIN

LABRADOR

NEWFOUNDLAND

Brest • FRANCE

NOVA SCOTIA

New York •
40°                                                                          40°
UNITED                                    SPAIN
STATES        • Norfolk                   Gibraltar
                                          • Casablanca
        *Bermuda*
                              *Azores*        AFRICA
                    *Madeira Islands*
                    *Canary Islands*
80°  *Bahama Islands*    40°        0°   © 2006 Jeffrey L. Ward

# · 1944–1945 ·

# 16

AND THEN IN MAY, AS SUDDENLY AND SURPRISINGLY as it had erupted, with the sinking of the liner *Athenia* on the first day of the war, September 3, 1939, the U-boat war dissipated and gradually died away.

On April 21, 1943, two U-boats were lost in action against Convoy HX 234. On May 5, in another convoy battle, seven U-boats were sent below. On May 9, three more subs were lost.

Radar was the reason. Radar had completely bewildered the U-boat effort. Dönitz noted of one of these convoy battles: "During this fog period alone fifteen boats were attacked with depth charges and six of them were located by destroyers, surprised on the surface and engaged with gunfire. The lack of any means of counteracting this radar location undoubtedly left the boats in an inferior and, indeed, hopeless position."[1]

He wrote of another convoy battle: "No less than eleven of

the boats in contact with the convoy were detected and driven off while it was still light. This is a very high percentage. It is obvious that the enemy must have detected all the boats in contact with astonishing certainty."[2]

By May 1943, so many factors in the Allied arsenal had grown up to loom over Dönitz's subs—aviation, new ships, new weapons, new technology—that the submarines were facing a new kind of war. But the U-boat admiral blamed radar; radar, he believed, was responsible for the stalemate of his submarines. He concluded: "While the U-boats continued to lack a receiver capable of picking up [radar] signals on these new wave bands, any further attacks on convoys in bad visibility would remain impossible."[3] On May 12, two more U-boats were sent below, two more on the 17th. By May 22, U-boat losses had hurtled out of all proportion. A total of twenty-seven subs had been sent below by May 22nd, far out of line with anything BdU had seen in the sinking statistics for the war to date. The losses simply stunned. By the end of the month a total of thirty-three subs had been sunk. The tallies defied understanding, too pronounced to explain in the long precedent and context of the campaign. Dönitz abruptly came to the conclusion in the wake of the May sinking statistics that he could no longer win the U-boat war.

"We had lost the battle of the Atlantic," he wrote later. "Events in May 1943 had shown beyond dispute that the anti-submarine organization of the two great sea powers was more than a match for our U-boats."[4] The overwhelming of his submarines had had a wrenching personal effect on Dönitz.

"When [a] boat was lost, Dönitz would sort of go into his private room and sort of cry about it," Eberhard Godt, the chief of operations at BdU, was quoted as having told other officers.[5]

The U-boat war disintegrated, then it collapsed. Dönitz

withdrew all boats from the North Atlantic and redeployed them to the Azores, to the south and the west. There they managed to score but meager successes. "He didn't have that many U-boats in the (Central) Atlantic. They very rarely found convoys," says Arnold Hague, the naval analyst. "It's very difficult to find a convoy unless you've got positive information."[6] The massive, draining contest which had resounded and rung across more than 2,000 miles of ocean, across 1,500 days, fell away.

In the weeks following these developments, Dönitz had to decide whether he should simply call off his U-boats and let the other branches of the armed forces fight on alone. Would such a cessation of the U-boat war permit the Allies to redistribute resources—industrial, manpower, fuel stocks—to other branches of the armed services, fostering an attack of still greater intensity on German citizens and Nazi Germany? If so, was it reasonable to ask his submariners to continue a fight that would necessarily entail enormous losses and sacrifices?

"I finally came to the bitter conclusion that we had no option but to fight on. The U-boat arm could not alone stand aside and watch the onslaught, of which it had hitherto borne the brunt, now fall in all its fury as an additional burden on the other fighting services and the civilian population," he wrote in his memoirs, *Ten Years and Twenty Days*.[7]

But Dönitz felt he must put the question to his men. He convened a summit at the headquarters of his senior officer, Submarines (West), Kapitän zur See Hans Rudolf Rösing, gathering there the commanders of his Biscay-based boats, the commanders of the 10th, 3rd, 9th, 7th, and 6th U-boat flotillas. In conference, he asked them whether the crews and they themselves believed it was worthwhile carrying on the U-boat war, despite its complete hopelessness, despite the severe sacrifice this would require. The commanders, to a man, told Dönitz they firmly believed, and were sure the crews would demand, that the U-boat service fight on.

"They were unanimous both in their conviction that the campaign must be continued and in their confidence that the great majority of the crews would be in agreement with the decision. The U-boat arm proved that their confidence was fully justified, and to the end of the war it fought with undiminished determination," Dönitz wrote.[8]

The conflict which had pitted some 1,200 fighting ships against each other and raged across 32 million square miles of Atlantic Ocean now downshifted. Though the Germans would fight with determination to the very last days of the war, they would never again return to the Atlantic with the strength and command they had gathered in 1942 and early 1943. The battle, ever circling, ever crossing back, had passed once again, this time into the hands of the Allies. The U-boat war would go on with substantial purpose, but Dönitz had effectively quit the central field of the North Atlantic.


In April, Paul Heineman took his last convoy across, HX 233, his swan song.

HX 233, the last run for the group that had come to be known as "Heineman's Harriers," was an almost effortless waltz across the ocean, an illustration of the changing fortunes of the Allied campaign.

HX 233 left New York April 6—most HX convoys had by now been shifted to New York departures—but about two thirds of the way across to the British Isles, roughly 750 miles off the coast of France, a U-boat on lonely picket duty, U-262, made contact with the convoy. The submarine, under Kptlt. Heinz

Franke, raised seven other boats. The hammer closed on Heineman on the night of the 16th; on the 17th, the U-boats attacked.

Kptlt. Heinrich Hasenschar in *U-628* led off the action at dawn, sending a tin fish slamming into the 7,100-ton British freighter *Fort Rampart*, which exploded with a deafening roar, rocking the convoy columns. The steamer settled and soon sank.

But three hours later, Heineman, on the *Spencer*, got a contact on *U-175* under Kptlt. Heinrich Bruns. Heineman tracked the U-boat for almost one hour; then, as Bruns was about to fire a spread of torpedoes, he was startled into alertness by the *Spencer* nearing. He frantically dove.

It was too late. Heineman dropped a pattern of eleven depth charges on the sub, fracturing the pressure hull, smashing gauges, sheering off bolts on the diesel engines, and tearing the wireless from its mounting. Bruns now blew to the surface, breaking out onto the waves. *Spencer* immediately opened fire with every gun that could bear, from her main 5-inch rifles to her 20mm cannon. The U-boat crew now rushed abovedecks, jumping into the water. The first ones were cut down by gunfire from the *Spencer* and other ships in the convoy. Bruns was hit in the head and stomach and killed instantly. One man was blown away by 20mm rounds; others were killed by the fusillade. Now the rest of the crew came streaming up on deck. The remaining dozens of sailors were luckier, and made it into the water alive. The *Spencer*, too, suffered casualties. Twelve sailors were injured by fire from a merchant ship taking part in the bombardment; one American coast guardsman, Radioman 3rd Class Julius T. Petrella of Brooklyn, was killed. William Walton, a correspondent for *Time* magazine, recorded the scene of Petrella's mortal injury in his article "Scratch One Hearse":

[Germans] were not the only men to die. On the *Spencer*'s bridge a radioman dropped, clutching his belly.... Two men fell headlong in the passage, others felt a sharp sting and reeled back from their posts.

"I'm bad hit," gasped the radioman, Julius Petrella... "Gimme something quick." As they picked him up gently a warm, thick gush spilled from his back staining the deck with a dark pool. In his eyes was the hurt surprise of a man looking into unexpected death. Hastily the sickbay was emptied of regular patients for the wounded.[9]

Julius Petrella was quiet, slender, five feet nine inches tall, and had many friends on the *Spencer*. He liked to gamble and play cards, often with Harold Rogers, the baker on the *Spencer* who had remarked on the hurricane during the Battle of Convoy SC 100.

"We used to get down in that hold, and then we'd close the hatch; hell, everybody smoked then; you couldn't see the cards for the smoke flowing," Rogers recalled. "[Petrella] liked to gamble.... He was a very unlucky gambler. He owed a ton of money."

Petrella was close to many of his shipmates. "He was a good guy.... He was a great person.... More or less he was on the quiet side. He wasn't loud or nothing like that," says Rogers.[10]

Petrella, Rogers, another sailor named Arnold Diamond and a second cook, D. C. Lynam, would often make up the core of a card game. Lynam was from Mobile, Alabama; everyone knew him as "Mobile." Finally, Mike Hall, the stocky veteran of SC 100 who rose to the rank of captain long after the war but was then an enlisted man, broke up the ongoing game. Petrella, the quiet, slight radioman from Brooklyn, gambled and owed a lot of money. Later, in a stiff wind, Petrella was given a burial at sea as the crew lined up in uniform. He is survived by a niece and a nephew.

The *Spencer* and the coast guard cutter *Duane* ultimately picked up the German U-boat crewmen struggling in the water. A boarding party tried to capture the sinking *U-175*, but the sub plunged below before the coast guardsmen could secure it. No other ship in Convoy HX 233 was sunk. The convoy steamed six days back to Liverpool.

For Heineman, Convoy HX 233 was a tidy swan song; his score on the crossing was nearly perfect. He lost only one ship; he took a sub down in return. It was a fitting end for the tireless, hard-driving American escort leader who had come through one convoy battle in a hurricane, and others of red-hot intensity. The forty-six-year-old SOE completed a total of twelve crossings in a little less than one year. Heineman came in for a spell ashore.

Abroad, other commanders continued the long, downfield rush. The war was picking up speed and new momentum, all across the traveling ocean front the Germans were disintegrating; the Allied navies were in a long, unbroken dash to the goal. The RN, the RCN, and the USN were in a contest of an entirely new stripe; they had turned the tide—the Atlantic was now to all intents and purposes cleared. Aircraft were scoring victories at a constantly accelerating rate, the main convoy routes would never again be as seriously threatened. The British, Americans, Canadians had surged through four years of pitiless battle; that drive had at last broken into the open.

The thrust which would ultimately bring around the great dynamos and engines of the war, all the assemblies, drive train, shafts, tappets, and gearings of the whole, great, 2,000-mile-wide war effort, had started, almost imperceptibly, at a welter of sites, months and months before, in the corridors of Western Approaches, in the offices and parade grounds of other military installations, in laboratories, factories, planning rooms—a dozen places. The drive involved many elements, many phases. One critical development was aviation, the advent of which totally altered the shape of the war. The Consolidated VLR Liberator bomber entered service. From 1943 on, better than half the U-boat kills in the Battle of the Atlantic were scored by aircraft. Antisubmarine technology developed and, meshing with the refinements of aviation, began to move ahead the British surge: radar, for aircraft and ships; Huff-Duff, radio locating of subs; the Leigh Light, for night bombing attacks. Better weapons came on the scene in 1943—the enormous one-ton depth charge; the Hedgehog, a forward-firing depth bomb launcher. The development of better escort tactics, better fighting, advanced naval capability, all contributed to the Allied dash.

In the face of the headlong Nazi onrush, the British had perfected, advanced, honed their cutting edge, metamorphosing into an array of new military capabilities in response to the German onslaught, evolutions which ultimately built their talent, whetted their talent, checked the German gains and decided the submarine war.

If it had a beginning point, if the British surge had a genesis that could be defined at all, that beginning took place, perhaps, in the labyrinth of Western Approaches. The point of inception was a naval officer named Captain Gilbert Roberts.

Roberts had been given a considerable task in early 1942. The German thrust at sea was barreling through victory after victory. The pressure was on for the Royal Navy and the Royal Canadian Navy to stop the hemorrhage of shipping, to bring to an end the ever-mounting losses among the convoys. Escort tactics at the time were still primitive, both rudimentary and ill-defined. The standard response to a submarine attack was little more than a confused, seat-of-the-pants charge ahead. Escort practice was largely an uncharted area.

Roberts was a gunnery officer with experience in submarines. He was handpicked to start a tactical school which would be much more than just a school—a think tank, a laboratory, an academy to develop escort warfare to a keen, high pitch and impart its lessons to the commanders at sea. A training base for escort officers had been established in 1941 on the island of Tobermory by Vice-Admiral Gilbert O. Stephenson—this was not to be confused with Stephenson's course. Roberts's school was to raise tactics to the finest tuning; it was to be called the Western Approaches Tactical Unit, WATU for short. It was housed in eight rooms at the top of Derby House in Liverpool.

The goal-oriented Roberts was advised of his project's critical importance in a meeting with Churchill and set about his mission with full purpose and speed.

He spoke with commanders at sea about battle, their actions and reactions in submarine attacks. With his staff of forty-five, he explored the patterns of combat experience and the thinking about escort strategy. Roberts's WATU was an inquiry into the exercise and conduct of antisubmarine combat warfare.

What resulted was a one-week training course in which, by the end of the war, over 5,000 officers from twelve navies had participated, including Harry Tait, Peter Gretton, and the Prince of Greece, later known as HRH Prince Philip, the Duke of Edinburgh. Roberts instructed, analyzed; he invented a mock war game which pitted an officer behind a screened booth—with a slit permitting him to see a dummy field with models representing convoys and escorts—against imaginary submarines. Young Wrens from the Women's Royal Naval Service pushed around the models representing ships, according to the moves made by players. The object was to defend the convoys against submarine attacks. A player had two minutes to think up his move.

WATU was far more than a one-week course, though. Roberts and his staff considered warfare and tactical situations with an eye to understanding their basic rules and elements. They explored, examined, investigated procedure in battle.

The team at WATU would re-create and study what had happened in U-boat attacks, also using models on map boards. They considered different types of attacks and what the best countermeasures would be. These new tactical measures were taught to escort officers, and the work began to reap rewards. Out there, where the battle was being fought, U-boat sinkings began to rise sharply—because of Enigma, because of airpower, because of radar, but also in part because of the work WATU had done. In 1941, the Allies sank nineteen U-boats. In 1942 they bagged thirty-five. By 1943, the number of U-boat kills had jumped to 150; in 1944, 111. WATU was one of many factors producing this advance in U-boat sinkings.

Roberts's school codified tactics, regimented, formalized them. Its stratagems were the first well-grounded, explicit countermeasures the Royal Navy had seen in the war. The revolution in tactics, thus, was the first phase in the gathering engine of war the British had begun to devise in 1942, which was so vital to the breakthrough in 1943. They learned how to fight better.

Then aviation arrived, changing everything. The first U-boat kill scored by an aircraft in World War II took place on March

11, 1940. It would be years before airpower attained its full potential, though.

RAF Coastal Command, alongside Fighter Command and Bomber Command, was the wing which waged the air war at sea. It started in 1939 with 300 fewer aircraft than it had fielded at the end of World War I. At its apogee, Coastal Command mustered an enormous flight of 793 planes grouped into fifty-four squadrons; they were varied, a broad array of types. The role of airpower across the Atlantic in World War II was twofold: reconnaissance, to get far out over the sea and locate U-boats, alerting convoys and headquarters ashore; and, offensive, to attack and sink U-boats with the variety of weapons carried by bombers.

The Sunderland flying boat was the backbone of Coastal Command; it looked something like the sleek, streamlined early Pan Am Clipper flying boats. It had a range of 3,000 miles and could carry 4,960 pounds of bombs or depth charges. Sunderlands had a top speed of 212 miles an hour and "long legs," they could wing out over great ocean distances.

Coastal Command flew many other models of aircraft—the Wellington, the Bristol Beaufighter, the Handley-Page Halifax, Whitleys, De Haviland Mosquitoes, Lockheed Hudsons. But the battling babe, the champion of all-around, long-range ASW—antisubmarine warfare—bombers was American, built in San Diego, California—the Consolidated B-24 Liberator. In the model which came into widest use, it was called the Very Long Range (VLR) Liberator. Powered by four Pratt & Whitney R-1830 Twin Wasp motors, fourteen-cylinder, air-cooled radial engines, the VLR Liberator had a cruising range of 2,850 miles, a top speed of 290 miles an hour at 25,000 feet, and could carry a payload of 8,000 pounds.

When twenty VLR Liberators were delivered to Coastal

Command in September 1941, they were modified for service by eliminating their guns, armor, and other equipment to lighten them and extend their range. They were found to be an ideal aircraft for ASW. An aerial attack on a U-boat was swift, summary, very often fatal. The attack by Fred Colborne of 5 Squadron, Royal Canadian Air Force, on *U-604* on February 23, 1943, was nothing short of masterful.

On that winter day, far out over the North Atlantic, Colborne, in a PBY Catalina, spotted *U-604* about six miles ahead of a westbound convoy in visibility that was exceptional for the season. Gunning his engines, Colborne plunged in a steep dive, hurtling from 3,000 feet to 800—and began his attack. He raced in at the U-boat at an altitude of about 300 feet, then swooped down just as the sub dove. The submarine slid beneath the waves; Colborne realized he was coming in too fast and too high. He cut, hesitated, then charged in. Goosing the throttles, Colborne roared down and over the sub, depositing his depth charges just as his plane sped over the U-boat's track. The pattern so badly shook *U-604* that compressors were torn off their mountings, her propeller shafts were displaced, the main clutches were jammed, the diesel clutches were severely damaged, and one of the main ballast tanks took a four-foot crack.

The U-boat limped home to Brest and was out of commission for several weeks while being repaired. Air attacks were punishing.

On the western side of the Atlantic, the air war was conducted by the U.S. Navy and the U.S. Army Air Force, as well as the Royal Canadian Air Force. Pilots from these services also destroyed U-boats with consummate virtuosity, none more handily than Lieutenant Harry Kane, 396th Medium Bombardment Squadron, United States Army Air Force.

On July 7, 1942, Kane came upon the unsuspecting *U-701*,

commanded by Kptlt. Horst Degen, lying in satisfaction and open pleasure on the surface, airing out its foul, fetid innards after having polished off nine ships on its current patrol, the last of them the American tanker *William A. Rockefeller*.

Kane, in a Lockheed Hudson, surprised the sub, which at once crash-dived. Lieutenant Kane now threw the Hudson into a sharp turn; and, with engines roaring, he veered down on the U-boat, releasing three 325-pound depth charges in a tight-cut triangle. With pinpoint precision, the charges straddled the sub, one charge landing astern and two others bracketing the conning tower bull's-eye-perfect. The depth charges went off, destroying the U-boat. The crew streamed up on deck and abandoned ship, swimming in the waters of the Atlantic for three days, lost on the sea. Finally, seven survivors of *U-701*, including Degen, were rescued. Airplanes could kill U-boats, as the Allies were fast learning.

Then, in 1943, airborne radar appeared everywhere, all at once. In 1943, ASV-III radar came in. It had taken many years to develop. It had taken laboratories, scientists, and many versions to perfect. ASV-I had appeared in January 1940; ASV-II had been introduced in spring 1940. Finally, ASV-III "centimetric" radar came on line, in 1943, its beam much more intensely focused, giving far more capability and power. ASV-III could see much farther. The Germans had countered ASV-I and ASV-II with Metox, a receiver which could warn of radar signals. Then had come Naxos U, a more advanced detector. But ASV-III was undetectable by either Metox or Naxos U. It was the most effective radar the Allies had and vastly increased the ability of aircraft to find and destroy.

CAM (Catapult Aircraft Merchantmen) ships had been inaugurated in 1941 and 1942. These were merchant ships fitted with a catapult to carry a single fighter. When the pilot finished his sortie, he could either fly to a land base, if within range, or ditch his plane near the convoy and parachute to be picked up out of the sea.

MAC ships (Merchant Aircraft Carriers) came into service in 1943. These were merchant ships converted with a flight deck and aircraft hangar to accommodate three to four fighters. Escort carriers came along in 1943—small, light, fast aircraft carriers bearing a score of fighter planes and traveling with the convoys. All these evolutions were highly successful ways of delivering air power far out over the ocean, to cover the convoys.

VLR Liberators—290 miles an hour fast, capable of a range of almost 3,000 miles—finally closed the Air Gap and sealed off the black pit which had swallowed so many freighters and invaluable tankers. Despite the repeated pleas of the British, U.S. Fleet Admiral King in 1943 remained as unwilling to part with American VLRs for Atlantic duty as he had been to institute convoy on the U.S. coast in 1942. In the wake of the spectacle of HX 229 and SC 122, the climactic convoy battle in March 1943, in which twenty-two ships were lost, Churchill appealed once more to Roosevelt to release the VLRs. At FDR's direction, King grudgingly sent one squadron to Newfoundland in April, reversing his disastrous blunder. By May, the Air Gap was closed. The bleak gully which the Germans had come to call the Devil's Gorge was no longer the prime hunting ground of the U-boats.

Airpower was to sweep into the vanguard of the Allied offensive from 1943 to the end of the war in 1945. From April 1943 to the end of hostilities, more than half of all U-boat kills were scored by aircraft. By the end of the war, Coastal Command aircraft had scored 192 victories in all theaters. VLR Liberators accounted for seventy of those kills.

Airpower surged, streamed, flooded through the Atlantic, becoming an indispensable counterpart to naval warfare on the sea below. Pilots like Colborne and Kane arrived to play a decisive role in the victory which waited at the end.

Lastly, there occurred a sweeping advance in weapons about 1943 which brought new kinds of devices and armaments, further contributing to the Allied race for victory. Critical new inventions, designs, prototypes went into ships and airplanes—many with odd, even bizarre, names—Hedgehog, Squid, MAD, retro bombs.

Depth charges, to begin with, underwent swift development. In 1942, the explosive minol replaced amatol as the active ingredient in depth charges, increasing the range of effectiveness. With amatol, a depth charge had to land within twenty feet of a U-boat to do any damage; using minol, the effective range expanded to twenty-six feet, so depth charges no longer had to be dropped as precisely on a sub. In January 1943, Mark 7 pistols were fitted to Mark 7 heavy depth charges for the first time, increasing the depth range of these charges from 550 feet to 700 feet. Later, a 900-foot depth capability was attained with some missiles. As the maximum safe depth for U-boat operation was roughly 700 feet, the new charges could get at U-boats even below their most extreme underwater capability.

Finally, the one-ton depth charge—2,000 pounds—was proven to be lethally effective. Introduced in 1942, it was designated the Mark X.

New types of depth charge throwers were introduced. Hedgehog was a forward-firing depth charge launcher which hurled a pattern of twenty-four projectiles in an oval shape all at once. The key advance of Hedgehog was that sonar was susceptible to a blind spot, as the attacking ship passed above and the sonar pod, beaming out forward, passed ahead of the sub. With a forward-firing launcher, the blind spot was eliminated—a destroyer could shoot precisely up to the last, positive contact. This made the Hedgehog system much more precise. Squid was another forward-firing launcher, linked to data from the sonar.

Aircraft also mounted new weaponry. Some devices flew down, some flew backward, some had ears. The air-launched acoustic homing torpedo was introduced and proved its worth. Its nicknames included Fido and Wandering Annie. Retro bombs went into service, bombs fitted with small rockets that fired backward, reducing the forward drift of a missile launched from a speeding airplane. MAD (Magnetic Anomaly Detector) was a device which could detect the magnetic field created by the submerged hull of a U-boat, not visible from above. Sonobuoys could detect the sounds emitted by a submarine in the water. All these devices increased the accuracy, capability, precision of antisubmarine tactics.

The year 1943 saw the convergence and meshing of all these separate phases—WATU, aviation, new weapons, new technology, like the hundreds of moving parts of a machine, falling together, turning over, winding as one. In the spring of 1943, a complex Allied engine of destruction had come into being and was roaring, thundering forward like a great, rumbling dynamo. The war at sea was now radically reshaped by these dozens of advances.

The burst of new technologies and techniques powered the Allied rush at an ever increasing pace; alongside that onrush, the tradition of proven, old-fashioned naval shiphandling and compass rose seamanship did as much in its own routine and regimen to propel the Allied sweep as any of the complex wizardry hatched in laboratories. The captains at sea, wielding their ships in the exchange and cross of battle, were as critical as the gadgets. Of the masters, of the weathered veterans, of the oilskinclad, leathery commanders, none were more tried and tested than the great aces, the U-boat slayers, the escort leaders who had scored the grooves of their own, individual techniques, their own variations of the hunt and the kill.

Captain F. J. "Johnnie" Walker was the best; his 2nd Support Group racked up no fewer than twenty U-boats sunk. Walker in his youth had been a middleweight boxer; he was husky, agile, with a dour face like a mine shaft, a rugged, sturdy, stomping bloodhound who once characterized a victory over a U-boat involving five separate attacks and the dropping of fifty-five depth charges with the comment: "I was tolerably certain that the Boche had been poleaxed." [11] Walker, who was by nature so intent on U-boat hunts that he would spend unbroken hours on his bridge, directing combat through a bullhorn, was famed for his unique and extraordinarily successful "Creeping Attack" strategy. Under this maneuver, one ship would act as the directing ship for a run, focusing its sonar on a sub, directing in a second attacking ship until the attacking ship had stolen up on the unsuspecting bear. Then the trap sprang shut. The depth charges were released.

"Nobody ever survived one in any way, shape or form," says the naval expert Arnold Hague about the Creeping Attack. "No individual, not any submarine. It was sheer, calculated murder. . . . It was cold-blooded murder. But it's war. You want to kill the enemy. He worked out how to do it." [12]

Walker was the best, a virtuoso of heft. He commanded the

respect and sentiments of all his men. He trained them rigorously, to a high pitch; on Walker's ships, depth charges could be ready in thirty seconds. A statue of him stands today at a busy spot along a popular stretch of Liverpool waterfront, brooding, his eyes hollow, surveying the clutter and sprawl before him.

Commander Donald Macintyre was next in the rack score, with his clearly recognizable style. Commander Peter Sturdee, who was a young sub-lieutenant under Macintyre at the time of the capture of Otto Kretschmer, remembers of the India-born escort leader: "He was a stickler for efficiency and routine, but very, very human. He didn't suffer fools gladly. . . . He wasn't slim. He was strongly built." [13]

"You knew he was very good, very efficient. He was a very competent man," says Ron Smith, who served as a leading seaman on *Hesperus* under "DMac." "You knew where you were with him. You knew you didn't take liberties with Macintyre." [14]

Yet the crisp SOE had a human side, too, a sense of humor. Once within Smith's earshot, a seaman lagged in carrying out engine adjustments. "Prat, prat, prat," said Macintyre. ("Prat" is slang for "silly boy.")

"That makes two of us," the seaman responded.

"You and your bloody opposite [in the engine room]" Macintyre shot back.

It was one of the instances when Macintyre showed his lighter side. "It was only on occasions such as this that we realized that he did" have a lighter side, says Smith.

Commander Peter Gretton was third, dashing, cutting a slender figure, a flinty edge. Gretton served on three destroyers, lost very few ships, and in his vigorous pursuit of the war he did as much to develop and perfect the science of stalking and killing U-boats as any other officer of the Royal Navy.

Commander Harry Tait, with his three wins, had been the

last of the great aces. For them there was no lineup of bluecoats, no gleaming swords, no salute in the sun on parade grounds. They carried no glinting armor, no coats resplendent. They wore the heavy duffle coats, the sea jackets, wool or cotton, stained with salt. None of them was really Hercules or Theseus; they do not really seem like heralded champions. The war was brutal and long. The war was dark and grim. Men from merchant ships perished in oil blazing on the surface, in ships which plunged from the surface in twenty seconds. The Germans, too, died grimly, crushed in imploding hulls sailing down and deeper down in the dark gloom of the depths. No officer from the Battle of the Atlantic is really remembered in glint of sun, in ceremony. They were the rumpled heroes. They were haggard, weather-beaten, battered.

In spring 1943, in the Pacific, the war in Burma and China had bogged down, though Allied naval forces had prevailed in the Battle of the Bismark Sea and were advancing to New Georgia and the Solomons. Across the world, at a scatter of different points, the cycle of seasons came around once more, bringing new settings, new landscapes to other lives.

Among other navy personnel, Paul Heineman moved to Washington. In May 1943, he came in from the sea and moved to headquarters, Atlantic Fleet, taking on a command-level job as antisubmarine warfare officer on the staff of the Atlantic Fleet, with additional duty commanding the Anti-Submarine Warfare Unit. In this post he was awarded a Gold Star in lieu of a fourth Legion of Merit. Heineman moved up from command of the U-boat war at sea to oversight of that war. Washington had tapped a man with much experience.

Six hundred fifty miles to the north, across the pine trees and cedars of the Northeast, at Bowmanville Prison Camp in the Canadian wilderness, Otto Kretschmer, the wolf in the muzzle of captivity, would increase his stature dramatically, adding to his status of adventurer-hero. That spring he embarked on a plot of derring-do: a bold escape attempt.

Prisoners had begun digging three tunnels that spring—a main escape passage from the prison barracks and two diversionary tunnels—through which Kretschmer and three other commanders planned to crawl out to freedom, then make their way to the coast, and a waiting U-boat sent by Dönitz. Kretschmer had communicated with Dönitz through coded letters home. The tunnel excavation was hidden by the doors of a false wardrobe constructed by the inmates to conceal the work.

In October, however, all the dirt from the digging, hidden in the ceiling of the barracks, caved in and fell through. Guards immediately rushed into the barracks; the two diversionary tunnels were discovered. The next day the main tunnel was found. The plot had failed.

Alarmed, in turmoil, Kretschmer dispatched Kptlt. Wolfgang Heyda in a hastily devised plot to escape and warn the waiting U-boat. Heyda managed to get out of the camp, but was picked up on the coast by shore patrols. There the entire scheme ended. Kretschmer's daring attempt had collapsed in total failure. Life returned to normal at Bowmanville. The days passed in torpor. The eagle in captivity would languish, pinioned, under the rifle stocks of the guards at Bowmanville Prison Camp.

And thousands of miles from Kretschmer in bondage, on the sparkling waters of the Atlantic, Macintyre was seabound. Macintyre was back squinting in the sun, directing his B-2 escort group with his usual trim correctness 3,000 miles away. That spring he scored his fourth and fifth kills.

The fourth victory, over *U-191*, occurred on April 23, 1943.

That afternoon, *Hesperus*, H-57, gained contact on the submarine, first by HF/DF, then by sonar. The destroyer lunged out on the chase, followed by a corvette, *Clematis*. The two hounds surged across the surface, on the hunt.

Macintyre was in his own element, on the face of the fair sea with an echo pinging, back on the trail of a Type IX C/40 U-boat. *Hesperus* and *Clematis* raced ahead, forging through the waves. David Mottistone, who was a young sub-lieutenant on *Hesperus*, recalls Macintyre's "sense" for finding U-boats:

> He spent [two years working on] improving the submarine detection capabilities of ships, [and] got a complete feel for how the asdic [sonar] could be used, where it was in difficulty—like for instance if there were temperature layers in the sea, if it was rough, and so on; and all the refinements of what the echoes sounded like, how you could tell, if you were any good as an asdic operator, whether your echo was probably of a submarine, but not of a shoal of fish, or not of a wreck if you were in shallow waters, and so on.[15]

Macintyre, the finely tuned ace, had an ear as sensitive as that of a musical composer—but his medium was the ocean depths, how sound traveled in and was affected by the cavernous fathoms of the sea. He could divine where a sub was. Now he was racing in hot pursuit. *Hesperus* and *Clematis* bounded across the sea. *U-191*, under Kptlt. Helmut Fiehn, had crash-dived by this time, but sonar conditions were ideal and Macintyre obtained a strong echo. They caught up; *Clematis* attacked; Macintyre loosed a Mark X depth charge; *Hesperus* went in one more time and hurled a pattern of Hedgehog. The salvos exploded; *U-191* plunged to the bottom of the ocean depths.

Macintyre's fifth victory followed twelve days later. It was just as neat. H-57 picked up a submarine, *U-186*, by HF/DF; the veteran destroyer attacked with three depth charge runs that plastered the ocean deeps and sent the sub below.

*U-186* was *Hesperus*'s fourth victory; she would go on to become one of the most fabled ships of the Royal Navy, compiling five kills. Macintyre had scored his fifth kill; the thirty-nine-year-old commander was part of the leading edge of the gathering British surge.

# 17

THAT SUMMER, AS THE CONVOYS ROLLED THROUGH the Atlantic, at Western Approaches Combined Headquarters in Derby House in Liverpool in 1943, the staff of 700 was busy assessing, sifting, deciphering, analyzing Dönitz's still expanding, though more slowly, U-boat force. In the byzantine sprawl of corridors, rooms, cubicles, and offices at the command, Admiral Sir Max Horton and his crew were sizing up a rapidly changing picture and presiding over a war suddenly broken wide open.

On the level of individual commanders and operations, along the quays and jetties of Liverpool, fleet strength—destroyers, sloops, corvettes—stood at 159 ships, seven British escort groups and four Canadian; and Captain F. J. Walker's 2nd Support Group had just been formed. On April 28, sortieing from port, Walker's flagship, HMS *Starling*, had left

Western Approaches with the five other sloops that made up the unit—*Wild Goose, Wren, Kite, Cygnet*, and *Woodpecker*. They were powerful ships, mounting three twin four-inch-high angle guns, an array of 20mm and 40mm AA cannon, and depth charge rails. They were in action almost immediately. The 2nd Support Group went to the assistance of an eastbound convoy, fending off the enemy, lunging in chase through the night to keep threatening U-boats away. Next Walker put the group through intensive training, drilling the men without mercy. Then, on June 24, 140 miles northwest of Spain, four ships in the squadron, *Wren, Woodpecker, Kite*, and *Wild Goose*, teamed up to detonate the sub *U-449*. It was the first in an unbroken string of Allied victories that season. In the summer, the Royal Navy, the Royal Canadian Navy, and the U.S. Navy performed like a McCormack reaper, shucking away subs, threshing the seas as if U-boats were so many stands of wheat. They mowed down the field and brought home the harvest which at last was theirs, a continuing, broad gathering of U-boats bagged.

Tempered by the flame of their zealotry, Dönitz and his submariners kept the ram of the U-boat war driving. Immediately, Dönitz pulled his boats from the North Atlantic; he was never to return again, with one exception in the autumn of 1943. He now deployed his subs in new areas, around the Azores, to distant points such as Africa, the Caribbean, and the Indian Ocean. Here, where the Allied presence was thinner, he hoped the submarines might fare better.

In the southerly waters of the Central Atlantic, the U-boats cruised and hunted, crisscrossing the ocean in groups or singly, in the wastes west of Gibraltar. Ultimately they never reaped great success there. Allied antisubmarine warfare by this time had become too finely honed, had achieved too keen an edge. As the new deployment to the mid-Atlantic unfolded, in the north, the U-boat war suddenly faced new obstacles.

In April 1943, RAF Coastal Command set into motion a massive new bid which hurtled through summer to hit the Germans hard at the source of their operations—the Bay of Biscay. The blitz on Biscay would attempt to strike in the approaches through which submarines had to pass to reach the open sea. The British would try to choke Dönitz at the bottleneck of his exit passage.

Dönitz, already keenly aware of the growing threat posed by aircraft, had previously armed his boats with AA batteries—20mm flak guns and rapid-fire 37mm cannon, referred to by the U-boat crews as the *Wintergarten*, or Bandstand. U-boat command had also put *Flakspezialisten*, antiaircraft gun teams, on the subs, and surgeons to deal with the heavy casualties expected from aerial combat. Thus, the U-boats were substantially beefed up for action against long-range bombers.

In April, the RAF lifted off its first squadrons and struck the Atlantic coast of France. The U-boats cocked their guns, trained their barrels; a pitched battle now ensued between submarines and aircraft for control of the bay.

The German U-boat defenses were imposing, but Coastal Command won clear superiority in the first round. RAF pilots soon became savvy in dealing with the antiaircraft batteries. Pilots often worked in tandem with destroyers, sloops, or other surface ships. They were adept at low-altitude runs. Almost from the outset, it became obvious that the bomb-wielding Liberators and Sunderlands were outgunning the U-boats. By the end of May, six subs had been sunk in the bay. Between July 20 and August 1, another ten submarines were destroyed. Coastal Command, as planned, was disposing of the Germans in the bottleneck of the bay.

The duel in Biscay went on. Dönitz now jacked up his defenses, outfitting special subs as floating AA citadels, dubbed by the Germans "Aircraft Traps" or "Flak Traps." Heavily equipped with defensive armament—two two-centimeter four-barreled cannon and a 3.7-centimeter rapid-fire AA gun—their purpose was not to evade aircraft, but to lure them out and then shoot them down. At first the fortified U-boats had notable successes, downing a Sunderland and a Martlet, and damaging several other airplanes. But Coastal Command soon outpowered even these seagoing fortresses and rendered them of little use. In one instance, one of these massive redoubts, *U-441*, was so badly hit that twenty-three casualties resulted, including the captain, leaving the ship's surgeon to bring the boat back to base.

With his Flak Traps outpowered, his subs being badly pummeled by the RAF, Dönitz now seized upon the tactic of ordering his boats to band together in teams, so that the concentration of their combined gunnery could throw up a wall of fire, repelling intruders. Initially, teaming the boats had some success, but again the RAF soon learned to deal with the new tactic. In one exchange, a group of five U-boats under fire from four aircraft suffered so many casualties that two of the subs were forced to head home. The air offensive kept on as the RAF continued pressing the subs.

In the closing stages of the contest, totally overwhelmed, Dönitz finally ordered his boats to run submerged by day, surfacing only to recharge their batteries. If aircraft harried the subs too badly by day, they were to surface only at night. Coastal Command had all but closed the bottleneck, though. Dönitz had no more cards up his sleeve. Convincingly bested by the British initiative, the chief of the German navy finally canceled temporarily all sailings from the Biscay bases on August 2.

The loss tally confirmed that the bay initiative had had a dramatic effect on U-boat activity. Between July 1 and August 2, eighty-six U-boats crossed the waterway, fifty-five were sighted, seventeen were sunk, six were forced to return to base. In addition, air patrols off Spain and Portugal sank three boats and damaged a fourth.

"It was therefore no longer possible to fight our way through the Bay of Biscay by means of U-boat AA fire," Dönitz concluded.[1] The submarines went back to diving as soon as their radar detectors warned of a contact. Homeward-bound boats got in the habit of hugging the coast of Spain, where they were less susceptible to aerial attack. By August, Coastal Command had had a substantial impact on submarine traffic.

According to plans, the subs that had managed to get out of the bay operated far off in the Azores, Gibraltar, and Africa. But Allied defenses had gotten too proficient. The boats were often unable even to find convoys; they managed few successes in the face of newly inaugurated U.S. Navy "Hunter-Killer" groups there. These were freewheeling, free-ranging task forces usually based around small aircraft carriers; they would strike out and go after U-boats. Their successes were notable.

As the U-boat war ran into continuing headwinds, and momentum slipped from its tapering advance, it was clear that the war would not be won by conventional boats. German hopes, slowly, by steps, came to fix far out ahead, off in the future, on the advanced "Walter" boats and the moment when they would arrive. Futuristic, eerily streamlined, the Walter subs by themselves held the capability for turning around the entire war at sea, for decisively changing the parameters of the conflict. The Walter boats would be able to outrun any merchant ship and most escorts with their underwater speed of 18 knots. The Walter boats—the Type XXI and Type XXIII—would reinvent naval warfare.

Now, in May 1943, Dönitz, convinced of the central role the Walter boat must play, set out to fast-track development of the revolutionary subs. He first called upon the German naval staff. Planners there came back with a timetable projecting delivery of the first two Type XXIs before the end of 1944, mass production, after testing was complete, one year later. This meant the wonder boats could be introduced in significant numbers by 1946.

But that was too slow. Dönitz was racing against time. The new submarines would have to be ready to launch far sooner. The submarine Admiral now turned to the reich's armament minister, Albert Speer, asking him whether production time could be dramatically accelerated. Speer, the czar of war production, in turn, passed the matter on to a top industrial engineer, Otto Merker. Merker came back with a projection that, by use of an advanced modular construction method—under which the submarines would be built in eight separate sections close to the steel foundries, then assembled at the shipyards—the schedule could be substantially pushed. Using Merker's advanced methods, the first of the Walter boats could be ready to go in just four and a half months. The subs could go into service in just one year. Dönitz had his inside track. Now, at the twilight of the Atlantic battle, the Walter boats began to take shape in Bremen, Hamburg, and Danzig. If they appeared in time, on the accelerated track Merker forecasted, then the German war at sea, the ardent Dönitz believed, might flash anew.

"The menace represented by the new U-boats and especially by the 1,600-ton Type XXI, was very real—if they got to sea in large numbers," wrote Roskill of the British assessment. The

Walter boats were the last hope, though not the last thrust, of the German navy, the last resort of Dönitz and the Naval High Command. The Walter boat program began to take form against the backdrop of stalling German fortunes. It was the last redoubt of the war at sea.

The Atlantic Ocean, the second largest, one half the size in its width and sprawl of the Pacific, extends south from the forbidding, icy tracts of Kujutilik, past Portugal, to its waist in the Azores at about the level of Gibraltar. It then flows past the hump of Africa and drops in a widening funnel, between the parting splay of Africa and South America to its southerly extreme in the Southern Ocean. It is wide, but greater by latitude than by longitude. In the spring, it has the tranquility of a vast wilderness in the lassitude and warmth of the sun. In the spring of 1943, riven by war, this immense region was effectively split into two sectors by the Allies to further, by dividing responsibilities, the drive against the Germans.

On March 1, Allied naval and air chieftains gathered under Admiral King's chairmanship at the Atlantic Convoy Conference in Washington. Over twelve days, participants in the meeting mapped strategy and concluded that the northern half of the ocean should be completely taken over by the British and Canadians, giving these forces control over the convoys most important to their peoples, and freeing U.S. forces for duty in the Central Atlantic and the Caribbean.

The U.S. Navy now took on its most important role of the war in the Atlantic convoy duty in the central sector. Navy responsibility extended to more than a dozen convoy series; in the act of defending these convoys, American ships and aircraft dispatched a precise total of 107 kills.

The sprawl and array and panoply of the U.S. Navy were now everywhere. American "tin cans" took convoys through U-boat country, big, fast "DDs," as they were called, with their raked twin funnels, high, slashed bows and elevating 5-inch gun mounts. The destroyers sped across the southern sector, hunting submarines, hurrying across the open passage of the Atlantic. The convoys they took were numerous, varied, all types, motley. UGS convoys were general convoys from North America to the Mediterranean; they crossed with twenty, forty, fifty ships. GUS convoys went the other way, back to America. UGF convoys went from North America to Oran, in Algeria, and Naples, Italy; they were smaller, groups of fifteen or twenty cargo ships. These fueled the war in the Mediterranean and southern Italy, where Allied troops were now fighting, bringing explosives, food, mail, stores, oil, ammunition, refrigerated meat, flour, and much more.

The Mediterranean had proved a stage of central importance to the Allies. Gibraltar was a British bastion, serving as an escort base and the home of the powerful naval Force H; it was a key jumping off point for attacks on North Africa. Malta was another vital British fortress and fleet base which endured a crushing siege until the end of 1942. By the time its assignment sent the U.S. Navy into the Central Atlantic and the Mediterranean, supplies were rolling to support the invasions at Sicily, Salerno, and Anzio. American destroyers took convoys to port in Gibraltar, Casablanca, Marseilles, elsewhere, feeding the Allied troops fighting up the "soft underbelly" of Europe.

Samuel Eliot Morison, who traveled with many U.S. Navy units and ships to complete his majestic fifteen-volume series, *History of United States Naval Operations in World War II*, captured with his brilliant eye the sight of one of these formations:

> A convoy is a beautiful thing, whether seen from a ship or viewed from the sky. The inner core of stolid merchantmen in column is never equally spaced, for each ship has individuality. Someone is always straggling or ranging ahead until the commodore becomes vexed and blinks angrily "Number So-and-so take station and keep station." Around the columns is thrown the screen like a loose-jointed necklace, the beads lunging to port or starboard and then snapping back as though pulled by a mighty elastic under the sea; each destroyer nervous and questing, all eyes topside looking, ears below waterline listening, and radar antennae like cats' whiskers feeling for the enemy. . . . It seems a fresh miracle every morning when the rising sun lights the same ships, in the same order as those dark shapes which faded in the deepening twilight the night before. And any vessel, even a Hog Islander or an average Norwegian tramp with more rust than red-lead topside, is transfigured to a fair argosy when flooded by the first rosy light from the sun rising out of Africa.[2]

U.S. Navy sailors defended these flotillas, often in battle.

In the summer of 1943, ships of the navy's Tenth Fleet went on the offensive. U.S. Hunter-Killer groups ranged out into the Central Atlantic, seeking to hobble Dönitz's renewed campaign in the south. From July to October, USN groups targeted BdU's network of enormous Type XIV "Milch Cow" submarines. These mammoth whales were huge tanker submarines—almost 1,700 tons as opposed to the 761-ton Type VIIs—from which conventional boats could refuel at sea, thus extending their range. All BdU's underlying strategy for the war now, the operations in distant areas, the Caribbean, West Africa, the Indian Ocean, depended on this network of tanker subs to replenish boats in the field, far out to sea, greatly expanding their cruising radius. In the summer, the escort carrier strike groups of the U.S. Navy swept across the Azores, disposing in succession of one Milch Cow after another.

USS *Core* kicked off the romp with a bag on the afternoon of July 13. Lieutenant (JG) Earl H. Steiger, scouting far ahead of the *Core*, in a Wildcat, sighted the tanker sub *U-487*, 720 miles south southwest of Fayal in the Azores. Steiger surprised the sub while its crew was relaxing and engaging in horseplay on the surface, recovering flotsam from the water. On Steiger's arrival, the Germans manned their guns and shot him down. Steiger was never recovered. But at the same time, the *Core*'s squadron commander, Lieutenant Commander Charles W. Brewer, showed up with three other planes and attacked *U-487*, loosing a stick of bombs which sent the behemoth below. The offensive went on without a letup.

Next up was the escort carrier *Santee*, which potted three U-boats, including a Type IX doubling as a reserve Milch Cow. Lieutenant (JG) Robert F. Richmond dropped two depth charges and a Fido acoustic homing torpedo on the boat, *U-43*. All found their mark and the sub was sent to the bottom.

On August 4, the Royal Canadian Air Force chipped in, dispatching *U-489*, another Milch Cow. Credit went to a Sunderland of the RCAF's 423 Squadron.

Three days later, the U.S. escort carrier *Card* went on the chase. She set out on a long winning streak beginning on August 7. At 6:48 that morning, Lieutenant (JG) A. H. Sallenger in an

Avenger bomber from the *Card*, spotted *U-117*, a Milch Cow, and a smaller boat, *U-66*. Sallenger waited for reinforcements; when they arrived he attacked the sub, which was later finished off by the *Card* team with several well-placed charges. The *Card* pilots had chalked up another, sending to the bottom a big Type X B. When Sallenger's aircraft and another piloted by Ensign John F. Sprague did not return, the *Card* forged ahead to the combat area looking for her pilots. Sprague was never recovered. But Sallenger and his gunner were found bobbing on their raft in the middle of the ocean. The *Card* grabbed them up.

On August 9 and 11, the *Card* further added to her record. Lieutenant (JG) G. G. Hogan found a Type VII U-boat, *U-664*, and dropped an instantaneous-fuze 500-pound bomb just ahead of the submarine, rattling her. Another aircraft, piloted by Lieutenant (JG) R. H. Forney, now released two shallow depth charges on the sub; she was later sent to the bottom by further strafing and bombing. Forty-four of the submarine's crew were picked up by the destroyer USS *Borie*, despite the disruption of another nearby U-boat. Two days later, the *Card* upped her total again, dispatching a Type IX C/40 U-boat west-northwest of the Azores.

The racing *Card* struck again in the autumn, this time with considerable drama. At 9:01 on the morning of October 4, a scouting pilot from the carrier happened upon a choice target—four subs, sitting together in a cluster on the surface. *U-460*, a Milch Cow, had just refueled the smaller *U-264*. Two other subs were awaiting replenishment. The pilot, Lieutenant R. L. Stearns, swept down upon the covey of U-boats and planted a 500-pound bomb in the path of *U-460*, which broke up, spewing out gruesome human remains. Later in the day, other *Card* units accounted for *U-422*, jacking up the *Card*'s record to a full six kills.

Finally, two more victories were scored in the carrier offensive—*U-378*, a Type VII C was accounted for by USS *Core*; and *U-220*, a 1,700-tonner, was sent below by USS *Block Island*.

By November 1, Dönitz's network of Milch Cows had been considerably thinned out by the American sweep through the southerly waters of the Atlantic. Only ten of the tanker submarines had been constructed; all were ultimately destroyed. The last of the Milch Cows was finally accounted for by aerial attacks from USS *Croatan* in April 1944. Deprived of his tanker sub network, Dönitz's strategy of distant operations crumbled. The operations in remote areas, Africa, the southern Atlantic, the Caribbean, had rested squarely on the network of tanker U-boats. Without the Milch Cows, the fresh strategy of distant operations was useless. Roskill writes: "Thus did Dönitz's new attempt to conduct protracted operations in the remote parts of the Atlantic end in utter disaster, and in return for the very heavy losses he had suffered few Allied ships had been sunk."[3]

The escort carrier "Hunter Killer" groups were not the only American units to see intense action that summer and fall. Battle broke out all across the Central Atlantic, involving many ships and groups, but no engagement was more valorous or memorable than the last stand of USS *Borie*—which had rescued the survivors of *U-664*—commanded by Lieutenant Charles H. Hutchins. The standoff was not much short of awe-inspiring.

On the night of October 31, 1943, far out in the void of the blackened Atlantic, the *Borie*, on the hunt for *U-91*, made contact with an unexpected submarine. Lieutenant Hutchins closed and attacked three times, saw the boat plunge and picked up an underwater explosion. This submarine was *U-256*; Hutchins thought he had sunk her; in fact he had only damaged her, but so badly that she had to quit the scene and hobble home to Brest.

The *Borie* continued in the windy black, ranging far and wide across the dark sea. Then, at about two in the morning on November 1, still stalking *U-91*, Hutchins picked up yet another sub on the surface by radar at 8,000 yards, this one *U-405*. The American destroyer closed to within a quarter mile, then attacked with a volley of depth charges that blasted the sub to the surface. The crew of *U-405* scrambled topside and manned their guns; there now ensued a pitched battle with torpedo and gunfire across the inky night. *Borie* turned on her searchlight and began blazing away with her main 4-inch guns and machine guns, then went in to ram. The Germans, fighting with determination, fired back, planting solid hits in the *Borie*'s engineering spaces and bridge; but the destroyer's machine guns took out many of the U-boat's crew and a direct salvo blew the submarine's biggest gun into the water.

The two ships now sailed straight ahead for a time across from each other, the *Borie* firing at the sub. Hutchins at this point turned to ram; he raced in, hit the sub straight on—and *Borie* ran straight up and onto the U-boat's main deck, where she lodged. With the two ships frozen thus in a death clasp, the *Borie* caught on *U-405*'s foredeck, there now followed a face-off between the two crews. Hutchins trained two of *Borie*'s main 4-inch guns and three 20mm machine guns on the Germans, firing point-blank at the decks of the sub. Other crewmen of the *Borie* all about took up tommy guns, pistols, shotguns, and rifles and raked the U-boat's crew. In the midst of the melée, one of *Borie*'s sailors flung a sheath knife at a German rushing to man his gun, which found its mark in his guts. Another crewmember, Chief Boatswain's Mate Walter C. Kruz, threw an empty 4-inch shell at another U-boat crewman, sending him over the side.

Each time the heavy seas surged past, the two ships rolled and grated against each other, locked as they were as one. *Borie*'s engine room flooded, but the engineering plant was kept alive and up by Engineer Officer Lieutenant Morrison R. Brown and others who worked in water chest deep.

After ten minutes of this close-order combat, *U-405* managed to pull away and slide out from under the *Borie*. The destroyer now circled the battered U-boat, firing away, steaming full. Hutchins launched a torpedo; it shot across the dark, sped through the water, but missed the submarine. The U-boat now tried to ram *Borie*, but the hurtling vessel was halted literally stopped in the water just six feet from the *Borie*'s stern by three well-placed depth charges. Lieutenant Hutchins now opened up again with his guns; one solid salvo blew the skipper and his bridge crew into the water, another hit the submarine's exhaust tube. *U-405* slid to a halt. German crewmen came rushing up from below, discharging white Very pistols as a signal of surrender. As some of the U-boat's crew still tried to man the guns, the *Borie* did not cease fire until cries of *Kamerad*! (Comrade, often a sign of surrender) were heard. Finally, at 2:57 A.M. on November 1, one hour and twelve minutes after Hutchins had first picked up the sub, *U-405* slid stern-first under the water and dove below. The *Borie*'s crew sent up a hearty shout all around.

But the *Borie* herself had been mortally wounded. She steamed away under one engine, Hutchins throwing overboard all spare equipment he could, attempting a last effort to return to his task force leader, the *Card*. The old destroyer's plates had been worn out by the death lock resulting from the pile-up on top of the submarine, and finally her last engine went out. At 11:00 A.M. on November 1, on the empty sea, keeping his transmitter running by mixing rapidly disappearing generator fuel with lighter fluid, kerosene, and rubbing alcohol, Hutchins radioed the *Card*: "Commenced sinking."

Captain Arnold Isbell aboard the *Card* released his last two destroyers to pick up *Borie* crewmen; they finally recovered seven officers and 120 men in extremely heavy seas. Twenty-four other men and officers were lost when they abandoned their life rafts and attempted to swim to the rescue ships.

At last, Captain Isbell determined it was necessary to break off recovery operations to avoid other U-boats in the area; he was forced to order the *Borie* sunk. It was the end of a fine, gallant ship. Four depth charges from one of Isbell's Avengers finished off the valiant old four-stacker, and the veteran fighting warship finally plunged below at 9:54 in the morning on November 2. She had taken one sub, and badly damaged another. The proud, defiant ship settled and sank in the vast ocean expanse between Cape Race, Newfoundland, and Cape Clear, Ireland. She left a legacy of grit and moxie.

Thus did the Allies, with great toughness and strength of purpose, campaign across the Central Atlantic, routing the Germans before them. The autumn saw an unfurling Allied aegis spreading across the southerly waters, sweeping the U-boats from the seas.

Geography was now the problem for Dönitz. The vast, unbounded charts of the Atlantic were blocked off in areas that had been closed. To the west, the entire reach of the North Atlantic, and the main convoy routes, had been sealed off, long before, by clear Allied superiority in the air and on the sea. To the south, operations in the remote areas had been barred to him by the elimination of the U-tanker fleet. Everywhere he looked on the vast, empty, broad table of the sea, each sector had in turn been closed to his submarines. He had nowhere to move next, yet he felt he must fight on. Where could he push his rook on the chessboard of the sea? He decided he would venture west once more. He would choose the North Atlantic one more time—as it turned out, for the last time. He set forth in August and September.

That autumn, ten Type IX submarines sortied from their seaport bases; they were soon followed by thirteen more boats from the Biscay ports, six more from Norway and Germany. The Norway boats were stationed at Trondheim, Narvik, and Bergen. After two weeks, on September 16, the flotilla of U-boats set up a north–south patrol line 625 miles east of Cape Farewell at the southern tip of Greenland. There Dönitz hoped again to kindle new victories.

At the outset, the venture seemed promising; the first convoy to pass the German necklace of patrol lost six ships and three escorts. One other escort was damaged. The U-boats had fared well, but in return for their grim harvest, RN escorts and RAF aircraft took three subs in revenge, with three others damaged.

Then, in the pause of two weeks' time, the air had slipped from the balloon. Three convoys passed without losing a single ship. Coastal Command—the cover of airpower—sent three subs to their grave. A fourth convoy crossing suffered the loss of one Polish destroyer and one merchant ship—but BdU lost three submarines, better than evening the score.

One last battle flared that fall in 1943, around two convoys crossing westbound; the Germans managed to sink one merchant ship, but lost a grand total of six subs.

The North Atlantic was closing to Dönitz. In September and October alone, fully 2,468 merchant ships had crossed to the

United Kingdom with only twenty sunk. By comparison, U-boat control had lost twenty-seven subs through the same period. The battle had tipped; the Germans could no longer score. In a November 12 log entry, Dönitz's staff gloomily summed up the prevailing opinion:

"The enemy holds all the trump cards. Far reaching air cover using location methods against which we have no warning" had bested the U-boats. "The air menace has curtailed the mobility of the U-boats . . . as they can no longer be fueled at sea they can spend far less time on patrol. The enemy knows all our secrets, and we know none of theirs."[4]

By spring of 1944, the North Atlantic adventure was over. Moreover, as the campaign had weakened, Dönitz had concluded that the fielding of U-boats in packs, in any large groups, was no longer practicable. Henceforth, he was reduced to deploying the subs only in small pods. Says Roskill: "Dönitz gave up working the U-boats in large, mobile groups, and dispersed his forces more widely. . . . The autumn of 1943 thus saw the second victory over the U-boats on the convoy routes, and the final defeat of the 'wolfpack' strategy which since its introduction in the winter of 1940–41, had caused us such grievous losses."[5]

Robbed now of his chief tactic, Dönitz's war abruptly contracted. *Rudeltaktik*—pack theory—on which he had relied for four long years, the cornerstone of his early victories, was done. The wolfpacks were finished.

By November 1943, Dönitz dispatched his boats in five small groups, teams of twos or threes, east of Newfoundland, then off Cape Farewell.

At last, by the onset of 1944, he had pulled eight subs and sent them to work the waters around Gibraltar; finally, by spring, he had yanked the last of his submarines altogether from the North Atlantic, never to return. The curtain had come down on the northern oceans and almost every other sector around Grand Admiral Dönitz. All that was left of his struggle was the fervor which possessed him, and some—though not all—of his U-boat crews. In the waters where they could still manage attacks, many were still committed, all would fight to the end.

# 18

"By stupendous efforts and in spite of all losses, about sixty or seventy U-boats remained in action until almost the end," wrote Winston Churchill in a grudging tribute to the last days of the U-boat war. "Their achievements were not large, but they carried the undying hope of stalemate at sea. . . . The final phase of our onslaught at sea lay in German coastal waters. Allied air attacks destroyed many U-boats at their berths. Nevertheless, when Dönitz ordered the U-boats to surrender, no fewer than forty-nine were still at sea. . . . Such was the persistence of Germany's effort and the fortitude of the U-boat service."[1]

The Germans never stopped thrusting, never stopped driving, never let up to the last, dying day of the war. Grand Admiral Dönitz, at the top of all naval command, tempered by his own fervent conviction, proclaimed in a message to the navy on

January 1, 1944: "The Führer shows us the way and the goal. We follow him with body and soul to a great German future. *Heil* our Führer!"[2]

As late as April 1945, when the war had only six weeks to run, he urged in a decree: "No one thinks of giving up his ship. Rather go down in honor. . . . The Kriegsmarine will fight to the end. Some day its bearing in the severest crisis of this war will be judged by posterity. The same goes for each individual."[3]

The final days of the U-boat war unfolded in the chill waters north of France, in the inner jutting reach of the eastern Atlantic, with scattered last sorties to the Americas, the Azores, and the Indian Ocean. Driven back from all other outlying ocean areas by clear Allied superiority, the U-boat service pressed the last stages of its faltering campaign in the hunting grounds off England. In these waters, the submarines raided convoy formations almost guerrilla-like, hit-and-run. To the end, the subs managed occasional victories; they thrust, unyielding, to the final hour.

German commanders wielded effective crews, though the life expectancy of a U-boat man had dropped to three combat patrols, and the average age of crewmen had dropped to under nineteen. The navy's situation was grave, but it was not hopeless. Despite the losses of 1943, German U-boat strength did not reach its peak until January 1944, although the number of boats at sea at any time declined. New technology continued to hatch fresh developments. The Walter boats began coming together at last on the building ways at shipyards in Hamburg, Bremen, and Danzig. Ultimately, they would arrive too late, in too few numbers, to make any significant difference in the faltering war. The Walter boat program would be doomed by labor shortages, failures in coordination among the yards assembling the subs, and the massive Allied bombings which would obliterate the U-boats on the building ways. In early 1944, though, the Walter boats, steely, spartan, eerily fast, awaited.

Then in February, a new device originally invented by a Dutchman, the "Schnorkel," was fitted to U-boats. The Schnorkel looked something like another periscope. It was a long tube which jutted above the water, sucking in air on which a sub's diesel engines could operate while submerged, concealed under the sea.

Air attack was a critical problem for submarines; the Bay of Biscay duel had demonstrated clearly the potential of airpower. The ability to run unseen by planes high overhead was a major breakthrough and the Schnorkel was an immediate success. Of 216 Schnorkel sightings between September 1944 and May 1945, postwar research showed that only eighty-eight were accurate. Analysis suggested that many of these errors had been no more than "willy-waws," the spouts thrown up by whales.

The clear advantages of operating with the Schnorkel, or "snorting" as the Germans put it, were displayed by the remarkable odyssey of a lone Type VII C, *U-482*, in the lee of Northern Ireland. The submarine, delivered by Deutsche Werke Kiel AG and commanded by Kptlt. Hartmut Graf von Matuschka Freiherr von Topolczan und Spaetgen sank four merchant ships and a corvette in one exhaustive patrol in 1944, which lasted nearly six weeks. Of a total of 2,729 miles traveled by the U-boat, only 256 were sailed on the surface. For the rest of the entire patrol, Graf von Matuschka had run submerged, out of sight.

The Schnorkel vastly increased the effectiveness of the U-boat. After 1944, a growing number of subs operated with the device, evading in the gloom of the depths the eyes of roaming aircraft. The Schnorkel breathing tube proved one of the most significant developments of the last, tapering campaign of the war.

Then on the night of June 5–6, elements of both American and British army units parachuted into Normandy, touching down in the fields of France. Both the American 82nd and 101st Airborne Divisions encountered stiff resistance and suffered many casualties, but quickly secured their objectives. The British 6th Airborne Division fared better, handily securing its targets.

Then, as dawn broke, at 6:30 on June 6, 1944, a vast array of 3,000 landing craft, backed by 2,500 other support vessels, transported a force of some 156,000 troops to the Normandy beaches. D-Day had broken. Within the first forty-eight hours of the invasion, 14,000 tanks and other wheeled vehicles rolled ashore. The amphibious assault was supported by an armada of some 500 naval warships which blanketed the invasion beaches with a continuous bombardment, covering the troops going ashore. Allied units, storming from their infantry and tank landing ships, waded ashore on Omaha, Utah, Sword, Gold, and Juno beaches.

The German navy could do little to defend against the attack; overriding responsibility for fending off the Allied landing rested chiefly with the army, under Field Marshal Karl von Rundstedt, commander-in-chief, west. The navy had a limited role in preparations for the assault. Considerable debate had occurred about where the coastal batteries—under the control of the navy—should be placed, close to the Normandy beaches, or further inland. Admiral Theodor Krancke, the chief of Naval Group West, favored placing his shore batteries close to the coast, so Allied forces could be confronted before they waded onto land, targeting as much of the amphibious invasion as possible before the assault hit the beaches. The army, however, favored positioning coastal batteries further inland. The heated debate finally reached all the way up to Adolf Hitler. After a protracted argument between staff officers lasting more than an hour, the führer cast his decisive lot with the army.

The total available naval flotilla under the command of Admiral Krancke was considerably outclassed; among its ranks were some thirty E-boat patrol craft, four destroyers, some minesweepers, and several experimental one-man subs. The surface force faced an overwhelming array of Allied seapower.

The U-boats, under separate command, represented a more substantial armada. Two groups had been readied in the days before D-Day. Early on the morning of June 6, a spread of sixteen other subs fanned out to a range of points around the Isles of Scilly and the Isle of Wight off the English Channel coast. Nineteen other boats formed a reconnaissance line in the Bay of Biscay. Five other boats were diverted to Brest. These squadrons, more than the sum of about three good-sized wolfpacks, formed the full defensive screen of the U-boats.

The immense Allied flotilla overwhelmed even the hope of any important role by the German navy. As the invasion unfolded, the German light surface squadron was either too meager to sortie for battle, or rapidly put out of commission. It achieved no significant results. Even the U-boats managed to score but trifling ticks of damage. The final total of Allied ships sunk by submarines during the D-Day period, between June 6 and the end of August, came to a mere twenty-eight ships, including twelve merchant vessels and five escorts, out of an Allied array of some 6,000. In return, Allied forces sent below twenty subs. As was the case on almost every other marine front by 1944, the U-boats had barely put a dent in the vast Allied assault.

One more event marked that spring and summer of broad, fair victory. It was not on the immense scale of a full amphibious landing, but it was nonetheless a significant tick on the naval rolls in that season of waning close. Macintyre scored his sixth and seventh victories; they were typical of the gathering Allied rush downfield.

Macintyre now skippered an American-built frigate named HMS *Bickerton*. His sixth kill occurred on May 5. It was, like all his kills, neat, swift. Early on the morning of the 5th, *Bickerton* picked up a U-boat on Huff-Duff. He and another escort, HMS *Bligh*, took off in pursuit. They chased the sub, *U-765*, across the sea, soon caught up, then they went in on a Creeping Attack. *Bligh* and *Bickerton* carried off the exercise painstakingly, elaborately, homing like bloodhounds on the sub. They finally finished off the U-boat with a precise pattern of depth charges and an assist from an aircraft. *U-765* plunged to the bottom of the sea.

The seventh victory followed the next month; it was just as neat. On the night of June 25, *Bickerton* picked up a sonar contact. Macintyre surged ahead in pursuit, chasing the sub across the sea, maintaining contact by the ever steady ping of his sonar. He raced after the U-boat, *U-269*, chasing it across the sea, finally caught up; and at first attacked with depth charges, loosing three salvos on the sub. "Almost immediately a submarine rose like Leviathan out of the sea and lay wallowing," Macintyre later wrote.[4]

In the next instant, the gunnery officer yelled: "Permission to open fire, sir?"

The escort leader opened up; 4.7-inch gunfire blazed down on the sub; tracers lit up the night. The rain of fire continued; at last, in the stab of *Bickerton*'s searchlight, the escort's crew could see men aboard the U-boat jumping into the water. The Germans kept struggling in the dark; the frigate went in to pick up survivors. Finally, after a time, in the windy black of the night, *U-269* went up by the bow, and slowly slid below to her grave. Macintyre had scored his seventh victory. The searchlight was flooding across the water.

The Allied sweep went on in a dozen other locations. Lieutenant Commander S. Darling aboard HMS *Loch Killin* accounted for *U-736* on August 6, 1944; HMS *Forester*, under Commander G. W. Gregorie, depth-charged *U-413* to her end on August 20. Scores of other skippers and aircraft pilots racked up victories as the three great Allied navies drove forward across the disintegrating German war machine. The final act had begun.

In August, the Allied armies pushed to the Biscay coast, threatening the U-boat bunkers and bases themselves; U.S. troops had reached St. Lo; Paris was liberated. The Royal Navy ran with the fortunes of swift favor. By May 1945, the war in Europe would be over. In the last round some of the cruelest losses came.

Lt. Richard G. Addis, RNVR, DSC., twenty-seven, fond of penning doggerel, was lost when his destroyer, *Laforey*, the class leader of the "Lightning Class" destroyers was sunk by a Type VII C U-boat, *U-223*, in a battle off the coast of Sicily. He left a wife of three years and a three-week-old son.

Lt. Addis, a corvette man, had sailed on the North Atlantic, then in the Mediterranean. He was a signals officer, somewhat jaunty. Once in London, he and Mrs. Addis had gone to the theater; the performance was interrupted by Winston Churchill's famous "We shall fight on the beaches . . . We shall fight in the fields . . ." speech. The couple listened to the great speech; the performance had gone on. Addis won his salt crust in five years' sea duty, wrote occasional songs, funny songs.

Addis was lost when *Laforey* was torpedoed and later sunk by *U-223*, commanded by twenty-one-year-old Oberleutnant zur See Peter Gerlach. Gerlach himself later was sent below in the same battle.

Gillian Dearmer Addis Warr recalls that Lt. Addis's loss seemed bizarre, almost odd to her. "Up until then, he'd been in much more dangerous places, and I had a feeling he was fairly safe," she says today. During the war she worked with the Free French. In time she remarried. She lives today in the house her mother lived in during the war, just off the bustle of the King's Road in London.[5]

D-Day marked another departure in the U-boat war, another spiraling down of scope, another fallback in extent: the submarine campaign was forced to withdraw one more ring. The curving crescent of U-boats descending from the Hebrides, in the north, to France, in the south, was forced to pull back yet again, further diminishing field. Henceforth, Germany's submarines would be confined to the tight circle of British coastal waters and the inshore zones of Norway and Germany. Here, thrown back on their last hunting grounds, the U-boats played out their final tapering stand. Though they fought with gritty determination to the close of their struggle, Allied superiority had by now blanketed virtually every square mile of sea and air in what was, effectively, total control.

By the close of 1944, Allied strength and mastery had become virtually dominant from mast to aileron. On the sea, Western Approaches had a commanding flotilla of 207 escort vessels, frigates, sloops, destroyers, corvettes—roughly twice what it had fielded in the tense months of 1942. By 1944, MAC ships, the merchant aircraft carriers, were regularly carrying the wingspan of airpower out to sea with the convoys; free-ranging support groups, led by Johnnie Walker's 2nd Support Group, were ranging across the ocean, carrying the hunt for subs on the offensive. RAF Coastal Command had a fleet of more than 790 aircraft; these were scoring victories at a rate superseding all German resistance. On air and sea, the press to the ground was nearly complete. Allied naval and airpower ruled almost everywhere.

The last run of the U-boats was fast, tempered, and futile. From January 1945 until the unconditional surrender, the submarines continued to score victories, though not in substantial numbers. Thirty-nine submarines remained at sea in January 1945; most were confined to the offshore waters around Britain. Here they fought with unyielding conviction to the last, desperate hour. They raided in the Irish Sea, off Scotland, in Liverpool Bay, but the curtain was already falling on the dark, pitiless battle they had waged for almost six years.

The U-boats were now based in Norway. The Biscay bases had been given up abandoned as the Allied advance threatened the Atlantic coast of France. The final phase of the fighting was confined to offshore waters. The futuristic Walter boats were nearing completion, almost all the subs coming on line on German building ways were Type XXIs and Type XXIIIs; but only a handful would get to sea in the last days before war's end. To suggest how close the wonder boats came to disrupting the Battle of the Atlantic, in January the first Type XXIII (*U-2324*) sailed from Norway; in March the first Type XXI to become operational (*U-2511*) sailed from Kiel to the Norway bases. The

Walter boats missed only by months. None got into action before hostilities ended.

The Germans kept fighting to the last hour of the war. On Christmas Eve 1944, *U-486*, commanded by ObltzS. Gerhard Meyer, torpedoed the frigate *Capel* and four merchant ships in the waters off France—including the American troopship *Leopoldville*, which went down with the loss of 800 American soldiers. From January 9 to 11, 1945, *U-1055*, under ObltzS. Rudolf Meyer, sank three ships in the Irish Sea. Off the Wales coast, *U-1172* sent down another merchant ship. But the tables of war had already tipped too dramatically; the fast Allied rush to the end overpowered the last holdouts.

By February 1945, commanding Royal Navy, RAF, and RCN mastery sent down a total of thirteen subs in one month alone in British waters and off the coasts of Norway and Germany. In March, another fourteen were bombed to their graves. In April, twenty-one more were sent below. In the last weeks of the war, a frantic exodus began of U-boats headed north for the Norwegian bases. But the move to group in Norway was in vain. The signature of doom was scrawled everywhere across the slate.

Then the close came swiftly, with definitive might. In the last weeks, aerial attacks drove home the last, decisive slashes of Allied victory. On April 1, rocket-firing Typhoons of the 2nd Tactical Air Force veered down on U-boats trying to transit north through the Skagerrak and the Kattegat above Denmark, raining mayhem down upon the remaining scuttling boats. In the next few days, Mosquitos of No. 18 Group and Beaufighters of No. 16 Group swept in, inflicting doom all across the north, in the Kattegat and the Belts, the straits between Denmark and Sweden. In these last devastating strikes, twenty-seven U-boats in the transit areas were taken out; eighteen were destroyed at dockside, in shipyards and bases. Finally, in the last rush to triumph, B-24 Liberators roared in, striking across northern Germany and in coastal regions, delivering the last, punishing raids. On the 3rd of May, six subs—including three Type XXIs—were sent below. Three more went to their graves on the 4th. On the 5th, Liberators destroyed six more submarines. Nazi Germany was rubble. The end had come.

In the last hours before he shot himself on April 30, 1945, Adolf Hitler appointed as his successor Grand Admiral Dönitz, to follow in leading Germany. Karl Dönitz was installed as the last führer. He would hold power only twenty-four days.

On May 7, the last U-boat sunk by the Allies in World War II was sent to the bottom. She was *U-3503*, under the command of ObltzS. Hugo Deiring. Frighteningly, she was a Type XXI, one of the few Walter boats which had gotten to sea in the last phases of the war.

The loss of *U-3503* coincided with the loss of the very last merchant ship to go down in the terrible conflict that had spread across six exhausting years. The final merchant ship to die in the last battle of the Battle of the Atlantic was the Canadian steamer *Avondale Park*, 2,878 tons, built in Pictou, Nova Scotia. She almost made it to harbor; she went down on the last day of the war.

The long, wearying struggle in which so many men and ships had participated was over. Twelve Allied navies could finally scatter home to the ports from which, six years before, they had set out.

# 19

On May 4, at precisely 3:14 p.m., Admiral Dönitz broadcast to all U-boats at sea an order to cease hostilities, stand down from patrol, and return to base. There were no more than forty-five submarines at large at this time; only eight obeyed Dönitz's order at once, but one by one they finally surrendered.

Then, at noon on May 8, the British Admiralty issued its famous signal to all ships and authorities declaring that the German High Command had been instructed to order all U-boats on patrol to surface, signal their position, and proceed to appropriate designated ports. Earlier, at 2:41 a.m. on May 7, at his headquarters in Reims, in northeastern France, General Dwight D. Eisenhower, supreme allied commander of the Allied Expeditionary Force, had accepted the capitulation of Germany from General Alfred Jodl, the chief of the operations staff of the

German armed forces, to take effect at midnight, May 8. The great, globe-rending war against Nazi Germany had ended, though the Japanese still remained to be defeated.

The six-year struggle by and against Nazi Germany's submarines and the Kriegsmarine was over. The Royal Navy, returning to port and rafting up hull to hull, finished at last with its fight, was an unrecognizable extrapolation of its former self. In driving through the war, it had grown from a fleet of 418 to a magisterial force of over 3,900 warships. The destroyer division had swollen from 184 ships to 274. There had been no corvettes in 1939; by 1945 there were 280. The Battle of the Atlantic was the last great victory of the historic Royal Navy, the 300-year-old force which had ruled the waves almost since the days of carracks. In the climate of the postwar world, England's defense obligations would be nowhere near as great as they had been in the first half of the twentieth century; nor would Britain support a fleet on the grand scale of Nelson, Jellicoe, or Max Horton. The U.S. Navy superseded the RN as the greatest navy in the world during the Second World War, growing to a boggling fleet of 6,768 ships and three million men. Today, the Royal Navy counts ninety-eight ships in the lean fleet which guards Britain. An age had closed with the Battle of the Atlantic; the last great victory, on a theater of global impact, had been won.

And the men, the rumpled heroes? They met the end of their wartime exploits variously, each completing the journey in his own way. Drawn by the strain of battle, Capt. F. J. "Johnnie" Walker died of a stroke in 1944. His body lay in state in the Western Approaches Flotilla Chapel, amid the crests of the Western Approaches Battle Fleets, with a lone Union Jack over his coffin. More than a thousand people—sailors, Allied officers, civilians, men of the 2nd Support Group—came to hear him eulogized by Admiral Sir Max Horton in the Liverpool

Cathedral. Then his coffin was placed onboard that intrepid steed HMS *Hesperus* for a burial at sea. *Hesperus* slipped her lines and proceeded slowly down the Mersey River. Passing ships dipped their flags to the destroyer which bore the great warrior. One convoy was arriving as the warship passed out the mouth of the river, another was coming in. When *Hesperus* reached the edge of the open sea, the weighted coffin of the man who had done so much in leading his countrymen was slipped down into the flooding sea.

Admiral Horton had said of the old commander: "Victory has been won and should be won by such as he. May there never be wanting in this realm a succession of men of like spirit in discipline, imagination and valor, humble and unafraid. Not dust, nor the light weight of a stone, but all the sea of the Western Approaches shall be his tomb."[1] A bust of Walker still stands in the Operations Room today at Western Approaches, now a museum.

Donald Macintyre returned to aviation. His naval career, ironically, ended on a sad note. He lost the American-built frigate *Bickerton*, of which he had become so fond. In August 1944, while acting in support of the escort carrier *Nabob*, *Bickerton* was torpedoed. Macintyre had had some hope of keeping *Bickerton* afloat and saving her. But when the group had to move ahead, the task proved impossible. A destroyer put a torpedo into the ship which "had shown that she could 'take it' and 'hand it out,' " as Macintyre later wrote, and she settled in the water and finally slid below.[2] It was a bittersweet end to a long, lustrous career. Macintyre's brilliance as a U-boat killer would be remembered long after his last command.

Immediately, Macintyre transferred as second in command, then commander, of two Royal Navy air stations. Later he became a historian. He found his second calling in the writing of naval histories, excellent ones, and authored more than fifteen books on the history of war at sea. It was a curious, cerebral, sedentary occupation for the salt- and wind-blown, rulebook, hard-driving destroyer ace who had spent his life hurling ships on compass points, at sharp, pinging sonar echoes, and dashing German U-boats.

Commander Peter Gretton rose after the war to the top of the Admiralty as a Lord Commissioner of the Admiralty, Deputy chief of naval staff and fifth sea lord.

Captain Paul Heineman was transferred to the Pacific. He finished World War II as commanding officer of the cruiser USS *Biloxi*, in which capacity he was awarded the Bronze Star with Combat V as well as another decoration.

Otto Kretschmer was still in captivity at another prison camp, Camp 130 in western Canada. He went on to become an admiral in NATO, married a doctor, and died in 1998.

But on May 8, 1945, V-E Day was still news across the world, the best news; and people greeted it in the broadest, most joyous ways they could. In the village of Frant, England, they rang church bells. The village hadn't been allowed to ring them in four years.

Edna Smith, the wife of Leading Seaman Ron Smith, the tough, little gunlayer who had served under Harry Tait and Macintyre, got the day off from work and went to the movies. "I can remember they very kindly gave us the day off. So I think a few of us went to the cinema in the afternoon. I've forgotten the title of the film, but it was Gary Cooper and Ingrid Bergman. . . . We were very happy."[3]

And Arnold Hague, who would become a naval expert and work for the British Ministry of Defence, was with his mother in London. He was fifteen at the time. "My mother and I went up to London," Hague recalls. They went to Buckingham

Palace, where hordes had assembled to cheer the news of V-E Day, stayed for a while with the pack, then turned and started walking toward Trafalgar Square and Charing Cross Station, where they wanted to catch a train home. The throngs were so thick, though, that they could not move, just moved where the crowd moved, going with the amble and flow of the thousands who had turned out. "We finally wound up in Trafalgar Square. You just shuffled along. The whole of the mall was just people, the crowd was so dense, so solid with people." The crowd was roaring: "We want the King! We want the King!"[4]

# APPENDIX A

# LOSSES IN THE NORTH ATLANTIC

# 1939–1945

## 1939

### ALLIED MERCHANT SHIP SINKINGS

|  | Tonnage | No. of Ships |
|---|---|---|
| September | 104,829 | 19 |
| October | 110,619 | 18 |
| November | 17,895 | 6 |
| December | 15,852 | 4 |
| Total: | 249,195 | 47 |

## Appendix A

### U-Boats Sunk

| | |
|---|---|
| September | 1 |
| October | 3 |
| November | 1 |
| December | 1 |
| Total: | 6 |

---

## 1940

### Allied Merchant Ship Sinkings

| | Tonnage | No. of Ships |
|---|---|---|
| January | 35,970 | 35 |
| February | 74,759 | 17 |
| March | 11,215 | 2 |
| April | 24,570 | 4 |
| May | 48,087 | 9 |
| June | 296,529 | 53 |
| July | 141,474 | 28 |
| August | 190,048 | 39 |
| September | 254,553 | 52 |
| October | 286,644 | 56 |
| November | 201,341 | 38 |
| December | 239,304 | 42 |
| Total: | 1,804,494 | 375 |

## Appendix A

### U-Boats Sunk

| | |
|---|---|
| January | 1 |
| February | 4 |
| March | 2 |
| April | 3 |
| May | 0 |
| June | 1 |
| July | 2 |
| August | 2 |
| September | 0 |
| October | 1 |
| November | 2 |
| December | 0 |
| Total: | 18 |

---

### 1941

---

### Allied Merchant Ship Sinkings

| | *Tonnage* | *No. of Ships* |
|---|---|---|
| January | 214,382 | 42 |
| February | 317,378 | 69 |
| March | 364,689 | 63 |
| April | 260,451 | 45 |
| May | 324,550 | 58 |
| June | 318,740 | 68 |
| July | 97,813 | 23 |

| | | |
|---|---|---|
| August | 83,661 | 25 |
| September | 184,546 | 51 |
| October | 154,593 | 32 |
| November | 50,215 | 10 |
| December | 50,682 | 10 |
| Total | 2,421,700 | 496 |

## U-Boats Sunk

| | |
|---|---|
| January | 0 |
| February | 0 |
| March | 5 |
| April | 2 |
| May | 1 |
| June | 2 |
| July | 0 |
| August | 3 |
| September | 2 |
| October | 0 |
| November | 1 |
| December | 3 |
| Total: | 19 |

# Appendix A

## 1942

---

### Allied Merchant Ship Sinkings

|           | Tonnage    | No. of Ships |
|-----------|-----------|--------------|
| January   | 276,795   | 48           |
| February  | 429,891   | 73           |
| March     | 534,064   | 95           |
| April     | 391,044   | 66           |
| May       | 576,350   | 120          |
| June      | 623,545   | 124          |
| July      | 486,965   | 98           |
| August    | 508,426   | 96           |
| September | 473,585   | 95           |
| October   | 399,715   | 62           |
| November  | 508,707   | 83           |
| December  | 262,135   | 46           |
| Total:    | 5,471,222 | 1,006        |

### U-Boats Sunk

|           |    |
|-----------|----|
| January   | 1  |
| February  | 1  |
| March     | 0  |
| April     | 1  |
| May       | 0  |
| June      | 0  |
| July      | 2  |
| August    | 5  |

| September | 4 |
|-----------|---|
| October | 11 |
| November | 5 |
| December | 5 |
| Total: | 35 |

## 1943

### Allied Merchant Ship Sinkings

| | Tonnage | No. of Ships |
|-----------|---------|--------------|
| January | 172,691 | 27 |
| February | 288,625 | 46 |
| March | 476,349 | 82 |
| April | 235,478 | 39 |
| May | 163,507 | 34 |
| June | 18,379 | 4 |
| July | 123,327 | 18 |
| August | 10,186 | 2 |
| September | 43,775 | 8 |
| October | 56,422 | 12 |
| November | 23,077 | 6 |
| December | 47,785 | 7 |
| Total: | 1,659,601 | 285 |

## U-Boats Sunk

| | |
|---|---|
| January | 3 |
| February | 14 |
| March | 11 |
| April | 12 |
| May | 33 |
| June | 12 |
| July | 15 |
| August | 6 |
| September | 4 |
| October | 23 |
| November | 14 |
| December | 3 |
| Total: | 150 |

## 1944

## Allied Merchant Ship Sinkings

| | Tonnage | No. of Ships |
|---|---|---|
| January | 36,065 | 5 |
| February | 12,577 | 2 |
| March | 36,867 | 7 |
| April | 34,224 | 5 |
| May | 0 | 0 |
| June | 4,294 | 2 |
| July | 15,480 | 2 |
| August | 5,685 | 1 |

| | | |
|---|---|---|
| September | 16,535 | 3 |
| October | 0 | 0 |
| November | 7,828 | 3 |
| December | 5,458 | 1 |
| Total: | 175,013 | 31 |

## U-Boats Sunk

| | |
|---|---|
| January | 12 |
| February | 13 |
| March | 10 |
| April | 8 |
| May | 10 |
| June | 20 |
| July | 8 |
| August | 16 |
| September | 3 |
| October | 1 |
| November | 3 |
| December | 7 |
| Total: | 111 |

# Appendix A

## 1945

### ALLIED MERCHANT SHIP SINKINGS

|          | *Tonnage* | *No. of Ships* |
|----------|-----------|----------------|
| January  | 29,168    | 5              |
| February | 32,453    | 5              |
| March    | 23,684    | 3              |
| April    | 32,071    | 5              |
| May      | 5,353     | 1              |
| Total:   | 122,729   | 19             |

### U-BOATS SUNK

|          |    |
|----------|----|
| January  | 5  |
| February | 13 |
| March    | 14 |
| April    | 21 |
| May      | 1  |

(In addition, another 17 U-boats were lost in transit from Germany to Norway at the war's end.)

Total sunk or lost:  71

(Sources: For merchant shipping statistics, Capt. S. W. Roskill, *The War at Sea, 1939–1945;* for U-boat statistics, Clay Blair, *Hitler's U-boat War, Vol. 1, The Hunters,* and *Vol. 2, The Hunted,* as cited in Spencer Dunmore, *In Great Waters, The Epic Story of the Battle of the Atlantic, 1939–1945.*)

# U-boat Fleet Strength

## 1939–1945

| | Total Fleet | Operational | In Atlantic Ocean |
|---|---|---|---|
| **1939** | | | |
| September–December | 57 | 12 | 5 |
| **1940** | | | |
| January–March | 51 | 11 | 5 |
| April–June | 49 | 10 | 7 |
| July–September | 56 | 10 | 8 |
| October–December | 75 | 11 | 9 |
| **1941** | | | |
| January–March | 102 | 20 | 12 |
| April–June | 136 | 25 | 15 |
| July–September | 182 | 30 | 17 |
| October–December | 233 | 35 | 16 |

**1942**

| | | | |
|---|---|---|---|
| January–March | 272 | 45 | 13 |
| April–June | 315 | 60 | 15 |
| July–September | 352 | 95 | 25 |
| October–December | 382 | 100 | 40 |

**1943**

| | | | |
|---|---|---|---|
| January–March | 418 | 110 | 50 |
| April–June | 424 | 90 | 40 |
| July–September | 408 | 60 | 20 |
| October–December | 425 | 70 | 25 |

**1944**

| | | | |
|---|---|---|---|
| January–March | 445 | 65 | 30 |
| April–June | 437 | 50 | 20 |
| July–September | 396 | 40 | 15 |
| October–December | 398 | 35 | 20 |

**1945**

| | | | |
|---|---|---|---|
| January–May | 349 | 45 | 20 |

(Source: S. W. Roskill, *The War at Sea, 1939–1945, Vols. 1–3,* as cited in Terry Hughes and John Costello, *The Battle of the Atlantic.*)

# ROYAL NAVY FLEET STRENGTH 1940–1945 (HOME WATERS)

## April 8, 1940

| | Capital Ships | Aircraft Carriers | Escort Carriers | Cruisers | AA Ships | Destroyers | Sloops, etc. | Mine-sweepers | Sub-marines | Total |
|---|---|---|---|---|---|---|---|---|---|---|
| Home Fleet | 5 | 1 | – | 12 | 2 | 54 | 1 | – | 19 | 94 |
| Rosyth | – | – | – | – | – | 8 | 12 | – | – | 20 |
| Nore | – | – | – | – | 2 | – | 5 | – | – | 7 |
| Western Approaches | – | – | – | – | – | 34 | 7 | – | – | 41 |
| Other Commands | – | – | – | – | – | 11 | 2 | – | 15 | 28 |

Total ships: 190

## May 21, 1941

| | Capital Ships | Aircraft Carriers | Escort Carriers | Cruisers | AA Ships | Destroyers | Sloops, etc. | Mine-sweepers | Sub-marines | Total |
|---|---|---|---|---|---|---|---|---|---|---|
| Home Fleet | 6 | 3 | – | 13 | – | 24 | – | – | 7 | 53 |
| Iceland | – | – | – | – | – | 11 | 16 | – | – | 27 |
| Western Approaches | – | – | – | – | 1 | 43 | 64 | 10 | 9 | 127 |
| Other Commands | – | – | – | – | – | 42 | 6 | 13 | 6 | 67 |

Total ships: 274

## June 15, 1942

| | Capital Ships | Aircraft Carriers | Escort Carriers | Cruisers | AA Ships | Destroyers | Sloops, etc. | Mine-sweepers | Sub-marines | Total |
|---|---|---|---|---|---|---|---|---|---|---|
| Home Fleet | 2 | 1 | – | 9 | – | 26 | – | 14 | 14 | 66 |
| Western Approaches | – | – | – | – | 1 | 39 | 58 | – | 10 | 108 |
| Other Commands | – | – | – | – | 1 | 42 | 6 | 30 | – | 79 |

Total ships: 253

## May 7, 1943

| | Capital Ships | Aircraft Carriers | Escort Carriers | Cruisers | AA Ships | Destroyers | Sloops, etc. | Mine-sweepers | Sub-marines | Total |
|---|---|---|---|---|---|---|---|---|---|---|
| Home Fleet | 5 | 2 | – | 7 | – | 29 | – | 8 | – | 51 |
| Plymouth | – | – | – | 2 | 1 | 6 | – | – | – | 9 |
| Western Approaches | – | – | 3 | – | – | 32 | 116 | 8 | – | 159 |
| Other Commands | – | – | – | – | – | 38 | 6 | 30 | 11 | 85 |

Total ships: 304

## January 21, 1944

| | Capital Ships | Aircraft Carriers | Escort Carriers | Cruisers | AA Ships | Destroyers | Sloops, etc. | Mine-sweepers | Sub-marines | Total |
|---|---|---|---|---|---|---|---|---|---|---|
| Home Fleet | 4 | 1 | – | 7 | – | 25 | – | 6 | – | 43 |
| Plymouth | – | – | – | 6 | – | 9 | – | 6 | – | 21 |
| Western Approaches | – | – | 9 | – | – | 35 | 163 | – | – | 207 |
| Other Commands | – | – | – | – | – | 33 | 6 | 46 | 10 | 95 |

Total ships: 366

## January 5, 1945

| | Capital Ships | Aircraft Carriers | Escort Carriers | Cruisers | AA Ships | Destroyers | Sloops, etc. | Mine-sweepers | Sub-marines | Total |
|---|---|---|---|---|---|---|---|---|---|---|
| Home Fleet | 1 | – | 4 | 7 | – | 20 | – | – | – | 32 |
| Nore | – | – | – | – | – | 24 | 31 | 38 | – | 93 |
| Po. and ANCXF* | 2 | – | – | – | – | 4 | 32 | 4 | – | 40 |
| Plymouth | – | – | – | – | – | 9 | 24 | 22 | – | 55 |
| Western Approaches | – | – | 3 | – | – | 11 | 156 | – | – | 170 |
| Other Commands | – | – | – | – | – | 17 | 6 | 9 | 7 | 39 |

Total ships: 429

*Portsmouth and Allied Naval Commander, Expeditionary Force.

(Source: Naval Historical Branch, Ministry of Defence, United Kingdom)

# NOTES

## PROLOGUE

For an introduction to the Battle of the Atlantic, see Terry Hughes and John Costello, *The Battle of the Atlantic*; and Spencer Dunmore, *In Great Waters: The Epic Story of the Battle of the Atlantic, 1939–1945*. For a discussion of Nazi Germany, see William L. Shirer, *The Rise and Fall of the Third Reich*. For the *San Demetrio*, see F. Tennyson Jesse, *The Saga of San Demetrio*; Calum Macneil, *San Demetrio*; and "Confidential, Report of an Interview with Mr. Charles Pollard, Chief Engineer, and Mr. Arthur C. Hawkins, Second Officer of the M. V. *San Demetrio*," Naval Historical Branch, Ministry of Defence, United Kingdom. This chapter also draws on interviews with Cpt. Christopher L. W. Page RN Rtd, Head, Naval Historical Branch, Ministry of Defence, United Kingdom; J. M. Wraight, Admiralty Librarian, Naval Historical Branch; and Arnold Hague, formerly of the Naval Historical Branch, London, March 5 and April 16, 2002.

## CHAPTER 1

For a general discussion of U-boat operations, see David Miller, *U-boats*, and Harald Busch, *U-boats at War: German Submarines in Action, 1939–1945*. For U-boat types and losses, see Axel Niestle, *German U-boat Losses During World War II*. For a discussion of the war career of Kptlt. Otto Kretschmer, see Terence Robertson, *The Golden Horseshoe: The Story of Otto Kretschmer, Germany's Top U-boat Ace*; and

# Notes

Stephen Howarth, *Men of War: Great Naval Captains of World War II*. For development of wolfpack strategy, see Barrie Pitt and the Editors of Time-Life Books, *The Battle of the Atlantic*; Grand Admiral Karl Dönitz, *Memoirs: Ten Years and Twenty Days*; Jak P. Mallman Showell, *U-boat Warfare: The Evolution of the Wolfpack*; Terry Hughes and John Costello, *The Battle of the Atlantic*. This chapter also is drawn from documents in the collection of the U-boat Archive, Stiftung Traditionsarchiv Unterseeboote, Altenbruch, Germany.

1. Chicago Museum of Science and Industry, *U-505* exhibit.
2. Ascribed in Barrie Pitt and the Editors of Time-Life Books, *The Battle of the Atlantic* (New York: Time-Life, 1977), p. 64.
3. Grand Admiral Karl Dönitz, *Memoirs: Ten Years and Twenty Days* (Cambridge, Mass.: Da Capo, 1997), p. 125.
4. Winston S. Churchill, *The Second World War, Vol. 2: Their Finest Hour* (Boston: Houghton Mifflin, 1949), p. 600.

## CHAPTER 2

For the U.S. presidential election of 1940, President Roosevelt's early policy shifts before the U.S. entry into war, and his relationship with British prime minister Winston S. Churchill, see Samuel Eliot Morison and Henry Steele Commager, *The Growth of the American Republic*; Doris Kearns Goodwin, *No Ordinary Time, Franklin and Eleanor Roosevelt: The Home Front in World War II*; James MacGregor Burns, *Roosevelt: The Soldier of Freedom, 1940–1945*; Kenneth S. Davis, *FDR: The War President, 1940–1943*; Frank Freidel, *Roosevelt: A Rendezvous with Destiny*; John Gunther, *Roosevelt in Retrospect: A Profile in History*; Joseph P. Lash, *Roosevelt and Churchill, 1939–1941: The Partnership That Saved the War*; Martin Folly, *The United States and World War II: The Awakening Giant*. For a discussion of Prime Minister Winston S. Churchill during the early war years and his relationship with President Roosevelt, see Martin Gilbert, *Finest Hour: Winston S. Churchill, 1939–1941*; Winston S. Churchill, *The Second World War, Vol. 2: Their Finest Hour*. The state of the Battle of the Atlantic in the early years is treated in Terry Hughes and John Costello, *The Battle of the Atlantic*; Spencer Dunmore, *In Great Waters*; and John Keegan, *The Price of Admiralty: The Evolution of Naval Warfare*. This chapter is also based on "State of the Fleet, 1939–1945 Royal Navy" Naval Historical Branch, Ministry of Defence, United Kingdom.

## CHAPTER 3

For a brief account of the battle of Convoy SC 11, see Clay Blair, *Hitler's U-boat War, Vol. 1: The Hunters, 1939–1942*. This chapter is also drawn

# Notes

from Convoy Data Sheets for Convoy SC 11 prepared by Arnold Hague
and the following documents from the National Archive, United King-
dom: File Adm. 199/56, Convoy A. 1. Form for Convoy SC 11; File
Adm. 199/1707, Secret, Enclosure "A" to Commanding Officer,
*Enchantress'* Report of Proceedings dated 25th November 1940, HMS
*Enchantress*; File Adm. 199/56, Report by Commodore of Convoy No.
SC 11; File Adm. 199/142, Track Charts of the Battle of Convoy SC 11;
and the following documents from the Naval Historical Branch, Ministry
of Defence, United Kingdom: Confidential, Report of an Interview with
Mr. P. F. M. Buchholtz, Apprentice of SS *Bradfyne*; Confidential, Report
of an Interview with Mr. H. Peters, Chief Engineer of SS *Justitia*; Report
of an Interview with Mr. H. E. E. Pedersen (Danish), Third Mate of SS
*Leise Maersk*; Confidential, Report of an Interview with Cpt. P. D.
Townsend, Master of SS *Alma Dawson*; and, from the National Archives
Microfilms Publications T-1022, Record Group 242: Kriegstagebuch
(KTB) of *U-100*, commanded by Kptlt. Joachim Schepke, Nov. 20–23,
1940.

1. British National Archive, file Adm. 199/56, Report by commodore of Convoy No. SC 11.
2. U. S. National Archives and Records Administration, Kriegstagebuch (KTB), *U-100*, Kptlt. Joachim Schepke.
3. Interview, James Woodhead, 8/7/2002.
4. Naval Historical Branch, Ministry of Defence of the United Kingdom, Report of an Interview with Mr. H. E. E. Pedersen (Danish),
   Third Mate of SS *Leise Maersk*.
5. Interview, James Woodhead, 8/7/2002.

## CHAPTER 4

For the career of Kptlt. Otto Kretschmer, especially his leave, see Terence
Robertson, *The Golden Horseshoe: The Story of Otto Kretschmer,
Germany's Top U-boat Ace.* For U-boat operations at this time, see Tim-
othy P. Mulligan, *Neither Sharks nor Wolves: The Men of Nazi
Germany's U-boat Arm, 1939–1945*; Andrew Williams, *The Battle of the
Atlantic*; Grand Admiral Karl Dönitz, *Memoirs: Ten Years and Twenty
Days.* For the *San Demetrio*, see F. Tennyson Jesse, *The Saga of San
Demetrio*; Calum Macneil, *San Demetrio*; Confidential, Report of an
Interview with Mr. Charles Pollard, Chief Engineer, and Mr. Arthur C.
Hawkins, Second Officer, of the M. V. *San Demetrio*, Naval Historical
Branch, Ministry of Defence, United Kingdom.

1. Donald Macintyre, *U-boat Killer* (London: Cassell, 1956), p. 10.
2. Interview, David, Lord Mottistone, 10/2/2003.
3. Terence Robertson, *The Golden Horseshoe: The Story of Otto*

*Kretschmer, Germany's Top U-boat Ace* (Charleston: Arcadia Publishing, 2000), Appendix D.

4. Terence Robertson, *The Golden Horseshoe*, p. 96.

5. Ibid.

## CHAPTER 5

For a general discussion of convoy practice and routine, merchant seamen and the merchant marine in World War II, see Barrie Pitt and the Editors of Time-Life Books, *The Battle of the Atlantic*; C. B. A. Behrens, *History of the Second World War: Merchant Shipping and the Demands of War*; G. H. Bennett and R. Bennett, *Survivors: British Merchant Seamen in the Second World War*; Terry Hughes and John Costello, *The Battle of the Atlantic*; and S. W. Roskill, *A Merchant Fleet in War, 1939–1945*. This chapter also draws on the National Archive, United Kingdom, File Adm. 199/5, Part 2, "Organisation and Conduct of British Convoys"; and interviews with Francis J. Dooley, Teaneck, N.J., Nov. 26, 2004; George E. Murphy, Teaneck, N.J., Nov. 26, 2004; James Bartuska, telephone, Feb. 9, 2004; Joseph E. Bodner, Massapequa, N.Y., Dec. 2, 2004; George Goldman, Teaneck, N.J., Nov. 26, 2004; Frank Dorner, Chicago, Il. Feb. 16, 2004.

1. Interview, Joseph E. Bodner, 12/2/2004.

2. Interview, George Goldman, 11/26/2004.

## CHAPTER 6

For a general discussion of the Battle of the Atlantic in 1940 and 1941, see Spencer Dunmore, *In Great Waters: The Epic Story of the Battle of the Atlantic*. This chapter also draws on Terence Robertson, *The Golden Horseshoe: The Story of Otto Kretschmer, Germany's Top U-boat Ace*; Donald Macintyre, *U-boat Killer*; Martin Gilbert, *Finest Hour: Winston S. Churchill, 1939–1941*; Terry Hughes and John Costello, *The Battle of the Atlantic*; and interviews with Horst Elfe, Berlin, Sept. 23, 2003; Volkmar König, Toronto, Aug. 29, 2003; and Cdr. Peter D. Sturdee, RN Rtd, Dorridge, England, Aug. 2, 2002.

1. "Confidential Report on Kretschmer Sent by Admiral Dönitz to Naval Headquarters in Berlin at the End of 1939," as cited in Appendix A, Terence Robertson, *The Golden Horseshoe: The Story of Otto Kretschmer, Germany's Top U-boat Ace*, p. 185.

2. Interrogation Report, Interrogation of Kptlt. Otto Kretschmer.

3. Interview, Horst Elfe, 9/23/2003.

4. Ibid.

5. Interview, Volkmar König, 8/29/2003.

6. Interview, Cdr. Peter D. Sturdee, RN Rtd, 8/2/2002.

# Notes

## CHAPTER 7

For a general discussion of British and Royal Navy developments during 1941, see Barrie Pitt and the Editors of Time-Life Books, *The Battle of the Atlantic*; Spencer Dunmore, *In Great Waters: The Epic Story of the Battle of the Atlantic*; Clay Blair, *Hitler's U-boat War, Vol. 1: The Hunters, 1939–1942*; and Arnold Hague, *The Allied Convoy System, 1939–1945*; W. S. Chalmers, *Max Horton and the Western Approaches: A Biography of Admiral Sir Max Kennedy Horton, GCB, DSO*; Arthur Herman, *To Rule the Waves: How the British Navy Shaped the Modern World*; Alfred Price, *Aircraft Versus Submarine: The Evolution of the Anti-Submarine Aircraft, 1912–1972*; Correlli Barnett, *Engage the Enemy More Closely: The Royal Navy in the Second World War*. For detailed material on British destroyers during World War II, see Maurice Cocker, *Destroyers of the Royal Navy, 1893–1981*. This chapter also draws on a tour of Western Approaches Combined Headquarters Museum, Aug. 2002; a tour of HMS *Cavalier*, Oct. 2003; "State of the Fleet, 1939–1945, Royal Navy," Naval Historical Branch, Ministry of Defence, United Kingdom; and interviews with Charles A. Edwards, Northampton, England, July 22, 2002; Arnold Hague, London and Hinchley Wood, England, March 2002–Sept. 2003; James Woodhead, Grantham, England, Aug. 7, 2002; and Roy Hemmings, Bristol, England, July 19, 2002.

1. Interview, Charles A. Edwards, 7/22/2002.
2. Interview, James Woodhead, 8/7/2002.
3. Interview, Roy Hemmings, 7/19/2002.

## CHAPTER 8

For a brief account of the battle of Convoy SC 26, see Clay Blair, *Hitler's U-boat War, Vol. 1: The Hunters, 1939–1942*. This chapter is drawn from: Convoy Data Sheets for Convoy SC 26 prepared by Arnold Hague; Convoy Information for Convoy SC 26 from Uboat.net; the British Admiralty War Diary for April 2, 1941; and the following documents from the National Archive, United Kingdom: File Adm. 199/55, Convoy A.1, Form for Convoy SC 26; File Adm. 199/55, Secret, Ocean Escort's Report of Proceedings, HMS *Worcestershire*; File Adm. 237/29, Convoy Form D, Report of Proceedings by Commodore of Convoy; File Adm. 237/29, Secret Report of Proceedings No. 35, HMS *Wolverine*; File Adm. 237/29, Secret, Intelligence Report, History and Sinking of *U-76*, HMS *Wolverine*; File Adm. 237/29, Secret, Home Fleet, Destroyer Form F., HMS *Wolverine*; File Adm. 237/29, Secret, Convoy Report of Proceedings from Commander (D), Sixth Escort Flotilla; File Adm. 237/29, Confidential, Enclosure No. 2 to *Scarborough* 3093. Narrative of attack on

*U-76*, 5th April, 1941; File Adm. 237/29, Extract from Report of Attack on *U-76*, 5th April, 1941, HMS *Arbutus*; File Adm. 237/29, Report of Proceedings, HMS *Hurricane*; File Adm. 199/1983, Secret, Analysis of Attacks by U-boats on Convoy SC 26 and HMS *Worcestershire* 2nd to 5th April, 1941; File Adm. 237/29, Secret, Translation of Letter Written in German by Steuermannsmaat Carl Becker of *U-76*, on board HMS *Arbutus*, Addressed to Frau Edith Becker, Wiesbaden, Wilhelminenstrasse 8, Dated Sunday, 6th April, 1941; Secret, Translation of a Diary contained in notebook belonging to Ordinary Telegraphist Günther Bruse of *U-76*; File Adm. 199/1983, Track Charts of Battle of Convoy SC 26; File Adm. 237/29, Confidential, Report of an Interview with Cpt. P. E. Birch, Master of SS *Thirlby*; the following documents from the Naval Historical Branch, Ministry of Defence, United Kingdom: Confidential, Report of an Interview with Cpt. A. Henney, Master of SS *British Reliance*; Confidential, Report of an Interview with Cpt. A. G. Phelps Mead, Master of SS *Alderpool*; Confidential, Report of an Interview with Mr. C. L. Robertson, A.B., of SS *Westpool*; Confidential, Report of an Interview with Cpt. G. Jones, Master of SS *Harbledown*; Confidential, Report of an Interview with Mr. A. Croft, 2nd Officer of SS *Welcombe*; Confidential, Report of an Interview with Cpt. E. W. Agnes, Master of SS *Athenic*; the following documents from the U.S. National Archives Microfilm Publications T-1022, Record Group 242: KTB of *U-69*, commanded by Kptlt. Jost Metzler, Secret, March 31 to April 5, 1941; KTB of *U-74*, commanded by Kptlt. Eitel-Friedrich Kentrat, April 2–5, 1941; KTB of *U-94*, commanded by Kptlt. Herbert Kuppisch, March 31–April 5, 1941; KTB of *U-73*, commanded by Kptlt. Helmut Rosenbaum, Secret, March 3–April 4, 1941; KTB of *U-98*, commanded by Kptlt. Robert Gysae, April 2–4, 1941.

1. U.S. National Archives and Records Administration, KTB of *U-74*, Kptlt. Eitel-Friedrich Kentrat.
2. British National Archive, File Adm. 237/29, Enclosure to ID Form AC. Attack by U-boats on Convoy SC 26 night of 2nd/3rd April 1941.
3. Naval Historical Branch, Ministry of Defence, United Kingdom: Report of an Interview with Mr. C. L. Robertson, A.B., of SS *Westpool*.
4. British National Archive, File Adm. 199/55, Ocean Escort's Report of Proceedings, HMS *Worcestershire*.
5. British National Archive, File Adm. 237/29, Enclosure to ID Form AC. Attack by U-boats on Convoy SC 26 night of 2nd/3rd April 1941.

6. U.S. National Archives and Records Administration, KTB of *U-74*, Kptlt. Eitel-Friedrich Kentrat.
7. Scrapbook of Ron Smith.
8. U.S. National Archives and Records Administration, KTB of *U-98*, Kptlt. Robert Gysae.
9. Ibid.
10. Naval Historical Branch, Ministry of Defence, United Kingdom: Report of an Interview with Mr. A. Croft, Second Officer of SS *Welcombe*.
11. U.S. National Archives and Records Administration, KTB of *U-94*, Kptlt. Herbert Kuppisch.
12. British National Archive, File Adm. 237/29, Enclosure No. 2 to *Scarborough* 3093. Narrative of attack on *U-76*, 5th April 1941.
13. British National Archive, File Adm. 237/29, Translation of Letter Written in German by Steuermannsmaat Carl Becker, of *U-76*, on board HMS *Arbutus*, Addressed to Frau Edith Becker, Wiesbaden, Wilhelminenstrasse 8, Dated Sunday, 6th April, 1941.

## CHAPTER 9

For U-boat operations and developments through 1941, see Jak P. Mallmann Showell, *U-boat Warfare: The Evolution of the Wolfpack*; Grand Admiral Karl Dönitz, *Memoirs: Ten Years and Twenty Days*; Spencer Dunmore, *In Great Waters: The Epic Story of the Battle of the Atlantic*; David Miller, *U-boats*. For a discussion of Grand Admiral Karl Dönitz, see Peter Padfield, *Dönitz, the Last Führer: Portrait of a Nazi War Leader*. For a discussion of Enigma, see Patrick Beesley, *Very Special Intelligence: The Story of the Admiralty's Operational Intelligence Center, 1939–1945*; Stephen Budiansky, *Battle of Wits: The Complete Story of Codebreaking in World War II*; F. H. Hinsley, *British Intelligence in the Second World War*. For the sinking of the *Bismarck*, see KBismarck.com.

1. Jak P. Mallmann Showell, *U-boat Warfare: The Evolution of the Wolfpack*, p. 69.
2. Grand Admiral Karl Dönitz, *Memoirs: Ten Years and Twenty Days*, p. 132.
3. Ibid., p. 135.

## CHAPTER 10

For a discussion of attacks on U.S. destroyers in the fall of 1941, see Samuel Eliot Morison, *History of United States Naval Operations in World War II, Vol. 1: The Battle of the Atlantic, September 1939–May 1943*; Spencer Dunmore, *In Great Waters: The Epic Story of the Battle of the Atlantic*; Terry Hughes and John Costello, *The Battle of the Atlantic*. For President Roosevelt's views and actions regarding involvement in World War II during 1941, see Martin Folly, *The United States and World War II: The Awakening Giant*; Winston S. Churchill, *The Second World War, Vol. 3: The Grand Alliance*; Jon Meacham, *Franklin and Winston: An Intimate Portrait of an Epic Friendship*. For U.S. destroyers on North Atlantic patrol, see Patrick Abbazia, *Mr. Roosevelt's Navy: The Private War of the U.S. Atlantic Fleet, 1939–1942*. For detailed information on U.S. Navy destroyer types and data, see Naval Institute Press, *U.S. Naval Vessels 1943*. For Kptlt. Otto Kretschmer and Cpt. Donald Macintyre, see Terence Robertson, *The Golden Horseshoe: The Story of Otto Kretschmer, Germany's Top U-boat Ace* and Donald Macintyre, *U-boat Killer*. This chapter also draws on an interview with Rear Adm. Erich Topp, Remagen, Germany, Sept. 22, 2003.

1. Terry Hughes and John Costello, *The Battle of the Atlantic*, p. 158.
2. Samuel Eliot Morison, *History of the United States Naval Operations in World War II: The Battle of the Atlantic, 1939–1943* (New York: Castle Books, 2001), p. 87.
3. Ibid.
4. Interview, R. Adm. Erich Topp, 9/22/2003.
5. Terry Hughes and John Costello, *The Battle of the Atlantic*, p. 185.
6. Interview, Cpt. Duncan Knight, RN Rtd, 9/8/2002.

## CHAPTER 11

For information on the Japanese attack on Pearl Harbor, see Robert J. Cressman, *The Official Chronology of the U.S. Navy in World War II*. For information on the German submarine attack on the U.S. East Coast, see Samuel Eliot Morison, *The Two-Ocean War*; Grand Admiral Karl Dönitz, *Memoirs: Ten Years and Twenty Days*; Stephen Howarth, *Men of War: Great Naval Captains of World War II*; and Sir John Slessor, *The Central Blue: Recollections and Reflections*. For a detailed treatment of merchant ship losses in 1942 off the U.S. East Coast, see Jürgen Rohwer, *Axis Submarine Successes, 1939–1945*. For the history of the Royal Navy, see Fred T. Jane, *The British Battle Fleet, Vols. 1 and 2*; Alexander McKee, *Against the Odds, Battles at Sea, 1591–1949*; Oliver Warner, *Nelson and the Age of Fighting Sail*; Roger Morriss, Brian Lavery, and Stephen Deuchar, edited by Pieter Van Der Merwe, *Nelson: An Illustrated History*; St. Vincent 200 Web site and "Royal Navy History." Official Web site of the Royal Navy. This chapter also draws on an interview with Arnold Hague, Sept. 29, 2003.

1. Robert J. Cressman, *The Official Chronology of the U.S. Navy in*

# Notes

*World War II* (Annapolis: The Naval Institute Press, 2000), p. 59.

2. Terry Hughes and John Costello, *The Battle of the Atlantic*, p. 197.

3. Samuel Eliot Morison, *History of the United States Naval Operations in World War II, Vol. 1: The Battle of the Atlantic, September 1939–May 1943*, p. 127.

## CHAPTER 12

For a brief account of the Battle of Convoy SC 100, see Clay Blair, *Hitler's U-boat War, Vol. 2: The Hunted, 1942–1945*. This chapter also draws on: Convoy data sheets for Convoy SC 100 prepared by Arnold Hague; Convoy Information for Convoy SC 100, Uboat.net; and the following documents from the National Archive, United Kingdom: File Adm. 237/197 Convoy A. 1, Form for Convoy SC 100; File Adm. 237/197, Confidential, Report of Escort of SC 100, USCGC *Spencer*; File Adm. 199/714, Confidential, Inclosure (A) to Commanding Officer, *Campbell*, Serial 032, Anti-Submarine Activities of USS *Campbell, C. G.*, on 24 Sept. 1942 while Escorting Convoy SC 100; File Adm. 237/197, Secret, SC 100, Report by HMS *Nasturtium*; File Adm. 199/714, Report of Proceedings, HMS *Bittersweet*; File Adm. 199/714, SC 100, Ship's Narrative, HMCS *Trillium*; File Adm. 199/714, Report on Sighting and Attack on U-boat when escorting SC 100, HMCS *Mayflower*; File Adm. 199/714, Report of Attack on U-boat, 20 Sept. 1311Z (1111 plus two), HMCS *Rosthern*; File Adm. 199/714, Action Sept. 20th, 22nd, 23rd, 24th, 25th, HMCS *Weybrum*; File Adm. 199/714, Report of Proceedings, HMCS *Lunenburg*; File Adm. 237/197, Secret, Preliminary Investigation of Attacks on SC 100; File Adm. 237/197, Confidential, Report of an Interview with the Master, Cpt. J. F. Travis of SS *Empire Hartebeeste*; File Adm. 237/197, Confidential, Report of an Interview with the Master, Cpt. J. D. Donovan of the MV *Athelsultan*; File Adm. 237/197, Confidential, Report of an Interview with Able-Seaman H. K. Neilsin of SS *Tennessee*; File Adm. 237/197, Affidavit of Alex Mitchell, Master of SS *Empire Opal*; File Adm. 199/714, Confidential, Anti-submarine Action by a Surface Ship, USS *Spencer*; File Adm. 199/714, Track Charts of the battle of Convoy SC 100; the following documents from the U.S. National Archives Microfilm Publications T-1022, Record Group 242: KTB, *U-617*, commanded by Kptlt. Albrecht Brandi, Secret, Sept. 22–24, 1942; KTB, *U-432*, commanded by Kptlt. Heinz-Otto Schultze, Sept. 22–24, 1942; KTB, *U-373*, commanded by Kptlt. Paul-Karl Loeser, Secret, Sept. 19–21, 1942; KTB, *U-596*, commanded by Kptlt. Gunter Jahn, Secret, Sept. 19–21, 1942; KTB, *U-221*, commanded by Kptlt. Hans-Hartwig Trojer, Sept. 21–26, 1942; KTB, *U-258*, commanded by Kptlt. Wilhelm von Mässenhausen, Secret, Sept. 24–25, 1942; and interviews with Mike Hall, USCG (Ret.), Baltimore, Md., Oct. 12, 2002, and Harold Rogers, Baltimore, Md., Oct. 13, 2002. This chapter also draws on data from the U-boat Archive, Stiftung Traditionsarchiv Unterseeboote, Altenbruch, Germany.

1. British National Archive, File Adm. 237/197, Signals to Commander, Task Unit 24.1.3.
2. Interview, Cpt. Mike Hall, United States Coast Guard (Ret.), 10/12/2002.
3. British National Archive, File Adm. 237/917, Report of Escort of SC 100, USCGC *Spencer*.
4. U.S. National Archives and Records Administration, KTB of *U-596*, Kptlt. Gunter Jahn.
5. U.S. National Archives and Records Administration, KTB of *U-373*, Kptlt. Paul-Karl Loeser.
6. British National Archive, File Adm. 237/197, Report of an Interview with Cpt. F. J. Travis of SS *Empire Hartebeeste*.
7. Interview, Harold Rogers, United States Coast Guard (Ret.), 10/13/2002.
8. Interview, Cpt. Mike Hall, United States Coast Guard (Ret.), 10/12/2002.
9. British National Archive, File Adm. 237/197, Report by HMS *Nasturtium*.
10. U.S. National Archives and Records Administration, KTB of *U-617*, Kptlt. Albrecht Brandi.
11. British National Archive, File Adm. 237/197, Report of an Interview with the Master, Cpt. J. D. Donovan, of the MV *Athelsultan*.
12. Ibid.
13. U.S. National Archives and Records Administration, KTB of *U-617*, Kptlt. Albrecht Brandi.
14. British National Archive, File Adm. 237/197, Report of an Interview with Able-Seaman H. K. Neilsin of SS *Tennessee*.
15. U.S. National Archives and Records Administration, KTB of *U-432*, Kptlt. Heinz-Otto Schultze.
16. U.S. National Archives and Records Administration, KTB of *U-617*, Kptlt. Albrecht Brandi.

CHAPTER 13

For information and background on the German winter offensive of 1942–1943, see Terry Hughes and John Costello, *The Battle of the Atlantic*; Samuel Eliot Morison, *History of United States Naval Operations in World War II, Vol. 1: The Battle of the Atlantic, September*

*1939–May 1943*; S. W. Roskill, *The War at Sea, 1939–1945, Vol. 2: The Period of Balance*; Spencer Dunmore, *In Great Waters: The Epic Story of the Battle of the Atlantic*; Grand Admiral Karl Dönitz, *Memoirs: Ten Years and Twenty Days*. For convoy statistics on losses during the 1942–1943 winter offensive, see Arnold Hague, *The Allied Convoy System, 1939–1945*. For material on life aboard U-boats, see: Jak P. Mallmann Showell, *U-boat Warfare: The Evolution of the Wolfpack*. For information on the sinking of *U-357*, see Donald Macintyre, *U-boat Killer*. For details on British destroyers, see Maurice Cocker, *Destroyers of the Royal Navy, 1893–1981*. This chapter also draws on archival materials of the Royal Navy, including "Confidential Record, Richard Courtney Boyle," "Confidential Record, Edward Campbell Lacy Day," information in Ubootwaffe.net; interview with Roy Hemmings, Bristol, England, July 19, 2002; interview with Cpt. Duncan Knight, RN Rtd, Guillards Oak, England, Aug. 8, 2002; interview with Ron Smith, Cardiff, England, Aug. 9, 2002; interview with Harold Rogers, Baltimore, Md., Oct. 13, 2002; interview with Horst Elfe, Berlin, Sept. 23, 2003; interview with Werner Hirschmann, Toronto, March 8, 2004.

1. Royal Navy, Confidential Record, Richard Courtney Boyle.
2. Royal Navy, Confidential Record, Edward Campbell Lacy Day.
3. Interview, John Raikes, 5/4/2002.
4. S. W. Roskill, *The War at Sea, 1939–1945, Vol. 2: The Period of Balance*, p. 218.
5. Ibid., p. 217.
6. Ibid.
7. Interview, Roy Hemmings, 7/19/2002.
8. Interview, Cpt. Duncan Knight RN (Rtd), 8/8/2002.
9. Interview, Harold Rogers, United States Coast Guard (Ret), 10/13/2002.
10. Interview, Ron Smith, 8/9/2002.
11. Interview, Werner Hirschmann, 3/8/2004.
12. Interview, Horst Elfe, 9/23/2003.
13. Jak P. Mallmann Showell, *U-boat Warfare: The Evolution of the Wolfpack*, p. 35.
14. Donald Macintyre, *U-boat Killer*, p. 85.
15. Ibid., p. 87.
16. Interview, Charles A. Edwards, RN, 7/22/2002.

## CHAPTER 14

For information on Enigma and the breaking of the Enigma code, see: Patrick Beesly, *Very Special Intelligence: The Story of the Admiralty's Operational Intelligence Center, 1939–1945*; F. H. Hinsley and Alan

# Notes

Stripp, *Code Breakers: The Inside Story of Bletchley Park*; Stephen Budiansky, *Battle of Wits: The Complete Story of Codebreaking in World War II*; Hugh Sebag-Montefiore, *Enigma: The Battle for the Code*; Jak P. Mallmann Showell, *Enigma U-boats: Breaking the Code*; Gordon Welchman, *The Hut Six Story: Breaking the Enigma Codes*; David Miller, *U-boats*; Bletchley Park Web site. For information on the Ships for Victory program, Liberty ships, shipbuilding, and maritime manning programs, see: John Gorley Bunker, *Liberty Ships: The Ugly Ducklings of World War II*; Terry Hughes and John Costello, *The Battle of the Atlantic*; Martin Folly, *The United States and World War II: The Awakening Giant*; Andrew Williams, *The Battle of the Atlantic*.

## CHAPTER 15

For information on the north Russia convoys and particularly on survivors of the SS *Washington* in the Battle of Convoy PQ17, see Samuel Eliot Morison, *History of United States Naval Operations in World War II, Vol. 1: The Battle of the Atlantic, September 1939–May 1943*; and also on the north Russia convoys, see Fred Herman, *Dynamite Cargo, Convoy to Russia*; Harald Busch, *U-boats at War: German Submarines in Action, 1939–1945*. For the end of the German winter offensive in 1942–1943, see Terry Hughes and John Costello, *The Battle of the Atlantic*; Arnold Hague, *The Allied Convoy System, 1939–1945*; Grand Admiral Karl Dönitz, *Memoirs: Ten Years and Twenty Days*; Clay Blair, *Hitler's U-boat War, Vol. 2: The Hunted, 1942–1945*; David Miller, *U-boats*; S. W. Roskill, *The War at Sea, 1939–1945, Vol. 2: The Period of Balance*. For London in 1943, see Peter Ackroyd, *London: The Biography*; Maureen Waller, *London 1945: Life in the Debris of War*; and Philip Ziegler, *London at War: 1939–1945*. Material on the battle of Convoy HX 229 and SC 122 is drawn from the following documents in the National Archive, United Kingdom: File Adm. 199/575, Remarks by Commodore Commanding Londonderry Escort Force Convoy HX 229; File Adm. 199/575, Secret, Convoy HX 229, HMS *Highlander*, Report of Proceedings, 12–22 March, 1943; File Adm. 199/579, HMS *Havelock*, Report of Proceedings, Convoy SC 122, 11–20 March 1943. This chapter is also based on interviews with Thomas Corrales aboard M/V *Lykes Motivator*, Feb. 14, 2002, and by telephone, June 10, 2005; and Arnold Hague, Hinchley Wood, England, Sept. 29, 2003.

1. Notes of Walker Taylor III, Wilmington, NC.
2. Interview, Thomas Corrales, Jr., 6/10/2005.
3. Photocopy of letter from War Shipping Administration, provided by Thomas Corrales, Jr.

4. Grand Admiral Karl Dönitz, *Memoirs: Ten Years and Twenty Days*, p. 312.

5. Ibid., p. 310.

6. S. W. Roskill, *The War at Sea, 1939–1945, Vol. 2: The Period of Balance*, p. 355.

7. Peter Ackroyd, *London: The Biography*, p. 732.

8. As cited in Philip Ziegler, *London at War: 1939–1945*, p. 233.

9. Interview, Arnold Hague, 4/16/2002.

10. Royal Navy, Confidential Record of Richard Courtney Boyle.

11. Clay Blair, *Hitler's U-boat War, Vol. 2: The Hunted, 1942–1945*, p. 266.

12. Samuel Eliot Morison, *History of United States Naval Operations in World War II, Vol. 1: The Battle of the Atlantic, September 1939–May 1943*, p. 344.

13. S. W. Roskill, *The War at Sea, 1939–1945, Vol. 2: The Period of Balance*, p. 370.

14. Interview, Arnold Hague, 9/29/2003.

## CHAPTER 16

For information on the collapse of the U-boat war in May 1943, see Grand Admiral Karl Dönitz, *Memoirs: Ten Years and Twenty Days*; S. W. Roskill, *The War at Sea, 1939–1945, Vol. 3: The Offensive Part 2*; Terry Hughes and John Costello, *The Battle of the Atlantic.* For information on the battle of Convoy HX 233, see W. A. Haskell, *Shadows on the Horizon: The Battle of Convoy HX 233*; "Scratch One Hearse," by William Walton, *Time* magazine. For information on Cpt. Gilbert Roberts, RN, and the Western Approaches Tactical Unit, see Mark Williams, *Captain Gilbert Roberts, RN, and the Anti-U-boat School.* For development of ASW technology, see Alfred Price, *Aircraft Versus Submarine: The Evolution of the Anti-Submarine Aircraft, 1912–1972*; Robert Buderi, *The Invention That Changed the World: How a Small Group of Radar Pioneers Won the Second World War and Launched a Technical Revolution*; Jennet Conant, *Tuxedo Park: A Wall Street Tycoon and the Secret Palace of Science That Changed the Course of World War II*; David E. Fisher, *A Race on the Edge of Time: Radar—The Decisive Weapon of World War II*; and Spencer Dunmore, *In Great Waters: The Epic Story of the Battle of the Atlantic, 1939–1945.* This chapter is also based on information drawn from Arnold Hague, *The Allied Convoy System, 1939–1945*; Terence Robertson, *Escort Commander*; Donald Macintyre, *U-boat Killer*; Terence Robertson, *The Golden Horseshoe: The Story of Otto Kretschmer, Germany's Top U-boat Ace*; "Vice-Admiral Sir Peter Gret-

ton," *The Book of Naval Obituaries*, Ministry of Defence, United Kingdom; "The Consolidated B-24 Liberator," U-boat.net; "Consolidated
B-24D 'Liberator'," United States Air Force Museum Web site; archival
material of the Royal Navy, Ministry of Defence, United Kingdom; and
interviews with Horst Bredow, Founder and Director, U-boat Archive,
Stiftung Traditionsarchiv Unterseeboote, Altenbruch, Germany, Sept. 25,
2003; Harold Rogers, by telephone, Aug. 2005; Cdr. Peter D. Sturdee,
RN Rtd, Dorridge, England, Aug. 2, 2002; and Ron Smith, Cardiff, England, Aug. 9, 2002.

1. Grand Admiral Karl Dönitz, *Memoirs: Ten Years and Twenty
   Days*, p. 339.
2. Ibid.
3. Ibid.
4. Ibid., pp. 341, 406.
5. Interview, Horst Bredow, 9/25/2003.
6. Interview, Arnold Hague, October 2005.
7. Grand Admiral Karl Dönitz, *Memoirs: Ten Years and Twenty
   Days*, p. 407.
8. Ibid., p. 408.
9. "Scratch One Hearse," *Time* magazine.
10. Interview, Harold Rogers, 10/13/2002.
11. Terence Robertson, *Escort Commander* (Garden City, N.Y.: Dou-
    bleday, 1979), p. 57.
12. Interview, Arnold Hague, 4/29/2002.
13. Interview, Cdr. Peter D. Sturdee RN, 8/2/2002.
14. Interview, Ron Smith, 8/9/2002.
15. Interview, David Lord Mottistone, 10/2/2003.

## CHAPTER 17

For information on Cpt. F. J. Walker, RN, see Terence Robertson, *Escort
Commander*. For information on German U-boat losses in 1943–1945, see
Axel Niestle, *German U-boat Losses During World War II*. For back-
ground and information on the closing phase of the Battle of the Atlantic,
1943–1945, see S. W. Roskill, *The War at Sea, 1939–1945, Vol. 3: The
Offensive, Part 1*; Grand Admiral Karl Dönitz, *Memoirs: Ten Years and
Twenty Days*; Terry Hughes and John Costello, *The Battle of the Atlantic*;
Spencer Dunmore, *In Great Waters: The Epic Story of the Battle of the
Atlantic*. For U.S. naval operations in the South Atlantic in 1943–1945 and
the last stand of USS *Borie*, see Samuel Eliot Morison, *History of United
States Naval Operations in World War II, Vol. 10: The Atlantic Battle
Won, May 1943–May 1945*. Statistical information for this chapter is
drawn from Arnold Hague, *The Allied Convoy System, 1939–1945*.

1. Grand Admiral Karl Dönitz, *Memoirs: Ten Years and Twenty Days*, p. 415.
2. Samuel Eliot Morison, *History of the United States Naval Operations in World War II, Vol. 1: The Battle of the Atlantic, September 1939–May 1943*, p. 99.
3. S. W. Roskill, *The War at Sea, 1939–1945, Vol. 3: The Offensive, Part 1*, p. 246.
4. Ibid., p. 50.
5. Ibid., pp. 47, 54.

## CHAPTER 18

For information on the closing stages of the U-boat war in 1944–1945, see Grand Admiral Karl Dönitz, *Memoirs: Ten Years and Twenty Days*; S. W. Roskill, *The War at Sea, 1939 to 1945, Vol. 3: The Offensive, Part 1 and Part 2*; Terry Hughes and John Costello, *The Battle of the Atlantic*. For D-Day, see Britannica Online. This chapter also draws on information in Donald Macintyre, *U-boat Killer*, "State of the Fleet, 1939–1945," Naval Historical Branch, Ministry of Defence, United Kingdom; interviews with Gillian Addis Warr, London, May 6, 2002, and Sept. 30, 2003.

1. As cited in Grand Admiral Karl Dönitz, *Memoirs: Ten Years and Twenty Days*, p. 429.
2. "Grand Admiral Karl Dönitz, German Navy," by Peter Padfield, in Stephen Howarth, *Men of War: Great Naval Captains of World War II*, p. 203.
3. Ibid., p. 205.
4. Donald Macintyre, *U-boat Killer*, p. 161.
5. Interview, Gillian Ware, 9/30/2003.

## CHAPTER 19

For the German stand-down from arms, see S. W. Roskill, *The War at Sea, 1939 to 1945, Vol. 3: The Offensive, Part 2*; and Terry Hughes and John Costello, *The Battle of the Atlantic*. This chapter also draws on information contained in Terence Robertson, *Escort Commander*; Donald Macintyre, *U-boat Killer*; "State of the Fleet, 1939–1945," Naval Historical Branch, Ministry of Defence, United Kingdom; and interviews with Edna Smith, by telephone, Aug. 2005, and Arnold Hague, Hinchley Wood, England, Sept. 16, 2002.

1. Terence Robertson, *Escort Commander*, p. 198.
2. Donald Macintyre, *U-boat Killer*, p. 169.
3. Telephone interview, Edna Smith, August 2005.
4. Interview, Arnold Hague, 4/16/2002.

# BIBLIOGRAPHY

## SECONDARY SOURCES

### Books

Abbazia, Patrick. *Mr. Roosevelt's Navy: The Private War of the U.S. Atlantic Fleet, 1939–1942*. Annapolis: United States Naval Institute, 1975.

Ackroyd, Peter. *London: The Biography*. New York: Doubleday, 2001.

Ambrose, Stephen E. *The Wild Blue: The Men and Boys Who Flew the B-24s Over Germany*. New York: Simon & Schuster, 2001.

Arthur, Max. *There Shall Be Wings: The RAF, 1918 to the Present*. London: Hodder & Stoughton, 1993.

Baker, Richard. *The Terror of Tobermory: An Informal Biography of Sir Gilbert Stephenson, KBE, CB, CMG*. Edinburgh: Birlinn, 1999.

Barnett, Correlli. *Engage the Enemy More Closely: The Royal Navy in the Second World War*. New York: W.W. Norton, 1991.

Baxter, James Phinney. *Scientists Against Time*. Cambridge: MIT Press, 1968.

Beesly, Patrick. *Very Special Intelligence: The Story of the Admiralty's Operational Intelligence Center, 1939–1945*. New York: Ballantine, 1977.

# Bibliography

Behrens, C. B. A. *History of the Second World War: Merchant Shipping and the Demands of War*. London: Her Majesty's Stationery Office and Longmans, Green, 1955.

Bennett, G. H., and R. Bennett. *Survivors: British Merchant Seamen in the Second World War*. London: Hambledon, 1999.

Bercuson, David J., and Holger H. Herwig. *The Destruction of the Bismarck*. New York: Overlook, 2001.

Blair, Clay. *Hitler's U-boat War, Vol. 1: The Hunters, 1939–1942*. New York: Random House, 1996.

———. *Hitler's U-boat War, Vol. 2: The Hunted, 1942–1945*. New York: Random House, 1998.

Brittain, Vera. *England's Hour*. Pleasantville, N.Y.: Akadine, 2002.

Buchheim, Lothar Günther. *Das Boot*. London: Cassell, 2002.

Buderi, Robert. *The Invention That Changed the World: How a Small Group of Radar Pioneers Won the Second World War and Launched a Technical Revolution*. New York: Touchstone, 1997.

Budiansky, Stephen. *Battle of Wits: The Complete Story of Codebreaking in World War II*. New York: Simon & Schuster, 2002.

Bunker, John Gorley. *Liberty Ships. The Ugly Ducklings of World War II*. Annapolis: Naval Institute Press, 1972.

Burns, James MacGregor. *Roosevelt: The Soldier of Freedom, 1940–1945*. New York: Harcourt Brace Jovanovich, 1970.

Busch, Harald. *U-boats at War: German Submarines in Action, 1939–1945*. New York: Ballantine, 1955.

Busch, Rainer, and Hans Joachim Röll. *German U-boat Commanders of World War II: A Biographical Dictionary*. London: Greenhill, and Annapolis: Naval Institute Press, 1999.

Cannadine, David, ed. *Blood, Toil, Tears and Sweat: The Speeches of Winston Churchill*. Boston: Houghton Mifflin, 1989.

Chalmers, W. S. *Max Horton and the Western Approaches: A Biography of Admiral Sir Max Kennedy Horton, GCB, DSO*. London: Hodder & Stoughton, 1954.

Churchill, Winston S. *The Second World War, Vol. 2: Their Finest Hour*. Boston: Houghton Mifflin, 1949.

———. *The Second World War, Vol. 3: The Grand Alliance*. Boston: Houghton Mifflin, 1950.

Cocker, Maurice. *Destroyers of the Royal Navy, 1893–1981*. London: Ian Allan, 1981.

Conant, Jennet. *Tuxedo Park: A Wall Street Tycoon and the Secret Palace of Science That Changed the Course of World War II*. New York: Simon & Schuster, 2002.

# Bibliography

Cressman, Robert J. *The Official Chronology of the U.S. Navy in World War II*. Annapolis: Naval Institute Press, 2000.

Davis, Kenneth S. *FDR: The War President, 1940–1943*. New York: Random House, 2000.

Dawidowicz, Lucy S. *The War Against the Jews, 1933–1945*. New York: Bantam, 1976.

De La Bedoyere, Guy. *The Home Front*. United Kingdom: Shire, 2002.

Dönitz, Grand Admiral Karl. *Memoirs: Ten Years and Twenty Days*. Cambridge, Mass.: Da Capo, 1997.

Dunmore, Spencer. *In Great Waters: The Epic Story of the Battle of the Atlantic*. Toronto: McClelland & Stewart, 1999.

Edwards, Bernard. *Attack and Sink: the Battle for Convoy SC 42*. United Kingdom: New Era Writer's Guild, 1995.

Fisher, David E. *A Race on the Edge of Time: Radar—The Decisive Weapon of World War II*. New York: McGraw-Hill, 1998.

Folly, Martin. *The United States and World War II: The Awakening Giant*. Edinburgh: Edinburgh University Press, 2002.

Freidel, Frank. *Roosevelt: A Rendezvous with Destiny*. New York: Little, Brown, 1990.

Gilbert, Martin. *Finest Hour: Winston S. Churchill, 1939–1941*. London: William Heinemann, 1983.

——. *Road to Victory: Winston S. Churchill, 1941–1945*. London: William Heinemann, 1986.

Goodwin, Doris Kearns. *No Ordinary Time. Franklin and Eleanor Roosevelt: The Home Front in World War II*. New York: Simon & Schuster, 1994.

Gretton, Peter. *Convoy Escort Commander*. London: Cassell, 1964.

Gunther, John. *Roosevelt in Retrospect: A Profile in History*. New York: Harper & Brothers, 1950.

Hague, Arnold. *The Allied Convoy System, 1939–1945*. Annapolis: Naval Institute Press, 2000.

——. *Sloops, 1926–1946*. United Kingdom: World Ship Society, 1993.

——. *The Towns*. United Kingdom: World Ship Society, 1988.

Hancock, W. K., and M. M. Gowing. *History of the Second World War: The British Economy*. London: His Majesty's Stationery Office and Longmans, Green, 1949.

Haskell, W. A. *Shadows on the Horizon: The Battle of Convoy HX 233*. Annapolis: Naval Institute Press, 1998.

Herman, Arthur. *To Rule the Waves: How the British Navy Shaped the Modern World*. New York: HarperCollins, 2004.

Herman, Fred. *Dynamite Cargo: Convoy to Russia*. New York: Vanguard, 1943.

Hinsley, F. H. *British Intelligence in the Second World War*. New York: Cambridge University Press, 1993.

Hinsley, F. H., and Alan Stripp. *Code Breakers: The Inside Story of Bletchley Park*. Oxford: Oxford University Press, 2001.

Howarth, Stephen. *Men of War: Great Naval Captains of World War II*. New York: St. Martin's, 1993.

Hughes, Terry, and John Costello. *The Battle of the Atlantic*. New York: Dial Press/James Wade, 1977.

Jane, Fred T. *The British Battle Fleet, Vols. 1 and 2*. London: Library Press, 1915.

Jesse, F. Tennyson. *The Saga of* San Demetrio. New York: Alfred A. Knopf, 1943.

Keegan, John. *The Price of Admiralty: The Evolution of Naval Warfare*. New York: Viking, 1989.

Kershaw, Ian. *Hitler, 1936–1945: Nemesis*. New York: W. W. Norton, 2000.

Larrabee, Eric. *Commander in Chief: Franklin Delano Roosevelt, His Lieutenants and Their War*. New York: Harper & Row, 1987.

Lash, Joseph P. *Roosevelt and Churchill, 1939–1941: The Partnership That Saved the War*. New York: W. W. Norton, 1976.

Lenton, H. T., and J. J. Colledge. *Warships of World War II*. London: Ian Allan, 1973.

Longmate, Norman. *How We Lived Then: A History of Everyday Life During the Second World War*. London: Pimlico, 2002.

Macintyre, Donald. *U-boat Killer*. London: Cassell, 1956.

Macneil, Calum. *San Demetrio*. Sydney: Angus & Robertson, 1957.

Mallmann Showell, Jak P. *Enigma U-boats: Breaking the Code*. United Kingdom: Ian Allan, 2002.

———. *The German Navy in World War II: A Reference Guide to the Kriegsmarine, 1935–1945*. Annapolis: Naval Institute Press, 1979.

———. *U-boat Warfare: The Evolution of the Wolfpack*. Annapolis: Naval Institute Press, 2002.

McKee, Alexander. *Against the Odds: Battles at Sea, 1591–1949*. Annapolis: Naval Institute Press, 1991.

Meacham, Jon. *Franklin and Winston: An Intimate Portrait of an Epic Friendship*. New York: Random House, 2004.

Miller, David. *U-boats*. Washington: Brassey's, 2000.

Morison, Samuel Eliot. *History of United States Naval Operations in World War II, Vol. 1: The Battle of the Atlantic, September 1939–May 1943*. New York: Little, Brown, 1947.

———. *History of United States Naval Operations in World War II, Vol. 10: The Atlantic Battle Won, May 1943–May 1945*. Boston: Little, Brown, 1990.

———. *The Two-Ocean War*. Boston: Atlantic-Little, Brown, 1963.

Morison, Samuel Eliot, and Henry Steele Commager. *The Growth of the American Republic*. New York: Oxford University Press, 1962.

Morriss, Roger, Brian Lavery, and Stephen Deuchar, edited by Pieter Van Der Merwe. *Nelson: An Illustrated History*. London: National Maritime Museum, Greenwich, and Laurence King Publishing, 1995.

Mulligan, Timothy P. *Neither Sharks nor Wolves: The Men of Nazi Germany's U-boat Arm, 1939–1945*. Annapolis: Naval Institute Press, 1999.

Naval Institute Press, *U.S. Naval Vessels 1943*. Annapolis: Naval Institute Press, 1943.

Niestle, Axel. *German U-boat Losses During World War II*. London: Greenhill, 1998.

Padfield, Peter. *Dönitz, the Last Führer: Portrait of a Nazi War Leader*. New York: Harper & Row, 1984.

Peterson, Pete, ed. *They Couldn't Have Won the War Without Us: Stories of the Merchant Marine in World War II . . . Told by the Men Who Sailed the Ships*. Galena, Ill.: Lead Mine, 1998.

Pitt, Barrie, and the Editors of Time-Life Books. *The Battle of the Atlantic*. New York: Time-Life Books, 1977.

Price, Alfred. *Aircraft Versus Submarine: The Evolution of the Anti-Submarine Aircraft, 1912–1972*. Annapolis: Naval Institute Press, 1973.

Robertson, Terence. *Escort Commander*. Garden City, N.Y.: Doubleday, 1979.

———. *The Golden Horseshoe: The Story of Otto Kretschmer, Germany's Top U-boat Ace*. Charleston, S.C.: Arcadia, 2000.

Rohwer, Jürgen. *Axis Submarine Successes, 1939–1945*. Annapolis: Naval Institute Press, 1983.

Roscoe, Theodore, designed and illustrated by Fred Freeman. *United States Destroyer Operations in World War II*. Annapolis: Naval Institute Press, 1953.

Roskill, S. W. *A Merchant Fleet in War, 1939–1945*. London: Collins, 1962.

———. *The War at Sea, 1939–1945, Vol. 2: The Period of Balance*. London: Her Majesty's Stationery Office, 1956.

———. *The War at Sea, 1939–1945, Vol. 3: The Offensive, Part 1*. London: Her Majesty's Stationery Office, 1960.

———. *The War at Sea, 1939–1945, Vol. 3: The Offensive, Part 2.* London: Her Majesty's Stationery Office, 1961.

Sebag-Montefiore, Hugh. *Enigma: The Battle for the Code.* New York: John Wiley & Sons, 2002.

Seth, Ronald. *The Fiercest Battle: The Story of North Atlantic Convoy ONS 5 22nd April–7th May 1943.* New York: W. W. Norton, 1962.

Shaw, Antony. *World War II Day by Day.* St. Paul, Minn.: MBI Publishing, 2000.

Shirer, William L. *The Rise and Fall of the Third Reich.* New York: Simon & Schuster, 1959.

Slessor, Sir John. *The Central Blue: Recollections and Reflections.* London: Cassell, 1956.

Sumner, Ian, illustrated by Alix Baker. *The Royal Navy, 1939–1945.* United Kingdom: Osprey, 2001.

Waller, Maureen. *London 1945: Life in the Debris of War.* New York: St. Martin's, 2004.

Warner, Oliver. *Nelson and the Age of Fighting Sail.* New York: American Heritage Publishing, 1963.

Welchman, Gordon. *The Hut Six Story: Breaking the Enigma Codes.* United Kingdom: M&M Baldwin, 2000.

Werner, Herbert A. *Iron Coffins: A Personal Account of the German U-boat Battles of World War II.* Cambridge: Da Capo, 2002.

Williams, Andrew. *The Battle of the Atlantic.* London: BBC Worldwide, 2002.

Williams, Mark. *Captain Gilbert Roberts, RN, and the Anti-U-boat School.* London: Cassell, 1979.

Ziegler, Philip. *London at War: 1939–1945.* London: Pimlico, 2002.

## Newspaper and Magazine Articles and Other Sources

Arnold Hague. "Comment on German Shipbuilding Capacity in 1939, and a Comparison with British Capability." Paper.

———. "Comment on Wartime Cargoes, Import and Export, Under British Control." Paper.

———. "Senior Officer of Escort—SOE, UK Ports, Formation of Convoys." Paper.

"Honour Amongst Warriors." *Liverpool Echo*, May 18, 1993.

"Macintyre, Donald George Frederick Wyville, 1904–1981." (Article), Oxford University Press.

"Noble, Sir Percy Lockhart Harnam Noble, 1880–1955." (Article), Oxford University Press.

"Obituaries, Admiral Otto Kretschmer, Atlantic Warrior." *Guardian* (Manchester), Aug. 21, 1998.

Scott T. Price. "The Coast Guard and the North Atlantic Campaign." U.S. Coast Guard Web site.

"Reminiscences of Captain D. G. F. W. Macintyre, DSO and two bars, DSC, Royal Navy, by Captain the Lord Mottistone, Royal Navy." As provided to Vice Admiral Sir Peter Gretton.

William Scharf. "Air Power and the Battle of the Atlantic." Research report.

——. "Derby House: The Home of Victory." Research report.

——. "U-boat Kills from 1943 Through the End of World War II." Statistical analysis.

"Veterans of Secret Unit Celebrate their War Hero: Radar." *New York Times*, Sept. 10, 2002.

William Walton. "Scratch One Hearse," *Time*, June 7, 1943.

## Interviews

James Bartuska, telephone, Feb. 9, 2004

Joseph E. Bodner, Massapequa, N.Y., Dec. 2, 2004

Horst Bredow, Founder and Director, the U-boat Archive, Stiftung Traditionsarchiv Unterseeboote, Altenbruch, Sept. 25, 2003

Clifton Brown, Gunner, USCG (Ret.), Baltimore, Md., Oct. 11, 2002.

Francis J. Dooley, Teaneck, N.J., Nov. 26, 2004

Frank Dorner, Chicago, Il., Feb. 16, 2004

Charles A. Edwards, Leading Seaman, Northampton (U.K.), July 22, 2002

Horst Elfe, 1st Watch Officer, *U-99*, Commander, *U-93*, Berlin, Sept. 23, 2003

George Goldman, Teaneck, N.J., Nov. 26, 2004

Arnold Hague, London, March 5 and April 16, 2002; Hinchley Wood (U.K.), March 22, April 16, 29, May 20, July 16, 2002, Sept. 29, 2003

Cpt. Mike Hall, USCG (Ret.), Baltimore, Md., Oct. 12, 2002

Roy Hemmings, Seaman-Torpedoman, Bristol (U.K.), July 19, 2002

Cyril Hill, Ordinary Seaman, Braintree (U.K.), Aug. 6, 2002

Werner Hirschmann, Chief Engineer, *U-190*, Toronto, March 8, 2004

Cpt. Duncan Knight RN (Rtd), Guillards Oak (U.K.), Aug. 8, 2002

Volkmar König, Midshipman, *U-99*, Toronto, Aug. 29, 2003

Russell Lewis, Boiler Tender 1st Class, USCG (Ret.), Baltimore, Md., Oct. 11, 2002.

Jak P. Mallmann Showell, Altenbruch (U.K.), Sept. 24 and 25, 2003

Cpt. David Lord Mottistone RN (Rtd), Cowes, Isle of Wight, Oct. 2, 2003

George E. Murphy, Teaneck, N.J., Nov. 26, 2004

Cpt. Christopher L. W. Page RN (Rtd), London, March 5 and 22, 2002

John Raikes, crewman, HMS *Wolverine*, Tonypandy (U.K.), May 4, 2002

Harold Rogers, Baker, USCG, (Ret.), Baltimore, Md., Oct. 13, 2002

Edna Smith, telephone, Aug. 2002

Ron Smith, Gunlayer, Cardiff (U.K.), Aug. 9, 2002

Warren Stricker, telephone, Jan. 29, 2004

Cdr. Peter D. Sturdee RN (Rtd), Dorridge (U.K.), Aug. 2, 2002

R. Adm. Erich Topp, Commander, *U-57, U-552, U-3010, U-2513*, Remagen, Germany, Sept. 22, 2003

Robert Wally, telephone, Feb. 2, 2004

Gillian Warr, London, May 6, 2002, and Sept. 30, 2003

James Woodhead, Chief Yeoman of Signals, Grantham (U.K.), Aug. 7, 2002

## PRIMARY SOURCES

### *Royal Navy*

"State of the Fleet, 3rd September, 1939–15th August, 1945"; "Atlantic Escort Groups—1 April 1943"; "The Organizations: The Admiralty and the Western Approaches"; "Biography, Admiral Sir Alan Scott-Moncrieff, KCB, CBE, DSO and Bar"; "Confidential Record, Alan Kenneth Scott-Moncrieff"; "Service Record, Capt. Donald G. F. W. Macintyre"; "Biography, Capt. Donald George Frederick Wyville Macintyre"; "Confidential Record, Capt. Donald George Frederick Wyville Macintyre"; "Service Record, Commander Arthur Andre Tait DSO RN"; "Confidential Record, Arthur Andre Tait"; "Confidential Record, James Marjoribanks Rowland"; "Confidential Record, Edward Campbell Lacy Day"; "Confidential Record, Richard Courtney Boyle"; "Confidential Record, Francis Babington Proudfoot"; Admiralty War Diary; Signals from the Admiralty War Diary; Documents pertaining to the development of depth charges; The Navy List; "HMS *Wolverine*, Summary of Service"; "HMS *Walker*, Summary of Service"; "HMS *Hesperus*, Summary of Service"; "September, 1942, Atlantic Convoy Instructions, General Section"; "September, 1942, Atlantic Convoy Instructions, Operations Section"; "Royal Navy History"; and all other documentary and archival sources of analytical and reportorial nature in the National Archive, United Kingdom, and U.S. National Archives listed in notes for chapters three, eight, and twelve.

### *U.S. Navy*

"Biography, R. Adm. Paul R. Heineman"; "Service record of R. Adm. Paul R. Heineman"; "Dictionary of American Naval Fighting Ships—USS *Reuben James* (DD-245)"; "Dictionary of American Naval Fighting

Ships, USS *Moffett* (DD-362)"; "Dictionary of American Naval Fighting Ships, USS *Biloxi* (CL-80)"; documentary material relating to Convoy ON 166; narrative of sinking of *U-606*; and all other documentary and archival sources of analytical and reportorial nature in the National Archive, United Kingdom, and U.S. National Archives listed in notes for chapters three, eight, and twelve.

### German Navy

"Staffing of the Staff up to October of 1939, Befehlshaber der Unterseeboote"; from Stiftung Traditionsarchiv Unterseeboote: "Locations of Boats Lost in Action According to Area of Loss"; "U-boat Food—'*U-150*' Menu for 15–21 August 1943"; "Staffing of BdU (Befehlshaber der Unterseeboote)"; "Locations of BdU, (Befehlshaber der Unterseeboote), from Jak P. Mallman Showell; "You Need a Feeling for It—Article on Otto Kretschmer," *Southeast Daily Post*, 4 June 1983; speech by Jupp Kassell, Sept. 22, 1986; from Uboat.net: "Top U-boat Aces, Otto Kretschmer"; "The Commander Interviews, Otto Kretschmer"; "Eberhard Godt"; "Top U-boat Aces, Erich Topp"; "Top U-boat Aces, Claus Korth"; "Top U-boat Aces, Adelbert Schnee"; "Top U-boat Aces, Johann Mohr"; "Top U-boat Aces, Wolfgang Lüth"; "Albrecht Brandi"; and photo research and all other documentary and archival sources of analytical and reportorial nature in the National Archive, United Kingdom, and U.S. National Archives listed in notes for chapters three, eight, and twelve.

# ACKNOWLEDGMENTS

Certain individuals played a key role in the development, research, and preparation of this book to the extent that, looking back, it is clear the project would not have been possible without their help. Arnold Hague RNR Rtd, formerly of *Jane's Fighting Ships* and the Naval Historical Branch, Ministry of Defence, United Kingdom, probably knows more about the Allied convoy system in World War II than anyone else alive. He is also an expert on world navies and gave invaluable assistance in countless interviews, guidance on research, photographs and data from his gigantic pool of computerized information on the roughly 25,000 Allied convoys of World War II. I owe him much involved gratitude and a great debt of thanks. Captain Christopher L. W. Page RN Rtd, Head of the Naval Historical Branch of the Ministry of Defence, United Kingdom, never begrudged time to see me, and helped me scout through the library of dossiers, volumes, card indexes, and archival materials at the Branch, to help in finding what he called "the right detail

Acknowledgments

a researcher might need." Much of the data and substance of this book go back in origin to his corner office. Mike McAloon of the Branch also was an unfailing source of data, information, and background.

Among those who were most helpful in my travels in Germany, Horst Bredow, Founder and Director of the U-boat Archive, Stiftung Traditionsarchiv Unterseeboote, was of important assistance in helping to arrange interviews with former U-boat personnel, and in welcoming me to the U-boat Archive. Jak P. Mallmann Showell, English language representative for the U-boat Archive and himself a prolific author on the U-boat war, gave me the benefit of his authoritative observations and his detailed knowledge of the U-boat arm.

Many sailors became friends as we talked and we grew to know each other; I could not come to the end of this project without mentioning the considerable contributions and kindness of Cdr. Peter D. Sturdee RN Rtd, Cpt. David Mottistone RN Rtd, Roy Hemmings, Charles A. "Bungey" Edwards, Ron Smith, James Woodhead, and Jack Raikes, all Royal Navy Rtd. In America, Mike Hall and Harold Rogers of the United States Coast Guard gave abundantly of their time. On the German side, I would be negligent if I did not mention the insights and generosity of Horst Elfe, R. Admiral Erich Topp, and Volkmar König.

My editor at Simon & Schuster, Bob Bender, was responsible for this book originally. From the start of the project and through the long incubation and preparation of the work, his support was of enormous importance, as well as his perceptions and his coaching. Michael Carlisle of Inkwell Management, my agent, was an indispensable comrade and key in guiding project and author from the inception of the work to its completion. I

330

owe Michael friendship and appreciate his attention and his own magic at hatching books. Ian Marshall and Emma Tait, my British editors, were loyal and astute guides and supplied invaluable support, wisdom, and editorial care.

I owe abundant thanks to Francis Lide, retired professor of German language, for his excellent translations of U-boat action reports, or KTBs, which were critical to completing this book. I also owe thanks to Will Scharf, a talented young researcher, whose three research reports were of great value.

Lastly, the project would not have been even conceivable, let alone attainable, without the intelligence, care, and particular gifts of my wife, Margaret, to whom the book is dedicated. Margaret played a critical role in the concept, development, research, and final shape of the book; over four years, her contributions were enormous, and extended from her wisdom and sense in forming the book, to the smallest matters of accuracy and sourcing. Her labors were legion. Finally, for my daughter, Margaret, thanks for constant good cheer, and for putting up with a frequently self-absorbed but devoted father, who drew on her pluck and support.

# INDEX

Page numbers in *italics* refer to maps.

# Index

# Index

# Index

# Index

# Index

# Index